DEMOCRACY'S OXYGEN

DEMOCRACY'S OXYGEN:

How Corporations Control The News

James Winter

BLACK
ROSE
BOOKS

Montréal/New York
London

Black Rose Books No. Z238
Hardcover ISBN: 1-55164-061-9 (bound)
Paperback ISBN: 1-55164-060-0 (pbk.)
Library of Congress No. 96-84480

Canadian Cataloguing in Publication Data

Winter, James P. (James Patrick), 1952-
Democracy's Oxygen: how corporations control the news

Includes bibliographical references and index.
ISBN 1-55164-061-9 (bound). –
ISBN 1-55164-060-0 (pbk.)

1. Mass media—Canada. 2. Journalism—Canada.
3. News agencies—Canada. I. Title.

P92.C3W55 1996   070.1'0971   C96-900293-9

BLACK ROSE BOOKS

C.P. 1258	250 Sonwil Drive	99 Wallis Road
Succ. Place du Parc	Buffalo, New York	London, E9 5LN
Montréal, Québec	14225 USA	England
H2W 2R3 Canada		

To order books in North America: (phone) 1-800-565-9523
(fax) 1-800-221-9985
In Europe: (phone) 081-986-485   (fax) 081-533-5821

A publication of the Institute of Policy Alternatives of Montréal (IPAM)
Printed in Canada

Dedication

To Kaeleigh & Kieran,
My Pride and Joy
and the future

and to Nanna & Poppa

CONTENTS

INTRODUCTION

> Few trends so thoroughly undermine the very foundations of our free society as the acceptance by our corporate officials of a social responsibility other than to make as much money for their shareholders as possible.— Milton Friedman

I was sitting at my computer on a Tuesday in February, 1996, working on this book, when I received a phone call. At the time I was editing a table listing chain ownership of Canadian daily newspapers, and the call came from Vince Rice, a reporter with the *St. Catharines Standard*. His newspaper had just been bought out by the Southam chain. Could I comment?

The Standard and its sister dailies, the Cobourg *Daily Star* and the Port Hope *Evening Guide*, were part of the Burgoyne Group, a small independent chain with a combined circulation of about 48,000. Four generations of the Burgoyne family have owned *The Standard* since 1892. The Southam chain which took it over is the largest chain in the country, controlled at the time by Conrad Black of Hollinger Inc., and Paul Desmarais of Power Corp.

Within a month we witnessed Black Saturday in Saskatchewan, as Conrad Black's Hollinger International bought the last two of the five Saskatchewan dailies, and laid off 182 staff. His encore a few weeks later involved gobbling up six dailies on the east coast and six in Ontario, all formerly Thomson papers. Before the dust settled on these takeovers, the cash-strapped Rogers Communications Inc. announced that its 10-newspaper Toronto *Sun* chain was on the sales block, with Pierre Péladeau's Québecor Inc. as the rumoured buyer. The feeding frenzy continued. By the third week in May, Black borrowed about $300 million to buy out Desmarais' shares in Southam Inc., raising his own minority controlling interest to 41 percent. He announced that he would pursue a majority of shares in the twenty-newspaper chain, with dailies ranging from the *Montréal Gazette*, to the *Ottawa Citizen*, *Windsor Star*, *Edmonton Journal* and the two Vancouver papers.

With 60 out of 104 dailies, Black now reaches 2.4 million Canadian households everyday: 43 percent of the national total. Of the 45 daily newspapers in the province of Ontario, 30, or 71 percent, are owned by one chain: Black/Southam. This dreadful situation actually looks good compared to some of the other provinces. In New Brunswick, the K.C. Irving family owns all four English-language daily newspapers, along with an estimated 300 corporations and much of the rest of the provincial economy, including many of the broadcast media. In Québec, ten out of eleven dailies are owned by Paul Desmarais, Conrad Black, and Pierre Péladeau, leaving *Le Devoir* as the only independent daily. Conrad Black owns all ten dailies in the provinces of Newfoundland (2), Prince Edward Island (3), and Saskatchewan (5).

In 1958, the three largest Canadian newspaper chains controlled about 25 percent of daily circulation. By 1970, the Special Senate Committee on Mass Media chaired by Liberal Senator Keith Davey reported the alarming fact that this figure had reached 45 percent. By the time of the Kent Royal Commission on Newspapers in 1980, it was about 57 percent. Today, the Southam-Hollinger chain alone controls 43 percent of circulation. When one adds in Thomson (12%) and the Toronto *Sun* chain (11%), the total is 66 percent for three chains.

Okay, so concentration is up. Aside from having to edit my table on newspaper chain ownership, so what? Isn't that the price of doing business in the global economy? It certainly reflects the economy at large, where small cartels are to be found in every sector. In 1995 Canada saw $77.4 billion in corporate mergers and acquisitions, up 60 percent from 1994, which in turn was up by more than 100 percent from 1993. Three record-breaking years in a row. Canadian companies made a record $95 billion in profits in 1995, up 19 percent from the year before. At about the same time they were reporting on these trends, the commercial news media were also reporting that: 1) corporations were continuing to lay off large numbers of workers, despite their huge profits; 2) wage increases for workers, well behind inflation, were not increasing along with corporate profits; 3) Jean Chrétien's federal Liberal government, elected in 1993 on the promise of creating jobs, was pleading with corporations to stop downsizing and create jobs.

For the news media, all of these events are as unrelated as they are inexplicable. GM Canada cut 2,500 employees in 1995, while realizing a record profit for any Canadian company, of $1.39 billion. The Big Five banks reported profits of $5 billion while laying off 2,800. Bell Canada slashed 3,200 jobs, while Inco Ltd. cut 2,000. According to the *Report On Business* of our so-called national newspaper, all of this could be explained by shareholder pressures for greater returns.[1]

The time-honoured tradition of concentration and monopoly dates back to 1588, when Jacques Cartier's nephew Jacques Noel obtained a monopoly on furs and mines in what was to become Canada. But, as concerned as we should be about concentration and monopolization in the economy more generally, news media are a special case. Although they are increasingly in the business of delivering readers to advertisers, their "product" is information and ideas. Despite the best efforts of journalists, concentration in ownership means less diversity in the news. This has serious ramifications for our democracy, such as it is.

Conglomerate ownership of the Southam Inc. variety inevitably results in a fixation on bottom line profits, which is incompatible with public service. Since 1988, Southam has cut its payroll in half, to a current level of about 7,300 employees. Some of these people's jobs were replaced by new technology, while some journalists were replaced by wire coverage. Moreover, the news hole shrank significantly. The absentee ownership of Southam means local news coverage, long the mainstay of daily newspapers, falls by the wayside. Early in the spring of 1996 for example, the Southam-owned *Windsor Star* supplied front-page wire-service coverage of a confrontational student protest against the Conservative government of Mike Harris at the Ontario legislature, all the while virtually ignoring a peaceful demonstration by 1,200 protesters at the University of Windsor which was given a paragraph or two on page three. Since Southam purchased *The Windsor Star* from the Graybiel family in the 1970s, its reputation as a quality newspaper has plummeted. Similar accounts surround the demise in quality at more recent Southam acquisitions such as the Kingston *Whig-Standard*, and the Kitchener-Waterloo *Record*.

Conglomerate ownership also heightens the potential for a conflict of interest in reporting the news. For example, how could one rely on the four English-language New Brunswick dailies, all owned by the Irving family, to report fairly on the strike by workers at Irving Oil Ltd. in Saint John N.B., which began in the spring of 1994 and is still going two years later? Or the blacklisting of those strikers which prevents them from being employed part-time elsewhere in the province? Or how could we rely on the Irving media to report on the "Irving Whale," the oil barge containing heavy oil and nine tonnes of polychlorinated biphenyls (PCBs) which sank 60 kilometres off Prince Edward Island in 1970? (In 1995, preparations for a lift operation on the barge cost about $12.8 million and the Irvings contributed about $2 million. The Irving family owned the barge when it sank, but their company denies liability, saying the barge was in international waters when it sank and the laws in 1970 did not require the vessel owner to pay for recovery operations).

Similarly, do newspapers controlled by Paul Desmarais tread lightly when covering Prime Minister Jean Chrétien, given the interconnections between the two? Chrétien's daughter France is married to Desmarais' son André. Chrétien himself was on the board of directors of Desmarais' Power Corp. prior to his election as leader of the official opposition in

1990. John Rae, older brother to former Ontario premier Bob Rae, is a vice president with Power Corp. and ran Jean Chrétien's leadership campaign in 1990 and the federal Liberal election campaign in 1993. Rae was also executive assistant to Jean Chrétien when he was Minister of Indian Affairs in the Trudeau government. Chrétien's son-in-law André Desmarais is president and CEO of Power DirecTv Ltd., and stood to benefit when the Chrétien cabinet took the unprecedented step of overturning a decision by the Canadian Radio-television and Telecommunication Commission, in the spring of 1995. The CRTC had awarded an effective monopoly on the so-called "death star" direct-to-home (DTH) satellite service, to Expressvu Inc., a conglomerate headed by giant BCE Inc. The Chrétien government reversed the CRTC decision, ordering that Power DirecTv also be licensed.

Chrétien dismissed the ensuing controversy over his cabinet's interference with the CRTC. "I have absolutely no conflict of interest," he told the House of Commons, saying that "the Prime Minister of Canada has the right to have his daughter well married." He indicated that he had personally stayed out of cabinet discussions on the matter, turning things over to deputy PM Sheila Copps. Recently, Power DirecTv announced that it was abandoning the DTH field due to what it described as the CRTC's costly restrictions on its license. But as we will see in chapter three, this fascinating case study raises serious concerns over conflict of interest, not just on the part of politicians, but the media conglomerates which report on them to us.

These corporate-political ties are one more reason why concentration of ownership of the press should be halted and rolled back to more acceptable levels. In the U.S., for example, eleven corporations control about half of the daily newspaper circulation. In Canada, one conglomerate controls 43 percent, two control 55 percent and three control 66 percent. This is unacceptable in what passes as a democracy with a free marketplace of ideas. How long can it be before one conglomerate controls all our news media? Legislation, as recommended by the Kent Royal Commission on Newspapers in 1981, is long overdue. What prevents the government from acting? Some answers follow.

***

In my previous book, *Common Cents: Media Portrayal of the Gulf War and Other Events*, in 1992, I attempted to describe the way in which the commercial media systematically distort the reporting of major events; how the narrow ideological perspective they provide becomes "common sense," the only sensible perspective on the part of the vast majority of their audiences. By closely scrutinizing the language of news media messages we can see the way they frame events, revealing the dominant perspective which they promote. I contrasted this mainstream view with alternative sources and ways of looking at the "same" events. I continue to do this in *Democracy's Oxygen*, but my primary purpose here is to go back a step to indicate who "owns" the news. I want to make clear what their ideology and ambitions are, the extent of concentration, the role of management influence, and how these and other related factors help to explain the reasons for the common sense perspective. *Common Cents* is about media content. It describes the news media's portrayal of five significant events. *Democracy's Oxygen*, on the other hand, answers the question of *why* news content is as it is.

At first blush, establishing who owns the news may seem like a silly exercise. We all "own" the news because we listen to, watch or read it. And besides, it is produced for us, with our interests in mind. But the reality of news media ownership, as indicated above, is one of tremendous concentration in the hands of the corporate elite: the likes of a handful of men with the names Conrad Black, Paul Desmarais, Ken Thomson, and Ted Rogers. As we will see, these men are all conservative ideologues. While they don't openly insist that their news media reflect their personal views, broadly speaking this is their ultimate goal and it is accomplished in a number of highly effective ways. John Bassett, publisher of the long defunct *Toronto Telegram*, was asked by a TV interviewer, "Is it not true you use your newspaper to push your own political views?" Bassett replied, "Of course. Why else would you want to own a newspaper?" This type of arrogant candour has now gone the way of the dodo bird. Instead we read and listen to denials and claims of editorial independence and charges of left-wing bias amongst journalists. But as (in my view) our premiere Canadian journalist Linda McQuaig points out, "We must always remember that virtually all media outlets are owned by rich, powerful members of the elite. To assume that this fact has no influence on the ideas they present would be equivalent to assuming that, should the entire media be owned by, say, labour unions, women's groups or social workers, this would have no impact on the editorial content."[2]

Far from providing democracy's oxygen, as they claim, the news media today legitimize a fundamentally undemocratic system. Instead of keeping the public informed, they manufacture public consent for policies which favour their owners: the corporate elite.

This book begins with an overview of the alarming extent of concentration of ownership in media industries. Case studies of two corporate media barons — Paul Desmarais and Conrad Black — demonstrate their neoconservative ideology, their broad influence and their quest for power. The news media mythology about dedication to the public interest contrasts with substantial evidence that the news is largely a corporate and management product. The result is "Media Think," group think on a vast scale which pervades the media and through which they promote narrow ideological dogmas about the world around us, including: globalization, privatization, and deficit hysteria.

A primary focus of this book is its description of the way in which the news media create the news. Morton Mintz, a former *Washington Post* reporter, summed it up: "The media tilt is the net result of a gamut of causes and motives, including bias, boosterism, careerism, cowardice, libel risks, economic imperatives, friendships, ignorance, lack of resources, laziness, protection of news sources, retreats from investigative reporting, stupidity, suppression, survival instincts, and the pro-business orientation of owners and of the managers they hire."[3]

The emphasis herein is on what I consider to be the main causal factors: ownership, hiring and management influences. From my perspective, many journalists are hard working and well-intentioned. They are, however, severely handicapped by the system which surrounds them, and by the conventional norms of journalism. As I demonstrate in interviews with journalists, editors and publishers, the constraints on journalists are tightening rather than loosening. Journalists themselves describe the impact of corporate cost-cutting, the bottom line, and management influence on the news. In contrast, I examine the public persona of journalism regarding such notions as freedom of the press, social responsibility, and the role an informed public plays in a democracy.

The book continues with a discussion of Project Censored Canada, and its top ten censored stories of recent years: what they were, and why they were under reported or omitted altogether from the mainstream news media. Special attention is paid to the role the media played in creating "deficit hysteria" which subtly legitimated the attack on social programs, workers and the poor. In this case, media boosterism contributed to the most successful propaganda campaign in recent Canadian history, and to the ongoing dismantling of our much-vaunted social safety net.

The final section is a humble effort to discuss what can be done about all of this; some proposed solutions which we can collectively work towards, in the interest of the majority rather than a small group.

I should like to indulge myself by briefly addressing my academic colleagues. This book has *not* been written for a small coterie of intellectual dilettantes pursuing what Noam Chomsky has called, "academic cults." For those of you who are wedded to these views at the outset, this book is not for you. Academic journals and texts overflow with perspectives such as these and you may dwell on them to your heart's content. Turn to those, and put this book back on the shelf.

This book provides some diversity. As a privileged group, we academics have an obligation to make our work accessible to the public. Thus, this book is written for the public: students, working people, retirees, the unemployed, all of the so-called "special interest groups" who make up the vast majority of our nation. It is written in a readable fashion, rather than being laden with high fallutin' words and academic jargon. It is not written solely for the converted, but for others who are still malleable, whose minds are still open despite the tremendous efforts and resources devoted to the contrary. It is not written with academic objectivity and neutrality, which are unattainable, but with the intention of informing people and helping to foment change. Above all, it is not written for those academics and journalists whose relentless function it is to indoctrinate others into Media Think, in their supposedly nonideological pursuit of the status quo. This book dissects the commercial media, heart chamber of the ideological system. A topic of no less interest, as I indicate very briefly herein, is the educational heart chamber of that same ideological system.

***

Endnotes

[1] See Gre Ip, "Shareholders vs. Job Holders: Downsizing: As politicians plead with business to add jobs, vocal shareholders are increasingly pressuring firms to cut costs and maximize profit," *The Globe and Mail*, March 23, 1996, B1.

[2] Linda McQuaig, *Shooting the Hippo: Death by Deficit and Other Canadian Myths* (Toronto: Viking, 1995), p. 12.

[3] Morton Mintz, "A Reporter Looks Back in Anger," *The Progressive*, December 1991, p. 29.

Chapter One

MEDIASAURUS

If you aren't careful the newspapers will have you hating
the people who are being oppressed and loving the people
who are doing the oppressing. — Malcolm X

Daily and perhaps hourly, Canadians are presented with information, ideas and viewpoints which help to describe and explain the events and indeed the very nature of the world around them. In this way we learn about the latest political election or about the economy, but also about wars or "conflicts" in faraway places, coups, earthquakes, and other selected events. This information builds upon our previous store of facts and values: what American journalist Walter Lippmann once called the "pictures in our heads" of the world around us.

In the global village, these pictures are almost entirely assembled and constructed by the news media, rather than resulting from personal experience. A sort of living montage, these media creations form our individual and collective world views. Thus, the news media are essential to the formation of attitudes, opinions, beliefs and values in our society.[1] They play an essential role both in reflecting our culture to us, and in creating that culture itself. Indeed, some authors such as Dallas Smythe have argued that the media play a significant role in determining our very consciousness.

Given this crucial role played by the media in our society, it is essential that a broad cross-section of the public owns them. Such broad-based ownership would greatly enhance the diversity of information and opinion. Indeed it is fundamental to democracy itself.

As I indicated in the introduction, Canada saw $77.4 billion in corporate mergers and acquisitions in 1995. This was up 60 percent from 1994, which in turn was up by more than 100 percent over 1993. Three record-breaking years in a row. In 1995, for example, Dutch Interbrew SA purchased John Labatt Ltd. for $2.9 billion; Seagrams of Montréal bought MCA Inc. for U.S.$5.7 billion; American MCI communications purchased computer company SHL Systemhouse Inc. of Ottawa for U.S.$1 billion; and Wallace McCain bought Maple Leaf Foods for $1 billion.

As I also indicated, such concentration of ownership and monopoly development have been a part of Canadian history since long before Confederation. In 1588, Jacques Cartier's nephew Jacques Noel obtained a monopoly on the furs and mines in what was to become Canada. This was one of the earliest monopolies granted by the French Crown, which was anxious to see established settlement in New France. In this early variation of trickle down theory, the Crown hoped that by eliminating competition, profits would accrue, which could then be used to establish a true colony, rather than simply a trading base. Oligopolies and monopolies have been built into the fabric of Canadian economic life; continuing through the Hudson's Bay Company charter in 1670, the Canadian Pacific Railway monopoly clause in 1880, and, as we will see, to present-day mass media.

Following the Canadian industrial revolution which took place in the latter half of the 19th century, the period between 1900 and 1914 saw mergers in such industries as textiles, tobacco, brewing, milling and paper. Between 1908 and 1912, 58 industrial mergers included approximately 275 firms with a total capital of $5,490 million. For example, between 1893 and 1923 in the canning business alone, 76 firms merged to provide Canadian Canners Ltd. with 75 to 80 percent of the market. By the 1930s, Imperial Tobacco had cornered 70 percent of all tobacco production, while five firms controlled 90 percent of pulp and paper production; two meat packing firms accounted for 85 percent; one cement company 90 percent; four copper companies 93 percent; and four agricultural machinery firms 75 percent.[2]

Other examples of concentration exist everywhere in Canada today, ranging from sugar refineries, to pulp and paper producers, corner convenience stores, grocery supermarkets, hardware stores, banks, bookstores, beer stores, video stores, and so forth. The Canadian economy is essentially made up of small cartels or oligopolies in virtually every sector. True competition remains a myth, a figment of someone's fervent imagination.

As illustrated by media and other corporations, the news media are owned by a small group of people. Every year, mergers and acquisitions continue apace. At this writing, *two corporations*, Hollinger/Southam and the Thomson Corp., *control 68 percent of all Canadian daily newspapers*, and 55 percent of the total circulation, and they are corporations with extensive interests outside the newspaper industry, run by the corporate elite. For example, Conrad Black of Hollinger International and Paul Desmarais of Power Corp. are the co-chairs of Southam Inc. and Canada's largest newspaper publishers. They also epitomize the Canadian corporate establishment.[3]

In the U.S., eleven companies control about half of the newspaper business there, a fact which caused two American observers to comment that the "media elite in this country...is [the] corporate establishment.

After a decade of mergers, takeovers, and newspaper closures, media power has concentrated into fewer — and more conservative — hands."[4] Americans are concerned about eleven companies with half of the circulation, versus two corporations in Canada with 55 percent. The largest chain in the U.S. has about 10 percent of national circulation, versus 43 percent here.

In Canadian television, five corporations reached 62 percent of viewers in 1993. In the cable industry, three companies now have 68 percent of the audience, up from 36 percent in 1983, even though the number of subscribers has increased by more than 40 percent. In radio, with 479 stations, just ten companies control 55 percent of the revenue share, up 50 percent in the past decade. In magazine publishing, the largest eight publishers controlled 52 percent of circulation in 1993-94. In book publishing and distribution, Statistics Canada reported that for 1991-92, just 21 out of 370 firms (6 percent) accounted for 51 percent of total sales.[5] A further breakdown of how many of these 21 firms are actually jointly held, was unavailable from Statistics Canada. As of 1993-94, sales of the 24 foreign-controlled book publishing firms came to 47 percent of the total market, while the remaining 292 Canadian companies accounted for 53 percent of sales.

Figure 1 indicates newspaper ownership concentration. Figure 2 on Canadian media corporation assets illustrates the growth in assets of the ten top media corporations in the country for the six-year period between 1988 and 1994. Over this period these corporations' assets grew from $16.9 billion to $37.1 billion, an increase of 225 percent. The percentage change in assets ranged from a drop of 25 percent by Southam Inc., to an increase of 646 percent by Rogers Communications Inc. In 1994, fourth-ranked Rogers swallowed up number third-ranked Maclean Hunter Inc., in a $3.1 billion takeover, vaulting into second place among media corporations, behind the Thomson Corp.

In 1958, the three largest Canadian newspaper chains controlled about 25 percent of daily circulation. By 1970, the Special Senate Committee on Mass Media chaired by Liberal Senator Keith Davey reported the alarming fact that this figure had reached 45 percent. By the time of the Kent Royal Commission on Newspapers in 1980, it was about 57 percent. Today, the Southam-Hollinger chain alone controls 43 percent of circulation. Adding in Thomson (12 percent) and the Toronto *Sun* chain (11 percent), the total reaches 66 percent for three chains. In New Brunswick, the K.C. Irving family owns all four English-language daily newspapers, along with an estimated 300 corporations and much of the rest of the provincial economy. Union leader Larry Washburn of the

Figure 1
Daily Ownership and Circulation

Corporation	# of Dailies (%)		Circulation	% Circ.
Hollinger	40	(38)	920,000	17%
Gesca/Power	4	(4)	307,000	6%
Southam	20	(19)	1,426,000	26%
Sub Total	64	(61)	2,653,000	49%
Thomson	11	(11)	666,000	12%
Toronto *Sun*	10	(10)	567,000	11%
Québecor	4	(4)	446,000	8%
Irving	4	(4)	135,000	3%
Nfld. Capital	2	(2)	50,500	1%
Independents	12	(11)	878,000	16%
Total	105	(100%)	5,395,500	100%

Figures as of May 1996. Hollinger is owned by Conrad Black. Gesca is owned by Paul Desmarais. Southam is controlled by Black (formerly with Desmarais). Source: Canadian Daily Newspaper Publishers' Association, (CDNPA), Canadian Advertising Rates and Data.

Communications, Energy and Paperworkers Union is quoted as saying, "Ah, Saint John. This is Irvingville in Irvingland. New Brunswick is the largest company town in Canada."[6] Irving employs an estimated one in every three working people in Saint John. In December 1992, 93 year-old billionaire K.C. Irving died, but his descendants carry on his empire. What follows is an excerpt from the lengthy obituary in *The Toronto Star* on K.C. Irving's death.

> The Irvings plant trees, cut them, saw them into lumber and make them into paper products. By one estimate, they own a quarter of New Brunswick's woodlands. They import oil, refine it and sell it at retail outlets. They own the trucks that carry Irving logs to Irving mills. The trucks fuel up at Irving gas stations, as do the Irvings' inter-city buses. They own the shipyards that are building Canada's new naval frigates. They make cement and steel. On the

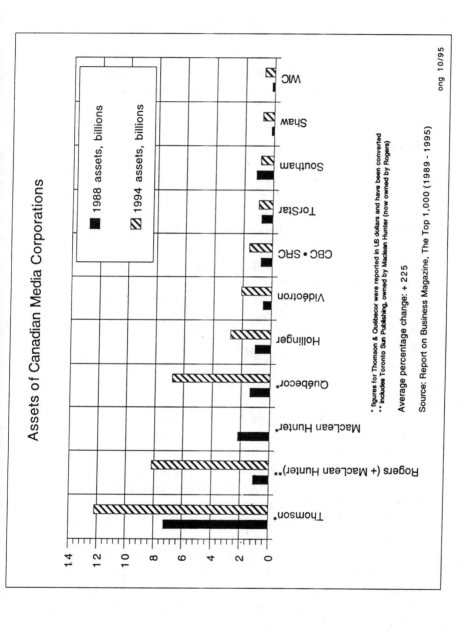

Assets of Canadian Media Corporations

1988 assets, billions
1994 assets, billions

Thomson*
Rogers (+ MacLean Hunter)**
MacLean Hunter*
Québecor*
Hollinger
Vidéotron
CBC • SRC
TorStar
Southam
Shaw
WIC

* figures for Thomson & Québecor were reported in US dollars and have been converted
** includes Toronto Sun Publishing, owned by MacLean Hunter (now owned by Rogers)

Average percentage change: + 225

Source: Report on Business Magazine, The Top 1,000 (1989 - 1995)

ong 10/95

retail market they sell building products, hardware and automotive products. They own every English-language daily newspaper in New Brunswick and some of its radio stations. The CBC itself is beholden to the Irvings. It broadcasts in New Brunswick through a [TV] station in Saint John, owned by the Irvings. Through their food company, Cavendish Farms, the Irvings have even taken on New Brunswick's other family of business barons, the McCains of french fry fame.[7]

The item didn't indicate what was left for the McCains or anyone else to own. It did say that, since 1971, K.C. Irving lived in the Bahamas and later Bermuda, for tax reasons. Over $5 billion in assets, second only to Ken Thomson, and no personal income taxes for the last 21 years! Yet who is left to complain, the New Brunswick news media? The potential for a conflict of interest in reporting on the Irving corporations by their own media boggles the mind.

In Québec, ten out of eleven dailies are owned by Paul Desmarais, Conrad Black, and Pierre Péladeau, leaving *Le Devoir* as the only independent daily. In Saskatchewan, PEI and Newfoundland, Black owns all of the dailies. Even in Ontario, with a total of 45 dailies, one chain (Black/Southam) controls 71 percent. (See Appendix F for a list of newspaper ownership by province, and Appendix C for individual dailies).

At this writing in May 1996, a huge legal buyout battle is taking place in Québec, between the Chagnon family's Groupe Videotron Ltée and the Audet's Cogeco Cable Inc. The two are fighting over the Pouliot family's CFCF Inc., which has television assets and 427,000 cable subscribers. For Videotron, winning CFCF would give it a lock on the Montréal cable market and adjacent cable services.

According to the news media, the concentration of ownership in their industries is an inescapable fact of life. Firm believers in the 'free marketplace,' the media see the development of oligopolies as an inevitable and natural process, whether in their own or other industries. The last thing that is needed is government interference. To hear them tell it, takeovers are exciting events, bordering on breathtaking, depending on the size, the billions of dollars and the major players who are involved.

The summer of 1995 brought an example in *The Globe and Mail*, drawn from an editorial in the conservative British magazine, *The Economist*. The editorial questioned whether Microsoft, owned by that "icon of American capitalism," Bill Gates, warrants the antitrust investigations under way in the U.S., investigations which, the editorial worried, "could delay the launch of the firm's new operating system, Windows 95." (In 1995 Gates topped the *Forbes* magazine list of the world's wealthiest non-monarchists, with a personal fortune estimated at U.S.$12.9 billion. Ken Thomson, owner of *The Globe and Mail* and 10 other Canadian dailies, ranked in seventh place and was the top Canadian, with a net worth of U.S.$6.5 billion.[8] A potential problem occurs when one company has exclusive rights to the operating system with which software must be compatible, at the same time that it is competing with other software companies. However, the article concluded that there is lots of competition and not to worry. It ended with a stirring defense of the free market: "A public desire for common standards, big-company muscle and sheer entrepreneurial flair are combining to create scary monsters with names like [Bill] Gates and [Rupert] Murdoch. The best way to deal with them is to watch them closely — *but never underestimate the capacity of natural economic forces to keep them in check, or of regulators' remedies to go wrong in practice.* Changing technology and the appetites of today's baby monsters should be enough to cope even with Gates" (emphasis added).[9]

A number of observations may be made about the thinking which lies behind this quote. First of all, there is the notion that "public desire" is in part driving the mergers and corporate concentration. Secondly, what to do about it? While we are permitted to "watch them closely," we know that "natural economic forces" will keep them in check. This is the "unseen hand" of the marketplace promoted by eighteenth century philosopher Adam Smith. Finally, the warning about the role of government: "regulators' remedies" which "go wrong in practice" are obviously never needed.

It's not clear whether the U.S. Justice Department heeded the advice of *The Economist*, or merely subscribes to the same philosophy. In any case, about a month later we learned that the antitrust action against Microsoft had been dropped.

Mr. Rogers' Country

A good example of the "breathtaking" coverage of media takeovers came in the spring of 1994, with the $3.1 billion takeover of Maclean Hunter Ltd. by Rogers Communications Inc. This merger created a new media giant, with the fourth-ranked Rogers buying up the third-ranked Maclean Hunter. The deal increased Rogers' cable audience by 71 percent, to 2.9 million subscribers. Rogers owns the Home Shopping

Network, 70 video stores, ten radio stations, one television station, the youth specialty channel YTV network, a one-third share of the long distance phone company Unitel, the Rogers Cantel cellular phone company, and Viewer's Choice, a pay-per-view cable service.[10] Maclean Hunter added to this ten newspapers (up for sale in 1996), including *The Financial Post* and the Toronto *Sun* chain, a string of weeklies, about 200 consumer and business periodicals including five of the ten top-selling magazines in the country, three TV stations, and 21 radio stations. In 1994, Rogers and its then-subsidiary Unitel contributed more than any other firm to the Liberal Party of Canada, just under $100,000.[11] This was the same year in which Rogers sought CRTC approval for its takeover of Maclean Hunter Ltd. In September of 1995, together with Shaw Communications, the number two cable firm, Rogers announced a joint venture launching the Sega Channel, a digital interactive video game specialty channel, for which they predicted 200,000 subscribers within a year.

So, the Rogers media behemoth encompasses almost every communications medium, from cable, video games, specialty channels, TV, and radio, to daily and weekly newspapers, magazines, and cellular phones. In some huge markets such as Ontario, Rogers now controls 75 percent of cable outlets. He controls 44 percent of the English language cable market, and about one-third of the country as a whole. For much of the press, the only concern over this takeover revolved around whether the $17 a share offer for Maclean Hunter was adequate to satisfy shareholders (it was eventually "sweetened" to $17.50); whether there would be a rival bid, and details on the way in which the conservative Maclean Hunter board was outmanoevered by the daring and expansive-minded Rogers. Harvey Enchin and John Partridge of *The Globe and Mail* were positively relieved that after two weeks of rumours and rhetoric, "Rogers Communications Inc. has finally put its money where its mouth is." Then their commentary degenerated into breathless anticipation. "If the offer is successful, it will solidify Rogers as by far Canada's biggest cable-television operator."[12] The deal also solidified the financial security of three Rogers executives, each of whom received a special cash bonus of more than $1 million for completing the transaction. Ted Rogers "earned" a bonus of $1.25 million; Vice Chairman Phil Lind drew a $1.2 million bonus, and chief financial officer Graham Savage received a $1.1 million bonus.[13]

A few stories reported ominous rumblings from the Canadian Radio-television and Telecommunications Commission (CRTC), which used to look askance at media concentration, especially cross-media ownership in the same market. But after a suitable delay and the usual show of public hearings, the CRTC went on to approve the takeover. This despite a recent CRTC study which warned of the dangers of media concentration. The study, released in November 1993, notes: "Concentration of ownership in Canadian media and broadcast properties has grown significantly in recent times and, if the trend continues, by the year 2000 the broadcasting system will be concentrated in very few hands."[14] As an aside, this is the very same CRTC which approved the privatization of the public educational television network in Alberta, at the request of Ralph Klein. In July, 1995, the CRTC approved the sale of the ACCESS Network in Alberta to a Toronto consortium which includes the CHUM Group and CITY-TV President Moses Znaimer.[15] The first thing to note is that this information was buried in the arts section; the second is the bubbly, favourable reaction which was reported, and the third is the precedent for other educational networks such as TV Ontario and the CBC itself.

When Rogers announced it would become an Internet access provider in the fall of 1995, "Internet consultant" Rick Broadhead told *The Globe and Mail* that Rogers' entrance into Internet services is a big plus. "I think with Rogers providing access...that's going to be a point at which the Internet will be taken very seriously. *Bell and Rogers are names people know and trust and feel comfortable with,*" Broadhead said (emphasis added).[16] No one indicated that the convergence in cross-media ownership and cosy cartels might conceivably provide any potential problem for the public. Apparently, being Canadian means knowing, trusting and feeling comfortable with our monopolies.

Returning to the Rogers takeover of *Maclean's*, Peter C. Newman of *Maclean's* magazine commented on his new boss' acquisition: "[Ted] Rogers' latest move, using the Maclean Hunter purchase as his entry point to building Canada's main electronic highway, is the most daring and far-sighted of his many ventures."[17]

But media reports which applaud concentration in their own industry are the norm. One of my "favourite" examples comes from a 1989 cover story in *Maclean's*, which carried Conrad Black on the cover. It was titled: "MEDIA WARS: The rise of the global owners, their battles for position and profit." Inside the issue, reporter D'Arcy Jenish enthused that, "with another big takeover, [Conrad] Black would be well on his way to becoming an international media giant."[18] Jenish's colleague Brenda Dalglish accepted the task of reporting on Rogers' takeover of Maclean Hunter, including *Maclean's*, in a story which put a smiling Ted Rogers on the cover of the magazine which he now, effectively, owned. She gushed that, "If the Canadian business community handed out awards in the same way that Hollywood bestows Oscars, Ted Rogers would walk away with an armful of statuettes this year." [19]

Other examples abound. When Southam Inc. announced plans to buy a majority share of the *Kitchener-Waterloo Record* late in 1989, fellow Southam newspaper *The Windsor Star* led its story with, "investment analysts generally applauded an announcement Friday." and went on to quote just one communications analyst with Merrill Lynch Canada, who said "it's a natural fit" within the Southam chain.[20] One wonders what it would take to make the acquisition unsuitable in the eyes of its sister newspaper. In chapter two we will examine some of the news coverage of Conrad Black's purchase of a dozen Thomson newspapers.

Muscle on Their Bones

A spate of American media mergers made the Canadian news late in the summer of 1995. In August, Walt Disney Co. spent U.S.$19 billion in the second largest takeover in U.S. history, to acquire the ABC television network. Disney acquired not only ABC Inc., but Capital Cities Communications, which had previously swallowed up ABC. The *Report on Business* said, "The new alliances should help lift the sagging fortunes of the big three networks while accelerating a new era in television programming." The article continued, "Disney's takeover agreement puts pressure on would-be acquirers to gobble up the remaining two networks."[21]

The very next day we read that Westinghouse Electric Corp. had purchased CBS Inc., the last remaining major independent network in the U.S., for $5.4 billion, in what was reported as a "widely anticipated" bid. The takeover was portrayed as a rescue mission which would "restore the sagging broadcaster" to its "former glory."[22] Buried deep within the article, on an inside page, we learned that shareholders would "have to wait for legislative changes to consummate the deal." Since Westinghouse already owned TV stations through its Group W broadcasting unit, the new company would own 15 TV stations, covering a third of U.S. viewers, whereas American laws prohibited one company from owning stations covering more than 25 percent of the U.S. market. But, the article noted, "a bill pending in Congress would raise [this limit] to at least 35 percent."

Just two days later The U.S. House of Representatives passed the Telecom Bill, which, as anticipated, deregulated the local telephone market and lifted most restrictions on the number of radio and TV stations a single company could own. Initially, U.S. President Bill Clinton threatened to veto the bill on the very evident grounds that it would result in too much concentration of power in the hands of a few large companies. But, by early in 1996, the bill received approval from both the Senate and Clinton.

Barely a month after the Westinghouse purchase, media giant Time Warner Inc. took over Turner Broadcasting System Inc. in a U.S.$7 billion stock transaction. *The Globe* quoted Ted Turner as explaining, "We were undercapitalized. We've always been undercapitalized...I'm looking forward to having a little muscle on our bones."[23]

So, to recap, Westinghouse Inc. owns CBS, General Electric owns NBC, Time-Warner owns Turner Broadcasting, and the Disney Corp. owns ABC.

This view that bigger is better, typified by *The Globe's* coverage in these cases, is by no means limited to the media. It is part of the broader neoliberal-conservative philosophy adopted by corporations and politicians alike, and has spawned rationalization, free trade and globalization. It represents the triumph of the so-called "free market," or Law of the Jungle. We will return to this topic in the concluding chapter.

Québecor Inc.

With 1994 assets of $6.8 billion, Québecor Inc. is the third largest media conglomerate in the country, behind Thomson Inc. at $12.2 billion, and Rogers at $8.2 billion (see Appendix A). Québecor has demonstrated phenomenal growth, with an increase in assets of almost 400 percent since 1988. Québecor controls four dailies with eight percent of national circulation, but is touted as a likely buyer (along with Power Corp). for the *Sun* chain, which Rogers put up for sale in May 1996, as this book was going to press. Owned by Québec's Pierre Péladeau, Québecor controls a tabloid empire comprised of *Le Journal de Montréal, Le Journal de Québec*, the Sherbrooke *Record*, and the *Winnipeg Sun*. If Péladeau is the successful bidder, the *Sun* chain would add nine dailies and bring him to about 17 percent ownership of national circulation. (Excluding *The Financial Post*, 20 percent owned by Conrad Black and 62 percent by the *Sun* chain. At this writing, Black is expected to buy *The Post*, which he has right to first refusal on). Hence, the sale of the *Sun* chain by Rogers, which is said to result from the need for cash, too much debt and no dividends on the horizon for shareholders, will decrease cross-media concentration but increase concentration of ownership within the newspaper industry itself.

Péladeau, who calls women reporters "darling" and was described by one as a "brash flirt who makes no apologies about his love of women," is reputed to interfere less in his papers than does Conrad Black. Charles Bury, editor of the Sherbrooke *Record*, who also worked for Black, said, "He certainly doesn't tell me what to write in editorial columns or news columns. He said to me once, 'You put out a nice little paper in Sherbrooke, keep on making me a little money, and you can do it for as long as you want.'" As we will see in chapter two, this contrasts with the interventionist approach taken by Black, about whom Bury says, "the [Toronto] *Sun* people...would be better off in the hands of Péladeau, by far. He wouldn't lay anyone off until he sees what each person does in the newsroom."[24]

Québecor is also the second-largest commercial printer in North America, printing the Canadian editions of *Time, TV Guide, Reader's Digest*, most Canadian telephone directories, and commercial flyers. As of 1994, it had 15,000 employees and 65 plants internationally, including Canada, the U.S., France and Mexico. Through its plant in Buffalo NY, Québecor publishes the Harlequin Romance novels owned by *The Toronto Star*'s parent company, TorStar Corp. Péladeau's net worth is about $359 million (see Appendix G).

To provide a brief indication of just who owns the Canadian media and some examples of their influence, we turn in the next two chapters to a case study in media ownership: Southam Inc. and its affiliates, which comprise Canada's largest newspaper chain. Southam co-Chairs Conrad Black and Paul Desmarais, with their respective media and corporate empires, receive special scrutiny for reasons which will become apparent.[25] As mentioned, the Southam conglomerate reaches four out of ten newspaper readers in Canada, on a daily basis. Before turning to the Southam case study, one media baron who requires special mention is Ken Thomson.

Ken Thomson's Fish and Chips

Ken Thomson, owner of *The Globe and Mail*, is the wealthiest Canadian, and with assets of about $10 billion (Canadian), was ranked seventh in the world by *Forbes* magazine in 1995. So, it was somewhat surprising to see him well down the list at number 33 in a 1996 *Report on Business* article on 50 chief executive officers who broke the million-dollar barrier.[26] His nominal salary of $1.5 million *would* place him in 33rd spot. But how does someone making "only" this salary amass a personal fortune of $10 billion? Thriftiness alone obviously would not suffice. The answer was to be found on the previous page of the business section that day, where we learned that Thomson planned to relinquish the title of CEO, while retaining his position as chairman of Thomson Corp. (Which, by the way, means that his salary likely won't be revealed for 1996, as only CEOs and the top five "money earners" are required to report). More than halfway through *this* story, is the fact that Thomson "earned about U.S.$220 million in [stock] dividends last year." This information was contained a mere page away from *The Globe's* assertion that Frank Stronach of Magna International was "in a class by himself," with his total compensation of $47.2 million.[27] By my calculations, Stronach made a paltry 14 percent of Thomson's compensation. Thomson alone made almost twice that of *The Globe's* total list of 50 top CEOs, with Frank Stronach thrown in for good measure. Just who is in a class by himself? And how can *The Globe and Mail* explain this oversight? Mere coincidence? One could argue that stock dividends are not a part of the corporate compensation package in a given year. But what does this say about the meaningfulness of the supposed list of "top CEOs?" Is the fact that Thomson makes hundreds of millions of dollars as the major shareholder *unrelated* to what he is willing to accept as compensation for acting as the CEO? Should any of these questions be raised in an article on the topic? What does Thomson's level of compensation, or for that matter Stronach's, do to the assertion in the article that the "bosses' pay [is] ruled by [the] market"? Isn't the bosses' pay ruled by the boss? Finally, just what is it that Thomson does, personally, to earn one-third of a billion dollars in a year? And shouldn't this question be posed somewhere alongside the pages so recently devoted to the salaries of Ontario public servants who made about three ten-thousandths of Thomson's earnings?[28]

Ken Thomson, Second Lord of Fleet, inherited his empire and his title from his father Roy, Lord of Fleet I, knighted by Her Majesty in 1964, in the name of the infamous and sensational newspapers of Fleet Street, in London, England. Roy Thomson once said: "I buy newspapers to make money to buy newspapers to make more money. As far as editorial content, that's the stuff you separate the ads with."[29] Ads whose revenue-generating power earned them the central role in his business; a business which began in Timmins, Ontario, where the elder Thomson got into radio broadcasting in order to promote the radio sets he was then selling. When his son, "young Ken" as he was affectionately known while his father was alive, announced the sale of the Timmins *Press* in 1996 — his father's first newspaper and the one where Ken got his start in the business as a reporter — he told *The Globe and Mail*, "You can't run a business, you know, on a basis of sentiment." *Globe* staff liked the statement so much it was used as the quote of the day.

In 1979 Thomson newspapers purchased *The Globe and Mail* and the rest of the FP chain. The next year, the company closed the Ottawa *Journal*, while Southam Inc. simultaneously closed the Winnipeg *Tribune*. A few days later, Thomson closed down the FP News Service. In total, 400 people were put out of work, and young Ken mused that: "Each has to find his own way in this world."[30] The Kent Royal Commission on Newspapers was struck as a result of the outcry over the closure of the two dailies in 1980. Ken Thomson appeared before the public hearings and said, "I believe in growing. I believe in growing in the newspaper business...I like to invest. I like my family's investments to grow...Newspapers I like very, very much." He went on to say, "look, we are running a business organization. They happen to be newspapers."[31] Vancouver publisher Stuart Keate told the Kent Commission, regarding the Thomson chain, "one has the feeling that they would be just as happy to own forty massive bank vaults or forty widget factories."[32] The Kent Commission noted that the family which owned *The Windsor Star* until the 1970s, (the Graybiels) "chose to allow only Southam to bid, because it was believed to take the public service objective seriously." The Commission commented, "nothing of the kind has ever been said of Thomson." The Davey Committee, a 1970 Special Senate Committee on media ownership, indicated that there are three types of newspapers: investigative ones, mediocre ones, and,

> There is a third kind of newspaper in Canada — The kind that prints news releases intact, that seldom extends its journalistic enterprise beyond coverage of the local trout festival, that hasn't annoyed anyone important in years. Their city rooms are refuges for the frustrated and disillusioned, and their editorial pages are a daily testimony to the notion that Chamber-of-Commerce boosterism is an adequate substitute for community service....A number of these newspapers are owned by K.C. Irving. A much larger number are owned by Roy Thomson.[33]

The cheapness and penny pinching of the Thomson chain have long made the Southam chain appear favourable by comparison, but as we will see, since Black and Desmarais' involvement, things have changed.

At the annual shareholders meeting in May, 1994, Ken Thomson confessed that Thomson Corp.'s newspaper group had been mismanaged and had to become as efficient as the rest of the corporation. Thomson Corp. is a diversified transnational with 136 companies. In 1994, it had $12.2 billion in assets (see Appendix A). "We let it get out of hand. I'll be honest with you, it was not being run right and it's going to be run right," Thomson said. The group's operating margins slipped to 16 percent in 1993, from as much as 30 percent just five years earlier.[34] Within three months, the company was reporting second quarter profits which leapt by 40 percent over those from a year earlier.[35] By 1995, as mentioned, Ken Thomson's shares would earn him $333 million in dividends to go along with his nominal $1.5 million in salary.[36]

Michael Johnston, CEO of the newspaper division resigned a year earlier, according to the Thomson-owned *Globe and Mail*, "because of intense pressure to improve profit from the corporate parent's reputedly even tougher New York-based President and CEO Michael Brown."[37] Brown told shareholders at the 1993 annual meeting that the company was investing heavily in training and executive development to improve its competitive position and growth rate. "It will give us a better bottom line," he said.

In the fall of 1994, Thomson closed the striking *Oshawa Times,* exposing as a myth the belief that one of the strengths of newspaper chains is their ability and willingness to support member papers through hard times. The Vernon (B.C). *News* is also slated to be closed in June, 1996. At Thomson's *Winnipeg Free Press,* ombudsperson Barry Mullin was fired in 1992 for criticizing the way his paper downplayed coverage of the Los Angeles riots, instead running what he called "softer features on a coloured braces fad or edible golf tees." Maurice Switzer, the new *Free Press* publisher at the time, laid off 50 people including the advertising and circulation directors, the general manager, and the production manager.[38] At the Thomson-owned Woodstock *Sentinel,* publisher George Czerny cut the Canadian Press newswire service effective January 1, 1993. This cost-cutting move made the *Sentinel* an "all local news" paper with no wire services and saved an estimated $90,000 annually.

Of Thomson's stingy newspapers — formerly 40 dailies, now reduced to eleven including the flagship *Globe and Mail* and once proud *Winnipeg Free Press* — even Peter C. Newman, chronicler of the rich and famous, indicated that they reflect "a blandness so pervasive that no self-respecting fish could bear to be wrapped in one of their pages."[39] Thomson's right-hand man John A. Tory candidly confessed that for

Canada's wealthiest billionaire and the seventh richest man in the world, "It's just very difficult for Ken to put his hand in his pocket and spend money."[40] This is no doubt one of the endearing characteristics which, by 1994, enabled the combined wealth of the world's 358 billionaires to equal that of the bottom 45 percent of the population of the planet.[41] One of Thomson's efficiencies includes the contracting out of newspaper printing. According to Michael Brown, president of the newspaper division, "If someone else prints a paper, they put up the capital, they take the union hassles. There's no messing around with ironmongering."[42]

The good news, as they say, is that Thomson has been selling off his newspapers and investing elsewhere. The bad news, as we will see, is that they are being bought up by Conrad Black. Thomson has diverse interests in publishing, travel and finance He lost out to an Anglo-Dutch conglomerate in a bidding war for the Lexis-Nexis on-line legal research service in 1994. However, early in 1996 Thomson bought West Publishing in the U.S. for $4.7 billion, or about four times its revenues. Almost all of the money for the takeover was borrowed from a consortium of nine banks. West produces college texts, CD-ROMs, and has a virtual stranglehold on the on-line provision of U.S. case law through its Westlaw on-line research service. Westlaw has a client list of almost every large and mid-sized law firm in the U.S. Also in 1996, Thomson bought the D.C. Heath school publishing business from Houghton Mifflin. These purchases reduced Thomson's newspaper revenues to a projected 14 percent of its total, reducing the company's reliance on advertising from a high of 90 percent to only 15 percent of revenues, according to Michael Brown.[43] But, a look at Thomson's quarterly report reveals that while sales from non-newspaper publishing and travel dwarfed that of newspapers in the revenue column, newspapers were the undisputed champion in the operating profit column.

If newspapers remain so profitable, the question is, what does Thomson know that Black doesn't? According to *Forbes*, Thomson Corp. is selling off its papers because of: the risks involved in depending on advertising in periods of recession; to focus on strategic regional markets and centralize printing and sales; to move into digital, electronic delivery and eliminate costs for vehicles and employees; and to tap the more lucrative market for specialized business information in law, finance, defense, science, medicine, engineering, education, and so forth.

Figure 3
Thomson Corp. Sales, Profits By Division
(In U.S.$Millions)

	1995		1994	
Division	Sales	Profit	Sales	Profit
Int'l Publishing	$514	$55	$407	$35
Financial	$313	$53	$278	$41
Newspapers	$327	$59	$301	$57
Travel	$674	$35	$594	$39
Total	$1828	$202	$1680	$172

Source: Casey Mahood, "Thomson profit drops 19%," *The Globe and Mail*, August 18, 1995, p. B7. For the quarter ending June 30, 1995.

The Thomson empire is run by John Arnold Tory, reputedly as sharp a businessman as may be found on Bay Street, and a man whom Ken Thomson doesn't merely like, but whom he "adores."[44] Tory's father John D. was also on the Thomson board with Ken's father Roy. John D. Tory founded the law firm Tory, Tory, DesLauriers & Binnington, where Ted Rogers articled. William DesLauriers, partner of the law firm, is on the board of Thomson Corp. John A. Tory is deputy chairman and director of Thomson Corp., but is also a director of Rogers Communications Inc., as well as being on the boards of Abitibi-Price Inc., the Royal Bank of Canada, and others. His son John H. Tory is a partner with Tory, Tory, DesLauriers & Binnington, but is also on the board of Rogers Broadcasting Ltd.; was the principal secretary to the Ontario premier and cabinet from 1982-1985; ran the Ontario election campaign of 1990; and the federal Tory election campaign in the fall of 1993. Hence, the man who runs the Thomson Corp. has close family ties through his son to the federal and Ontario Conservative Parties. His law firm of Tory, Tory, DesLauriers & Binnington also contributed $12,519 to the Liberal Party of Canada in 1994. Ken Thomson's subsidiary, the Woodbridge Co., contributed $15,000 to Jean Chrétien's Liberals.[45]

Thomson Corp. is a diversified multinational corporation which, in addition to its newspaper and publishing holdings, owns the Hudson's Bay Co., Simpsons, Zellers, a travel agency, and much more. This leaves the newspaper chain in a position of conflict of interest when reporting on the other corporate holdings, much the same situation as the Irving family of New Brunswick, as mentioned in the introduction.

The close connections amongst the current Canadian Family Compact which runs our corporations, media and government, are evident. Ken Thomson and Ted Rogers, two of our country's billionaires who also happen to own two of our largest "competing" media empires, are virtually indistinguishable when seen through family, business and political ties. Not surprisingly, this is reflected in the content of their news media outlets. Although the main focus in this book is on Canada's largest newspaper publishing conglomerate, Southam Inc., these other media barons are not that different.

With this very brief overview of the news media ownership situation, we now turn to our case study of Southam News, beginning with its current co-Chairmen Conrad Black and Paul Desmarais.[46] Black, the subject of chapter two, is the driving force behind all of Southam, in addition to the Hollinger and Sterling branches of his growing media empire.

***

Endnotes

[1] The news media do not do this alone, of course. Other media industries which create films, books, TV entertainment, magazines and so forth also influence our values. Similarly, the formal education system has a tremendous impact on the creation and reinforcement of values. For the most part this book will not address these other cultural apparatuses, which, while they deserve special attention, largely tend to work in concert with rather than against the mainstream news media.

[2] See Robert Picard, James Winter, Max McCombs and Stephen Lacy, eds., *Press Concentration and Monopoly: New Perspectives on Newspaper Ownership and Operation* (Norwood, NJ: Ablex:, 1988), pp. 105-106.

[3] As this book was going to press in May 1996, Black bought out Desmarais' shares in Southam, increasing his own stake to 41 percent. Black indicated he would move toward and beyond 50 percent, further concentrating ownership.

[4] Ben Bagdikian, *The Media Monopoly*, 4th ed. (Boston: Beacon Press, 1992), p. ix. See also Jeff Cohen and Norman Solomon, *Adventures in Medialand* (Monroe, NY: Common Courage Press, 1993), p.5. By way of comparison, as reported in the Kent Royal Commission on Newspapers, in 1970 40 percent of our English-language newspaper circulation was in the hands of independents, with 53 percent controlled by the three chains: Southam, Thomson and FP Publications. By 1980, the independents had dropped to 26 percent, Thomson had swallowed up FP and, together with Southam, it controlled 59 percent of English-language circulation.

[5] For a detailed account of concentration as well as corporate and political interlocks, see James Winter and Amir Hassanpour, "Building Babel: No wonder government, business

and the media speak the same language — they're run by the same group of friends," *The Canadian Forum*, Jan./Feb. 1994, pp.10-17.

[6] Murray Campbell, "Strikers struggle in 'Irvingville,'" *The Globe and Mail*, February 24, 1996, B1.

[7] From *The Toronto Star* obituary on K.C. Irving, reprinted in *The Windsor Star*, Dec. 14, 1992, p. A10.

[8] Reuters and AP, "Microsoft chief ranks No. 1 in Forbes billionaire survey," *The Globe and Mail*, July 5, 1995, p. B12. Also, "The World's 10 Richest People," *Forbes*, July 17, 1995.

[9] Editorial, "How dangerous is Microsoft?" *The Globe and Mail*, reprinted from *The Economist*, July 10, 1995, p. A11.

[10] In August, 1995, Rogers wrote off its 29.5 percent share in Unitel, taking a loss of $99 million. The next month it was announced that AT&T and three major banks would buy Unitel for $250 million. Lawrence Surtees, "AT&T, banks to buy Unitel," *The Globe and Mail*, September 27, 1995, p. B1.

[11] *The Monitor*, published by the Canadian Centre for Policy Alternatives, April 1996, p. 1. The figures were obtained from the Chief Electoral Officer of Canada.

[12] Harvey Enchin, John Partridge, "$17 a share bid for Maclean Hunter," *The Globe and Mail*, February 12, 1994, p. A1.

[13] This information was buried within an article in the *Report On Business* (ROB). See Harvey Enchin, "Rogers prepares for huge writeoff," *The Globe and Mail*, March 27, 1995, p. B1.

[14] Jim Bronskill, CP, "CRTC study warns about media concentration dangers," *The Halifax Chronicle-Herald*, Sept. 19, 1994.

[15] Christopher Harris, "CRTC approves sale of ACCESS Network," *The Globe and Mail*, July 21, 1995, p. C2.

[16] Geoffrey Bowan, "Net means business now," *The Globe and Mail*, December 4, 1995, p. B1.

[17] Peter C. Newman, "Life in the fast lane," *Maclean's*, March 21, 1994, p. 43.

[18] D'Arcy Jenish, "In the Black," *Maclean's*, July 17, 1989, p. 34.

[19] Brenda Dalglish, "King of the road," *Maclean's*, March 21, 1994, p. 36.

[20] See CP, "Paper's purchase called 'natural fit,' *The Windsor Star*, November 25, 1989, p. A9.

[21] Jacquie McNish, "Disney changes TV picture," *The Globe and Mail*, August 1, 1995, B1.

[22] Harvey Enchin, "CBS bought in $5.4 billion deal," *The Globe and Mail*, August 2, 1995, B1.

[23] Brian Milner, "Time Warner wins Turner in $7 billion deal," *The Globe and Mail*, September 23, 1995, B1. *"The Globe"* and *"The Globe and Mail"* are used interchangeably throughout this book..

[24] Quoted in Ann Gibbon, "Péladeau sets sights on *Sun*," *The Globe and Mail*, June 6, 1996, p. B6.

[25] As mentioned, Black bought out Desmarais' interest in Southam as this book was going to press. However, Power Corp. still retains extensive media holdings. An earlier,

much shorter version of these chapters was published in James Winter and Amir Hassanpour, "Building Babel: No wonder government, business and the media speak the same language — they're run by the same group of friends," *The Canadian Forum*, January/February 1994, pp. 10-17.

[26] John Saunders, "A league of their own," *The Globe and Mail*, April 13, 1996, p. B1.

[27] Ibid.

[28] The above constitutes a slightly rewritten letter to the editor of *The Globe and Mail* which I submitted in mid-April, 1996, that I am still waiting for the editors to run.

[29] Quoted in Wallace Clement, *The Canadian Corporate Elite* (Carleton University Press: Ottawa, 1975), p. 288.

[30] Doug Smith, "Man Bites Newspaper," *This* magazine, September 1992, p. 17.

[31] Tom Kent, Laurent Picard, Borden Spears, *Royal Commission on Newspapers*, (Ottawa: Ministry of Supply and Services, 1981), pp 91-92.

[32] Ibid, p. 102.

[33] Keith Davey, *The Uncertain Mirror: Report of the Special Senate Committee on Mass Media*, Vol. I (Ottawa: Information Canada, 1970), p. 85.

[34] Casey Mahood, "Greater efficiency goal at Thomson newspapers," *The Globe and Mail*, May 20, 1994, p. B1.

[35] Casey Mahood, "Thomson profit climbs 40%," *The Globe and Mail*, August 12, 1994, p. B5.

[36] Casey Mahood, "Thomson to relinquish chief executive title," *The Globe and Mail*, April 13, 1996, p. B3.

[37] John Partridge, "Thomson Newspapers chief quits," *The Globe and Mail*, May 11, 1993, p. B1.

[38] Doug Smith, "Man Bites Newspaper," p. 18.

[39] Peter C. Newman, "The Private Life of Canada's Richest Man," *Maclean's*, October 14, 1991, p. 49.

[40] Ibid.

[41] Maude Barlow and Bruce Campbell, *Straight Through the Heart: How the Liberals Abandoned the Just Society* (Toronto: Harper Collins, 1995), p. 45.

[42] Marcia Berss, "Greener Pastures," *Forbes*, October 23, 1995, pp. 56-60.

[43] Quoted in Casey Mahood and John Saunders, "Thomson buys U.S. giant," *The Globe and Mail*, February 27, 1996, p. B1.

[44] Quoted in Peter C. Newman, "The Private Life of Canada's Richest Man," p. 49.

[45] *The Monitor*, CCPA, April 1996, p. 7. Figures are from the Chief Electoral Officer, for 1994.

[46] These men still are co-chairs at this writing but as mentioned earlier Black arranged to buy up Power Corp.'s shares in Southam for about $300 million, just as this book was going to press late in May 1996. Power Corp. has retained its three members on the board of Southam.

Chapter Two

THE BLACK MARKET

The most powerful force for liberalism and democracy is information....Power ultimately depends on assumptions, and assumptions are intimately tied to information. — William Thorsell, editor, *The Globe and Mail*.

As a young man travelling in Spain in the 1960s, Conrad Black read a biography of American publisher William Randolph Hearst. According to his travelling companion at the time, Black was transfixed. He reportedly began to go on about Hearst, quoting him "endlessly."[1] Hearst inherited fabulous wealth from his parents, was expelled from Harvard university, established an influential newspaper chain, was elected to the U.S. Congress, and in the early years of this century, subsequently ran unsuccessfully for mayor of New York City, Governor of New York, and the U.S. Presidency. Hearst, who was given an unflattering depiction in the Orson Welles' 1941 film *Citizen Kane*, and consequently curtailed the film's distribution, is remembered for the grotesque opulence of his castle at San Simeon, California. His xenophobic militarism directly influenced the declaration and conduct of the Spanish-American War, and some blame him for starting it. He is renowned for his pursuit of power and prestige, above all else.

As 1995 drew to a close, two more ho-hum newspaper acquisitions by Conrad Black received passing mention in the news. Black purchased two Saskatchewan dailies, the Regina *Leader-Post* and the Saskatoon *StarPhoenix* from the Sifton family, which in 1979 sold its FP chain of newspapers to Thomson. This seemingly minor event deserved more attention for several reasons, most notably that Black now owned all five daily newspapers in the province of Saskatchewan. NDP premier Roy Romanow tried to look on the bright side. He was quoted as saying, "I just don't see Conrad Black picking up the phone to somebody at the *Leader-Post* and saying, 'This must be your editorial policy toward the NDP government.'" Premier Romanow should qualify for the Pollyanna of the year award. While Black wouldn't pick up the phone himself, as we will see, he began influencing the newspapers' content indirectly a day or so after the purchase closed. But Romanow was not content with that remark, he went on to describe Black as "well-read, intelligent and willing to listen to opposing arguments." He even claimed to have made a "strong pitch" to Black to have him relocate Sterling Newspapers' headquarters to Saskatchewan from Vancouver.[2]

James Bruce, publisher of *The Windsor Star* and, as a result, an employee of Black at Southam said "I don't believe that there were too many people in the industry who were really happy with what happened in Saskatchewan. In my opinion, the centralization of the entire daily press in Saskatchewan is not good. As a publisher, I think it is a very unhealthy situation."[3] It proved unhealthy for 182 employees at the Saskatchewan dailies when they were laid off on "Black Saturday," March 2, 1996, one day after the Hollinger purchase closed. The Saskatchewan dailies were profitable, but not profitable enough, according to the new owners. Professor Gerry Sperling, head of the political science department at the University of Regina, also was less circumspect than Premier Romanow. "It certainly makes a difference to the appearance of those papers, which weren't very good in the first place and are really rotten now," he told *The Globe and Mail*.[4] And a content analysis by journalism students at the University of Regina found a marked reduction in local reporting after the layoffs. Journalism professor Jim McKenzie said "you can't fire a quarter of the staff...and not expect to notice a difference." He said "we found quite a marked deterioration in the quality of news coverage...I think the paper is clearly weaker. They're filling it up with wire copy and pictures of kids in swimming pools."[5]

When the Kent Royal Commission on Newspapers reported in 1981, Black had less than one percent of the daily circulation in Saskatchewan. Now he has 100 percent. Those dailies, when added to the 19 that he bought from Ken Thomson in the summer of 1995, and the dozen in the spring of 1996, and his takeover of Southam Inc., all helped to put Black in the position of top Canadian press baron, with control of 60 out of 104 dailies, or 58 percent.

The fact that Black has now locked up the dailies in three Canadian provinces will be played out in political terms, much in the same way that Black has bragged about using the London *Daily Telegraph* to support Margaret Thatcher's government. The news media were instrumental in bringing down Bob Rae's NDP government in Ontario in 1995.[6] They played a significant role in the resignation of NDP premier Mike Harcourt in B.C., with a relentless media campaign over a tempest in a teapot.[7]

A "Media Supernova"

Black's Hollinger Inc. controls about 650 daily and weekly newspapers on four continents, with a combined circulation exceeding ten million. He owns London's *Daily Telegraph*, Israel's *Jerusalem Post*, and *The Chicago Tribune*. In Canada, he also owns 20 percent of *The Financial Post*, as well as *Saturday Night* magazine and a chain of newspapers, including *Le Soleil* and *Le Droit*. In 1992 he added a controlling interest (19 percent, increased to 41 percent in 1996) in Southam Inc., Canada's largest-circulation newspaper chain. Southam owns 20 dailies stretching from *The Gazette* in Montréal to the Vancouver *Sun* and *Province*. Black has since noted that his three-year partnership with the like-minded Desmarais meant that the two had obtained a controlling interest at a bargain. "We had bought half a loaf for the price of a quarter of a loaf," Black said.[8] According to *The Globe and Mail*, "Newspaper publisher Southam Inc. initiated major staff cuts shortly after Hollinger Inc., known for cutting jobs and boosting profits aggressively at newspapers it acquires, became one of its largest shareholders in 1992."[9]

Southam and Black also retain about a 12.5 percent share of Coles Bookstores, which merged with SmithBooks in September, 1994, to form Chapters Inc., a megachain of 430 bookstores with about 35 percent of the national book market.[10] Such concentration is not without its effects. Jacquie NcNish of the *Report on Business* notes that "Chapters now employs one team of only nine buyers for about 400 stores. That leaves publishers with no national alternative if Chapters shows little or no interest in a book."[11] In April 1996, employees of Chapters' warehouse and distribution centre in Toronto's west end walked out over the company's attempt to roll back their wages by eight percent, lay off between six and eight of 48 employees, and establish a joint committee of employees and management "to resolve disputes in lieu of the right to file a grievance or arbitrate."[12]

In February 1996 Chapters implemented placement fees for the prominent display of titles in prime locations throughout their stores. As explained in "Cooperative Advertising Opportunities," a document mailed to publishers, they will now pay from $1,500 to $3,500 per title for front-of-store, cash desk and end unit displays. These charges are effective for all Coles and Smithbook stores. For small publishers and the authors they represent, this could mean that no matter how good a book is, if the placement fees are not paid it will be relegated to the back shelves.[13]

In the summer of 1995 when publishing giant Thomson Newspaper Corp. was looking to sell off some of its small dailies, Black and Hollinger Inc. stepped in, gobbling up 34 of Ken Thomson's newspapers: 19 in Canada and 15 in the U.S.[14] As mentioned, just before year's end in 1995, Black acquired the Regina *Leader-Post* and the Saskatoon *StarPhoenix* from the Sifton family, giving him ownership of all five dailies in that province. Then, in April 1996, Black purchased a further six eastern Canadian dailies from Thomson. The next month he bought six more Ontario dailies. Then he devoured the remainder of the Southam chain. The Thomson chain was the largest in Canada in terms of the number of newspapers owned, but with this purchase Conrad Black quietly donned the mantle of Canada's premier newspaper baron. In its story on the summer of '95 purchases by Hollinger, the Canadian Press (CP) wire service in Toronto (which is carried by newspapers across the country), quoted Peter Desbarats, respected dean of the graduate school of journalism at the University of Western Ontario. Desbarats told CP that the sale brings a new player to a Canadian market that had been dominated by Thomson and Southam. "It diversifies ownership," Desbarats said.[15] It is not clear how this transfer from one media baron to another creates any diversity.

Pressed on the matter subsequently in personal correspondence, Desbarats admitted that he may have been too hasty. "The quote...was accurate," Desbarats said. "My initial reaction was that this did diversify to some extent a heavily concentrated industry. However, it was an extemporaneous comment made without much time to think about it, and I haven't given a lot of thought to it since." He said that he is more concerned with "the viability of newspapers over the long term," and the "other forms of media which are emerging to replace them."

This transfer from one media baron to another limits rather than increases diversity, since the dominant media player, the Black-Desmarais-Southam group, has added outlets at the expense of its smaller competitor. It also illustrates the convergence of media industries which reflects the direction of future information providers. After all, Thomson is moving further into such areas as financial services, distance education and electronic publishing. In the meantime, the quote from professor Desbarats provided nodding approval of the takeover for readers of the Canadian Press across the country.

When Black took over Southam in May 1996, Desbarats wrote an op-ed column in the *Globe*, referring to Black as "a media supernova." Although the takeovers represented a "nightmare scenario" from the perspective of the Kent Commission which Desbarats worked on in 1981, he said the times have changed.

> In the light of the 1981 royal commission report, Mr. Black's new control of Southam should be seen as a national disaster with ominous consequences for freedom of the press, political discourse and the very cohesiveness of the country. But this isn't 1981, or even 1984, and many things have changed in the intervening years.[16]

What has changed, according to Desbarats, is that "circulations have stagnated or declined, costs have increased and profits have deteriorated," which is the reason why Thomson Corp. is shifting its emphasis elsewhere. He then went on to portray Black in a very positive light:

> No one understands this better than Conrad Black, one of the few modern newspaper proprietors who enjoy dealing in ideas as well as newspaper shares. He has always been a writer as well as an entrepreneur, and he approaches the newspaper business with zest.

Desbarats then provided the ultimate rationalization for Conrad Black's motives and methods, helping Black to design the employee-free newspaper:

> If you were starting a daily newspaper from scratch in 1996, it wouldn't make sense to construct it on the old model. A nucleus of senior editors and designers would be the only permanent staff required. *Almost everything else could be done on freelance contract, often at the end of a modem.* Conrad Black may be working his way toward this type of structure (emphasis added).

There you have it: the newspaper equivalent of a garment workers, with non-unionized freelance home workers gratefully accepting piecework. One of the tragedies here is that this is not just Black's model, but one which is being promoted publicly by academics and in academia where those very piecework journalists will be trained. To give Desbarats his due, he expressed some discomfort over this model. "For older journalists like me, this is a difficult media world to imagine...

Emotionally, many of us can't really accept this," he wrote. But our hands are tied because the picture is "more complex" and the "answers are more elusive" than they were in the days of the Kent Commission, he concluded. Desbarats' lament aside, the picture really is no more complex now than before, and the answers remain transparent. As we will see in the concluding chapter, it is a matter of whether we are content with merely throwing up our hands and allowing the Conrad Blacks to determine our future, or whether we wish to take action ourselves, in our own collective interest.

When it came to reporting on Hollinger's purchase of the Saskatchewan dailies, the news media were subdued. The attitude seemed to be that since the Irving family owned all four English-language dailies in New Brunswick, there was nothing wrong with Black taking over Saskatchewan. Then, when Hollinger added monopolies in two more provinces to his stable in April 1996, the fact was noted in the business pages and brushed off. The *Report on Business* interviewed Tom Kent, chairman of the Royal Commission on Newspapers in 1981.

> Moreover, the deal may make no real difference from the readers' point of view, said Kent..."The Thomson papers are sufficiently thinly staffed to begin with that I doubt whether even Conrad Black can make them much thinner, so I don't think I can honestly say that there's any inevitable decline in quality in the way that there had been with some takeovers."[17]

But recent examples indicate otherwise. The Cambridge (Ontario) *Reporter*, with a circulation of about 10,000, was purchased by Hollinger from Thomson in fall, 1995. One reporter with that paper called in to CBC Ontario's *Radio Noon* phone-in program in May 1996 to describe the changes under Hollinger. She spent six years as an editor under Thomson, but was demoted to reporter with the Hollinger cutbacks, which amounted to 30 percent of the staff. Under Thomson, reporters were expected to write 40 stories each, per month. Under Hollinger, this has doubled, "plus editorials and taking pictures and writing opinion columns," she said. As for local news content, she said "They have people there who are doing nothing but rewriting press releases and [they are] tossing these off as local news."[18]

The lesson here is that we must never underestimate Black's ability to go where no man has gone before when it comes to "demanning" in the interest of profits. This case study illustrates the answer to the question posed by pundits who wonder how it is that Black can actually buy Thomson papers and make more money with them. Thomson is notoriously stingy, while Black is ruthless. The irony is that the pundits then go on to heap accolades on Black because of his evident "commitment" to journalism, as evidenced by his willingness to buy papers that even Ken Thomson is shedding.

In its story on Black's purchase of a dozen papers from Thomson, the *Globe* went on to say that some observers thought there should be a public inquiry, while others dismissed the idea. The article then went on to the question of Conrad Black.

> For his part, Black mocks the idea that he is gaining too much power in the newspaper business. "Yeah, that's right, of course, and Corner Brook [Nfld.] and Bathurst [N.B.] and New Glasgow [N.S.] are of course the way to do that. I mean, that's what I'm doing, sure."[19]

End of discussion. All of the newspapers in three provinces locked up, 40 nationwide, and through Southam, a total of 60 out of 104 newspapers. No cause for alarm? The *Globe* reporters should have had a closer look at Black's autobiography, as we will see. As for *The Toronto Star*, it commented (again, in the business section) that "Conrad Black is fast becoming the dominant player in a rapidly changing industry."[20] At what point will he finally *arrive* in a dominant position? In addition, the *Star*'s story included a colour graphic of a map of Canada, with ownership by newspaper chain. Small black "H"'s (nice touch!) covered the map, representing the geographic location of dailies owned by Black's Hollinger Inc. But the accompanying pie chart showed Black with just 14 percent of national circulation, which would lead one to conclude that any concerns are unwarranted. Most readers would be unaware that Black and Paul Desmarais share a controlling interest in Southam Inc. The *Star* buried this information on the turnover page, in the twenty-fifth paragraph of the story. Hence, a more accurate depiction would combine Black's 14 percent (17 percent by my calculations) with Southam's 26 percent and Power Corp.'s six percent, for a total of 49 percent of national circulation, and 64 of 105, or 61 percent of the newspaper titles. Is this an acceptable amount for one conglomerate to control?

The journalists who are union leaders *are* concerned, because they are aware of these facts. Gail Lem of the Southern Ontario Newspaper Guild said the Hollinger takeovers were "a frightening and dangerous development." She said that "Canadians should be put on alert that one man, Conrad Black, is making a relentless bid to control the press in Canada." These comments were reported in *The Globe*, where Gail Lem is a reporter, and were followed immediately by Black's denial. "Black said the union's statements were 'a complete load of rubbish,' and argued that many of his deals had increased the diversity of newspaper ownership in Canada," the paper reported.[21] Just how, neither Black nor *The Globe* explained. Not content with this, Black wrote a letter to the editor in which he bashed the unions and recommended therapy for the unemployed journalists.

> It is even more galling to endure the alarmist claims of spokesmen [sic] for organized labour who by their feather-bedding greed and irresponsibility have done more than any other group or interest to imperil the newspaper industry...Those who practice or profess print journalism should seek whatever therapy is necessary to overcome the trauma of past abrasions and learn to distinguish the friends of the craft from its enemies."[22]

With friends like Black, who needs enemies?

The Far (Right) Side

When Black was looking around in search of a publisher for his autobiography, his gaze ultimately, effectively, came to rest upon himself. *Conrad Black: A Life in Progress*, was published in the fall of 1993 by Key Porter Books, which is partially, indirectly, owned by Black, through his investment in Key Publishers Co. Ltd. Tremendous media fanfare helped to hype the book onto the best-seller lists, including exclusive excerpts in the *Report on Business Magazine*, for which Black was once a columnist, *Saturday Night*, which is owned by Black, and *The Globe and Mail*. In subsequent reviews the ROB called it "the most interesting and entertaining business book of the season," while *The Globe* found it "hard to put down," and "perversely enjoyable."

If these characterizations are accurate, then what business finds entertaining truly is perverse. Black's right-wing views are so extreme that former British Prime Minister Margaret Thatcher once remarked that she found herself on his left, politically. In a world inhabited by Mike Harris, Ralph Klein and Newt Gingrich, Black has managed to blend the right wing with the Neanderthal. For example, his autobiography recounts how, when he was buying up dailies to form the Sterling newspaper chain in the early seventies, he had to visit a lot of small towns such as Prince Rupert, B.C. "At Prince Rupert," he blithely states, "the highlight of our visit was a fistfight between two native (Indian) ladies in front of a liquor store."[23]

In 1987, a controversy erupted between Conrad Black and Linda McQuaig, the journalist and author, most recently of the best selling *Shooting The Hippo: Death By Deficit and Other Canadian Myths*.[24] In a column in the Toronto *Sun* in 1987, Black wrote that she was a "weedy...not very bright, left-wing reporter," over her reporting on a bribery scandal involving the government of David Peterson and developer Elvio Del Zotto. He went on to label investigative journalists in general as "swarming, grunting jackals."[25] In his 1993 autobiography Black puffed that McQuaig "would have had trouble successfully suing me [for libel] even if I had written that she was a vampire bat specializing in child molestation."[26] But in an interview with Peter Gzowski, promoting his book on *Morningside*, Black surpassed himself, saying "I thought McQuaig should have been horsewhipped, but I don't do those things myself and the statutes don't provide for it."

In *A Life in Progress*, Black explained how he was kicked out of Upper Canada College, not just for cheating, but for copying exams and selling them to his classmates. I guess that is his definition of entrepreneurial spirit. He excused his actions on the basis that the teachers at Upper Canada College were gay men whom he said derived great sadistic, indeed sexual pleasure from physically beating the boys. There "were a few teachers who were quite sadistic. One or more were rather active fondling homosexuals."[27] They were "sadists...aggressively fondling homosexuals...numerous swaggering boobies who had obviously failed in the real world...[who] all gradually produced in me a profound revulsion." According to Black, he was merely striking back at a brutal system. As he walked in disgrace from the school property, Black recounts how "Mrs. [Cedric] Sowby," the wife of the headmaster of the college, "with all of her facial hair," said to him, "you realize your life is over."[28] Hence, the title of his book: *A Life in Progress*. As had his hero, William Randolph Hearst, Black would prevail.

"Demanning" and Journalistic Autonomy

Black somewhat immodestly described how he parleyed a $500 investment in two tiny Québec weeklies into the Hollinger empire. His account of himself glosses over the $7 million inheritance left to him by his wealthy parents. Building media empires isn't easy. Black tells how, at his first daily, the Sherbrooke *Record*, he "instituted frugalities that vastly transcended anything I have seen unearthed in the [Ken] Thomson organization or elsewhere." He describes the approach taken by himself and his two partners, Peter White and David Radler. "David kept a copy of William Taylor's famous early-19th-century manual on industrial relations and regularly recited the opening sentence, which asserted that any such study must start from the premise that all employees are slothful, incompetent, and dishonest."[29]

Black described one scheme he struck upon for hiring penitentiary convicts as a means of "reducing salaries with an impeccable cover of good intentions." Another highly offensive part is where he bragged, "I eventually devised what I described as the elastic compensation system for the reporters and debated with them at the end of each week what they "deserved" on the basis of the volume and quality of their journalistic production. It was an outrageous system, of course."[30] Black described how he monitored his newspaper employees at the Sherbrooke *Record*:

> When one reporter marched into David [Radler's] office to present a petition of grievances, David fined him two cents, deducted from his weekly pay cheque for wasting a sheet of paper. When, on the night of NDP leader Allan Blakeney's first victory in Saskatchewan in 1971, the same reporter raised the two-finger V-for victory sign to David, he too raised up two victorious fingers and said, "That just cost you two," and deducted $2 from his next pay cheque, "for provoking the owners."[31]

Black confided that "many" of the journalists who have worked for him "had neurotic and familial problems that David [Radler] and I were always happy to help with if asked." Of Radler, Black has written that he ran their newspapers "with a fanatical determination that regularly produced [profit] margins more than twice those achieved by Southam in its comfortable metropolitan monopoly markets."[32] Radler told the Kent Commission on newspaper ownership that the greatest contribution by himself and Conrad Black to Canadian journalism was "the three-man newsroom and two of them sell ads."[33] Probably not an inaccurate depiction of their emphasis.

More recently, following the Southam Inc. annual board meeting in April of 1995, Black said he liked the company's improved performance,

having doubled its profit to $44 million in 1994, but he added that it
could have happened faster. Black, as quoted in the *Report on Business*,
said "Southam could be still more efficient." For instance, the total
number of more than 10,000 employees will gradually drop, "but I don't
anticipate anything Draconian," he said.[34] Earlier, he had written in his
autobiography that at his first Southam board meeting in February of
1993, "I proposed a further $80 million allocation for demanning to
remove 1,000 superfluous employees." He went on to write that
"Southam's newspaper division employed 7,500 people, clearly a third
of whom shouldn't have been there."[35]

And Black has been as good as his word. The 1995 Southam annual
report indicates that in 1992 the newspaper division had 7,787 full-time
employees. By the end of 1995 that figure had been reduced by 18
percent. A further reduction of 750 employees between 1996 and 1998
will total 27 percent, very near to the third which Black predicted in
1993.

By the time of Black's remarks in April, 1995, the number of
Southam employees — encompassing its magazine and business
communication interests in addition to newspapers — was fewer than
8,000 compared with twice that number in 1988.

Figure 4

Southam Revenues, Profits, Employees

Year	Revenues	Profits	# of Employees
1988	$1.7B	$ 73M	16,000
1992	$1.2B	-$ 263M	11,500
1993	$1.0B	$ 22M	10,800
1994	$1.2B	$ 44M	8,000

Source: The *Report on Business Magazine*, 1989-1995.

All of this is in keeping with Black's methods over the years,
stretching from the early days with the Sterling chain, to his acquisitions
of UniMedia in Québec, American Publishing in the U.S., the London
Telegraph, *The Jerusalem Post*, the Fairfax chain in Australia, much of

the Thomson chain, and now Southam Inc. When he purchased the UniMedia chain in the late 1980s from Jacques Francoeur, it included *Le Droit*, the French-language Ottawa daily founded by the Oblates to combat Bill 17, which banned French-language instruction in Ontario during World War I. Said Black, "The Oblates had conceded the softest and richest contracts to production workers I have seen in the newspaper industry (not excluding Fleet Street and New York City) and Francoeur had not made any progress in the fourteen years of his ownership." In early 1988, journalists at *Le Droit* struck. Black termed this "a serious tactical error, as we produced the newspaper without them and achieved the settlement we sought. Journalists at a Franco-Ontarian newspaper that had lost money for forty years were not the most intimidating work force to deal with." Within a couple of years under his ownership, according to Black, "extensive demanning was achieved and generously paid for [in severances]."[36]

In the fall of 1992 a protracted strike over journalistic autonomy and the hiring of freelance reporters hit *Le Soleil* in Québec City. According to Black, "progress in demanning at *Le Soleil* was slow, as Québec journalistic and production unions had to be approached with caution and at a statelier pace than in Britain and other jurisdictions where we were active."[37] Doug Smith, media critic for *Canadian Dimension* magazine, wrote in 1992 that "after purchasing *The Jerusalem Post*, in 1989, Black forced that paper's most senior and respected staff members to quit, provoked the rest into striking, and eventually reduced the work force by 190." According to Black's own account, "obviously, we thought, economies could be effected, no matter how difficult Israel's labour laws were." He saw a confrontation with the managing editor at *The Post* as "an opportunity for relatively inexpensive demanning so we peremptorily rejected [their] demands] and happily received the uncompensated resignations of fifteen journalists."[38] According to Radler's account, "I never fired anyone. No one was fired. Thirty-two resigned. Now, it was convenient for me, because there were 32 too many people, if not more, in the editorial department at that time."[39]

Of course, when people won't quit of their own accord, they have to be fired. Take for example the situation at the Saskatchewan dailies Black negotiated to buy late in 1995. Two days after the purchase closed, in March 1996, his ownership took its toll when, in one fell swoop, 182 jobs were eliminated at the new dailies. At the *Leader-Post*, 25 percent of the staff was fired: 89 of 350 employees. According to one fired reporter, Bill Doskoch, "it was an awesome display of capitalism at its ugliest."

They told us Friday of a big meeting Saturday. When we showed up, we were all shuttled into four different rooms. One problem was some people were sent to the wrong rooms. Two of my newsroom colleagues were among those who ended up going out of the Death Room....I was actually pretty calm as they told us that we were losing our jobs and would not be returning to the *Leader-Post* ever (there's security guards there now to keep us out). But people who were more in denial about the risk of big layoffs under Hollinger's ownership took it that much harder...My colleagues going to work this morning are doing so knowing full well that if Hollinger doesn't think it's making enough money in six months (or whenever), more people will be thrown in the street.[40]

At its sister newspaper, the Saskatoon *StarPhoenix*, similar events happened. Wilfred Popoff, a former managing editor who was fired after thirty years of serving three generations of the Sifton family, said, "I was fired not because of anything I did or didn't do, but because of the need to cut costs in the quest for fantastic profits." On the way in which employees were told, Popoff said it was militaristic, a characterization which would no doubt please Conrad Black, who is enamoured with the military. "The arrangement was reminiscent of military occupations portrayed in countless movies: The vanquished are summoned to the market square where officers of the occupying army register all people and direct them to various camps." On being locked out of the company, Popoff said, "I felt like a criminal. In my time I had managed large portions of this company, had represented it the world over and, until the previous day, had authority to spend its money. Now I couldn't be trusted not to snitch a pencil or note pad."[41] Popoff later told *The Toronto Star* that the mass firing was "a tragedy of major proportions." He said, "you can't take 24 bodies out of a newsroom of 63 and not affect quality."[42] According to Black, in a letter to the editor of *The Globe and Mail*,

The Saskatchewan newspapers that we bought from the Sifton family a few months ago employed half the work force of the London Daily and Sunday *Telegraphs* to produce six-day newspapers of 12 percent of our London

circulation and a fraction of the *Telegraph's* quality by any
measurement.[43]

The population of Saskatchewan being what it is, the two dailies in
question had a much smaller circulation than their London counterpart.
However, to put things in a different perspective, with half the workforce
of the *Telegraph*, the *Leader-Post* and *StarPhoenix* produced not just
one, but two separate dailies in two cities. With no Sunday edition, they
turned out 12 issues a week to the *Telegraph's* seven.

The massive layoffs in Saskatchewan are of course in keeping with
Black's views on what he calls demanning. But the extremity of his
position surfaced during an earlier incident in 1989 at the London
Telegraph, when management put out two editions of the paper during a
36 hour strike by editorial personnel. Black wrote in his autobiography
that the two days' newspapers produced by management exposed what
he called "one of the greatest myths of the industry: that journalists are
essential to producing a newspaper."[44] But then Black has never held
journalists in high regard. In the late 1970s he wrote:

> My experience with journalists authorizes me to record
> that a very large number of them are ignorant, lazy,
> opinionated, intellectually dishonest, and inadequately
> supervised. The "profession" is heavily cluttered with
> abrasive youngsters who substitute "commitment" for
> insight, and, to a lesser extent, with aged hacks toiling
> through a miasma of mounting decrepitude. Alcoholism is
> endemic in both groups.[45]

Whatever journalists' problems *might* be, Black, Radler *et al.* are
adding massive doses of unemployment. When Hollinger bought out
Power Corp.'s shares of Southam in May 1996, Hollinger President
David Radler indicated that Desmarais, Southam management and
independent directors were holding up some of the further staff cuts he
and Black wanted to make. There was just a "difference as to timing and
the swiftness of action," Radler said. Hollinger indicated in a news
release that it was "confident that further cost-cutting can still occur [at
Southam] and that significant enhancements to revenue will be
achieved."[46] One of the other measures which Black is reported to be
imposing at Southam is drastic cutbacks to — or the elimination
altogether of — the Canadian Press wire service, to which Southam
contributes $8 million annually. Black and Radler have denied the

rumours, indicating that they are committed to CP, but say it must be cut back by more than the 36 percent proposed by Southam management. "We want to promote reforms at Canadian Press to ensure its survival," Black told shareholders at Hollinger International's annual meeting in Chicago in May. CP is the national cooperative news agency with 88 member papers. In the past decade it has trimmed its editorial staff to about 260 journalists, from 400. It is not clear how local editorial autonomy can be retained if the owner pulls the plug on, or even drastically pares down the national news agency.

Black's paring continued with the "independent" members of the board of directors at Southam, most of whom were invited to resign following Hollinger's takeover in May. The independents were not openly aligned with either Power or Hollinger, and included corporate heavy-hitters such as Adam Zimmerman, former chair of Noranda Inc., and Tom Kierans, president and CEO of the C.D. Howe Institute. According to news reports, Black and Radler became increasingly frustrated with holdups to cutbacks. The final straw came when the independent directors spearheaded the rejection of a compromise proposal which would have given Black 10 of the 20 Southam dailies, including the *Montréal Gazette* and the *Windsor Star*, in return for his 19 percent stake in the company. Half of the dailies, in return for less than one-fifth of its shares. When this deal fell apart in May, an "increasingly irate" Black arranged instead to buy out Desmarais and take over Southam.[47]

In the U.S., through American Publishing which is a subsidiary of Hollinger Inc. (both were folded into Hollinger International Inc. in 1995), Radler and Black have acquired nearly 300 small-circulation dailies, weeklies and shopping guides in 29 states. According to journalist Jennifer Wells, "day to day, the papers of American Publishing are run by 18 district managers."[48] These are the people about whom Black has said,

> [T]hese smaller [newspaper] units could be successfully managed by recourse to careful and constant electronic monitoring of pay roll, advertising, and circulation, which had not been possible until recently, and by maintaining a flying squadron of fixer-counsellors, [travelling] around between the centres on our airplane, encouraging, advising, imposing controls or conducting surgery, like frontier marshals.[49]

In a refreshingly candid interview David Radler, president of Hollinger Inc., initially laid to rest the myth of editorial autonomy at chain-owned newspapers. In 1992, Radler told Peter C. Newman of *Maclean's* magazine that "I am ultimately the publisher of all these papers, and if editors disagree with us, they should disagree with us when they're no longer in our employ."[50] By 1995, with Hollinger's purchase of 19 Canadian newspapers from Thomson, Radler was singing the same refrain of supposed editorial autonomy that we hear from other newspaper chain owners.

In 1992, Radler told Peter C. Newman how he went about finding newspaper bargains.

> I visit the office of each prospective property at night and count the desks. That tells me how many people work there. If the place has, say, 42 desks, I know I can put that paper out with 30 people, and that means a dozen people will be leaving the payroll even though I haven't seen their faces yet.[51]

Just like the faceless employees in Saskatchewan. In 1994, Radler's advance man for their American newspaper purchases, Arthur Weeks, told journalist Jennifer Wells that

> Radler would turn to Weeks, as he did at the time of their first U.S. purchase, of the *Wapakoneta Daily News* in Ohio, and say, "Arthur, count the chairs." Radler distrusted vendor body counts, wary as he was of part-time workers, corporate America's zebra mussels — subsurface and astonishingly plentiful.[52]

By 1995, Radler told the *Report on Business* the following:

> Radler said Hollinger intends to continue to maintain salaries and benefits at the current level for employees at the newspapers, *and he doesn't expect there to be layoffs.* "It's a local publisher's decision on how many people work at the place, and it may surprise you *there may actually be some additions*," he said (emphasis added).[53]

Radler, whom Black affectionately calls "the refrigerator" because of his coldness, neglected to explain why, if hiring was "a local publisher's decision," he flies around the continent counting desks and dismissing people, sight unseen. Indeed, after the Saskatchewan firings, former publisher Michael Sifton maintained that it was not Hollinger's doing and that the cutbacks had been planned all along. One fired reporter said that it was untrue. "When the sale was announced, [Sifton] told people that selling to Hollinger would provide 'career opportunities' for the staff. There was never any mention of 'restructuring.'"

At the 1995 Southam annual meeting, the board backed Black and Paul Desmarais, and voted 88 percent in favour of ending a "poison pill" scheme, prompting the two largest shareholders to consider increasing their share of ownership.[54] The shareholders rights plan was set up in 1990 to make a hostile takeover bid difficult. Ironically, one of the persons whom the plan was designed to keep at bay was none other than Conrad Black, who has revealed that he bought *Saturday Night* magazine in 1987 "partly to quiet the Canlit set in the event that we assaulted the unholy and uneasy [poison pill] alliance between Southam and Torstar."[55] Parenthetically, Black planned the purchase of *Saturday Night* as early as the summer of 1973, when he wrote to U.S. conservative William F. Buckley, indicating his intentions, and asking advice. Black wrote: "we would like some advice from you as we [at *Saturday Night*] will at least partially emulate your example at *The National Review*."[56]

Political Connections and Ambitions

Black is close to Brian Mulroney, whom he has known for thirty years. When Mordecai Richler wrote an unflattering farewell to Mulroney for *Saturday Night* magazine, Mulroney called Black to see if the article could be changed. According to Black,

> I didn't think there was anything wrong with saying I would read it and call him back and I did read it and called him back and I said "You won't like it but I'm not changing it." I wouldn't ask for it to be changed. It couldn't be changed anyway. If I tried to change it, Mordecai would take it elsewhere and probably make it a good deal more antagonistic. And anyway, I wouldn't do that. But I did [call] because Mulroney's an old friend of mine.[57]

What this indicates is that if someone less famous than Mordecai Richler had written the article, it would have been stillborn. For his part, Richler subsequently wrote that the incident was a disturbing one, given that Mulroney was eventually appointed to the board of the Freedom Forum, an American foundation which is supposedly dedicated to promoting freedom of the press, and which is wholly supported and run by the Gannett newspaper chain in the U.S.

> I for one am proud that Mulroney is now going to swing his big bat in defense of ink-stained wretches. The truth is this represents a genuine change of heart, for in 1993, busy as he was running our country, Mulroney still found time to make editorial suggestions to [*Saturday Night*] magazine. When he heard that I was to write an appreciation of his years in office...he phoned Peter White, his former principal secretary and a director of Hollinger Inc., primary owner of *Saturday Night*, to ask if they couldn't get somebody more objective to celebrate his contribution to Canada. Say, Mila. I recently phoned White and asked, "Did Mulroney actually try to stop publication of my piece?" "No," White said, "but he did object to certain phrases." "Are you telling me that you showed him an advance copy of my article?" "It's so long ago, um, I don't remember all the details. However, no editorial changes were made in your article."[58]

Indeed, Black himself came storming to the rescue of his friend Mulroney when Stevie Cameron's book, *On The Take* topped the best-seller lists in the fall and winter of 1994-95. Cameron's book meticulously documented the patronage, corruption and even the crime of the Mulroney years.[59] Writing in *Saturday Night* magazine, Black dismissed the book as a "sophomoric smear-job." He said the book's revelations were insignificant, and that Mulroney's problems were merely due to poor public relations, which in turn were due to his "misplaced sanctimoniousness." Black wrote that possessing the courage of his convictions would have been sufficient to overcome Mulroney's problems, but instead he "didn't have the self-confidence to acknowledge that part of government is taking care of one's friends."[60] For Black, the arrogance of former Québec premier Maurice Duplessis (about whom he has written a biography) was both preferable and more effective.

Black and Mulroney share a very close friend and advisor in Peter White, whom Mulroney also called to complain about Mordecai Richler's article. As Graham Fraser of *The Globe and Mail* has noted, since the 1960s "White's career has been entwined with those of both Mulroney and Toronto financier Conrad Black." With Black, White purchased the *Sherbrooke Daily Record* in 1969, soon adding the Sterling newspaper chain. By 1973, Sterling was worth $20 million, and was 42 percent owned by Black and 25 percent by White. In 1986, they sold Sterling into Hollinger for $37 million.

White worked tirelessly for Mulroney in his PC leadership bids in 1976 and 1983, by, among other things, running Mulroney's campaign newspapers. Black notes in his book that "as the [1983] campaign progressed, our companies supported Brian not only with large donations, but also in picking up Peter White's bills as he travelled and worked with the candidate."[61] After Mulroney took over the opposition leader's office, White joined his staff, and was made appointments chief in the prime minister's office (PMO), replacing Liberals with Conservatives. After resigning from the PMO in 1986, White headed the Dominion Stores chain for Black. In that year, Black withdrew a $38 million surplus from a pension fund for unionized employees of Dominion Stores, prompting Ontario NDP leader Bob Rae to describe Black as "bloated capitalism at its worst." The Ontario Supreme Court eventually ordered Hollinger to return the money to the fund with interest. In 1990 Black repaid $44 million. In his memoirs Black brags regarding Dominion that "I recommended that a scythe be taken through the ranks of the low-lives at the warehouse, and it was."[62]

When Black purchased *Saturday Night* magazine in 1987, he installed White, then vice chairman of Hollinger Inc., as publisher. But, by July of the next year White was back in the PMO, this time as Mulroney's principal secretary. (Much later when Allan Gotlieb, whom Brian Mulroney appointed Ambassador to Washington, returned to Canada, Black appointed Gotlieb publisher of *Saturday Night*).

Although Black supported Claude Wagner in the 1976 PC leadership race, after Joe Clark's victory Black appointed Brian Mulroney to the boards of several of his holdings, including Standard Broadcasting and Hollinger North Shore Exploration Ltd.

Black gained notoriety over his 1978 purchase of Argus Corp., the holding company founded by E.P. Taylor. Ironically, Paul Desmarais failed in a bid to take over Argus, just two years before. Black sold Massey Ferguson and Dominion Stores, former Argus holdings, in the 1980s.

The board of directors for his firm, Hollinger International, includes Peter Bronfman, Peter Munk, and conservative international advisors such as: Henry Kissinger, Zbigniew Brzezinski, William F. Buckley Jr., and George Will.

The attitudes and actions related to newspapers and journalism on the part of Black and Radler recounted above, do not bode well for the future of Canadian journalism. But perhaps what is most disturbing about "the Establishment Man," as Peter C. Newman labelled Black in the book by the same name, is his all-consuming quest, not only for property, newspapers, and profits, but for political power. In the words of Laurier LaPierre, his former teacher at Upper Canada College,

> I don't think Conrad wants to be prime minister, but he really *does* want to be the power behind the throne and feels his money will buy him that. I don't think he will handle very well being thwarted or being denied that kind of role, and I don't think he will use his authority wisely. He is one of the few people I know for whom attaining power is an all-consuming goal. What Lord Acton meant in his famous epigram is that absolute power corrupts absolutely because there is no room for love. Once Conrad has finished consolidating his economic environment, he will attempt to create a significant political environment for himself. In the James Bond and John le Carre stories, there is always some weird genius who has a nuclear bomb and is threatening to use it to sanctify mankind. Conrad is like that: he will apply his economic clout politically to repress what he considers the moral wrongs of the world.[63]

Perhaps Black unintentionally endorses this assessment in his autobiography. Respecting his takeover of Southam Inc., he states: "Our corporate destiny is now disclosed, if not manifest...Newspapers, especially quality newspapers, remain powerful outlets for advertising and information (and Political influence)."[64]

Despite his recent denials, Black is buying newspapers for political influence in addition to profit. "Black not only has these dailies, but he has strong political views. There is some feeling he will use his views to influence content, as he is said to have done with *Saturday Night* magazine," says Jim Fleming, a former cabinet minister in the Trudeau government of the early eighties. Fleming, who was the minister responsible for newspapers, followed the Kent Report with his own hearings, and drafted legislation in 1983 which watered-down Kent's mild proposals. However Fleming's *Canada Newspaper Act* did limit chains and would have prevented Conrad Black's takeover of Southam Inc. Subsequently Fleming, a former *Toronto Star* reporter and broadcast journalist, was removed from the cabinet and the legislation never saw the light of day. Was he yanked over the Newspaper Act? Fleming, who now runs his own public affairs consultancy, remains uncertain to this day.

"I have no idea. *I know that Southam put pressure on some senior cabinet ministers from Montréal.* I just don't know" (emphasis added). Fleming said in an interview that, at the time, "I was warned by some senior bureaucrats that I was taking on something very dangerous," because of the political power and influence of the newspaper chain owners. He put together a preliminary package on how to proceed with the Kent Report's recommendations, including some ideas for legislation, and "somebody released it to [former Conservative MP, now CBC President] Perrin Beatty." The news media got hold of this and had a field day, which, from the start, "made it very difficult to proceed with the legislation." Kent's recommendations went "too far from the practical reality," said Fleming, whereas he "tried to do something which was workable."[65] So, here is evidence of successful political pressure exerted by media owners.

Fleming eventually resigned and went to work for the Toronto *Sun* as a columnist in the mid-80s, when it was edited by his former school chum Barbara Amiel, now Hollinger board member and VP in charge of editorial for her husband's newspaper empire. Amiel, whom he described as "extremely right wing," cut him back from three to two columns per week and cut the salary he negotiated with publisher Donald Creighton.

As we will discuss in the concluding chapter, it is this very political influence on the part of media owners Black, Desmarais, Ted Rogers, Ken Thomson and Québecor's Pierre Péladeau, which makes the likelihood of broader public political action remote under the current system.

***

Endnotes

[1] Quoted in Richard Siklos, Shades of Black: Conrad Black, Reed Books, Toronto, 1995.

[2] Quoted in Mitch Diamantopoulos, "Blackout: Conrad Black buys all five Saskatchewan Dailies," *The Prairie Dog*, monthly, Regina, Saskatchewan, February 1996, p. 3.

[3] Taken from the transcript of an interview with Michelle Pisani, Lanie Hurdle and Brad Milburn, April 1996.

[4] Quoted in John Saunders and Casey Mahood, "New layout, same story," *The Globe and Mail*, May 4, 1996, p. B5.

[5] David Roberts, "Takeover cited for 'weaker' newspaper," *The Globe and Mail*, May 28, 1996, p. A5.

[6] For a description of the media's role in the early years, see the chapter on the "Socialist Hordes" in James Winter, *Common Cents: Media Portrayal of the Gulf War and Other Events* (Montréal: Black Rose, 1992).

[7] See Terry Glavin, "Mugged by the Media: How journalists and their bosses brought down Mike Harcourt," *The Canadian Forum*, January/February 1996.

[8] Conrad Black, *A Life in Progress*, (Toronto: Key Porter Books, 1993).

[9] Greg Ip, "Shareholders vs. Job Holders," *The Globe and Mail*, March 23, 1996, p. B4.

[10] See Val Ross, John Heinzl, "Coles, SmithBooks to merge," *The Globe and Mail*, September 8, 1994, p. A1; John Heinzl, Val Ross, "SmithBooks-Coles deal okayed," *The Globe and Mail*, March 22, 1995, p. B1.

[11] Jacquie McNish, "Book Wars," *The Report on Business*, September 9, 1995, B1, B3.

[12] Val Ross, "Teamsters picket Chapters' executives," *The Globe and Mail*, May 6, 1996, p. C1.

[13] John Kennedy, "Chapters sets placement fees," *Quill & Quire*, May 1996. Credit for this example goes to Karen McRorie, in her unpublished paper, "Great Books are Just the Beginning: A Case Study of Chapters Inc.," Communication Studies, University of Windsor, 1995-96.

[14] See Casey Mahood, "Black buys 19 Thomson newspapers," *The Globe and Mail*, July 28, 1995, p. B3; Oliver Bertin, "Thomson sells 12 U.S. dailies," *The Globe and Mail*, August 8, 1995, p. B1; "Conrad Black buying three more Thomson dailies," *The Globe and Mail*, August 29, 1995, p. B3.

[15] Heather Scoffield, "Hollinger buys more papers," *The Windsor Star*, July 28, 1995, p. D7.

[16] Peter Desbarats, "Conrad Black and the newspaper universe," *The Globe and Mail*, May 28, 1996, p. A17.

[17] John Saunders and Casey Mahood, "New layout, same story," *The Globe and Mail*, May 4, 1996, B1.

[18] Quoted from CBC Ontario's *Radio Noon* program, May 31, 1996.

[19] Quoted in John Saunders and Casey Mahood, "New layout," p. B5.

[20] Dana Flavelle, "Fade to Black?" *The Toronto Star*, May 11, 1996, E1.

[21] Casey Mahood, "Thomson to sell 14 papers," *The Globe and Mail*, May 1, 1996, p. B1.

[22] Conrad Black, "Black advises therapy for print journalists," *The Globe and Mail*, May 8, 1996, p. A15.

[23] Conrad Black, "The Apprenticeship of Conrad Black," *The Report on Business Magazine*, October, 1993, p.59.

[24] Linda McQuaig, *Shooting The Hippo: Death by Deficit and Other Canadian Myths*, (Toronto: Viking, 1995).

[25] When these phrases were edited out of his column in *The Financial Post*, which Black partly owned, he resigned from his column in protest. This account is taken from John DeMont, "An Emerging Media Baron," *Maclean's*, July 17, 1989, p. 28. Black continues to own 20 percent of *The Post*, and has the right to first refusal on its sale by Ted Rogers, so he is the likely buyer, giving him a presence in the Toronto market.

[26] Black, "*A Life in Progress*," p. 399.

[27] Quoted in "Telling tales out of school," *Toronto Life*, October, 1994, p. 40.

[28] Ibid, p. 42.

[29] Conrad Black, "The Apprenticeship" p. 55.

[30] Ibid, p. 53.

[31] Ibid, p. 53.

[32] Black, *A Life in Progress*, p. 377.

[33] Quoted in Black, *A Life in Progress*, p. 378.

[34] Quoted in Ann Gibbon, "Southam ends poison pill," *The Globe and Mail*, April 26, 1995, p. B3.

[35] Black, *A Life in Progress*, p. 498.

[36] Ibid, p. 382.

[37] Ibid, p. 383.

[38] Ibid, pp. 393-394.

[39] Quoted in Jennifer Wells, "Paper Chaser," *Report on Business Magazine*, August 1994, p. 28.

[40] Bill Doskoch, personal correspondence, March, 1996.

[41] Wilfred Popoff, "One day you're family; the next day you're fired," *The Globe and Mail*, March 14,

[42] Quoted in Dana Flavelle, "Fade to Black?" *The Toronto Star*, May 11, 1996, p. E8.

[43] Conrad Black, "Black advises therapy"

[44] Black, *A Life in Progress*, p. 405.

[45] Conrad Black, "A view of the press," *Carleton Journalism Review*, Winter, 1979-80.

[46] Allan Robinson, Michael Den Tandt and Andrew Bell, "Conrad Black doubles stake in Southam," *The Globe and Mail*, May 25, 1996, p. A1.

[47] John Saunders, Casey Mahood and Paul Waldie, "Black reigns," *The Globe and Mail*, June 1, 1996, p. B13.

[48] Jennifer Wells, "Paper Chaser," p. 27.

[49] Conrad Black, *A Life in Progress*, p. 377, 378.

[50] Peter Newman, "The inexorable spread of the Black empire," *Maclean's*, February 3, 1992, p. 68.

[51] Quoted in Peter C. Newman, "The inexorable spread of the Black empire," *Maclean's*, February 3, 1992, p. 68.

[52] Jennifer Wells, "Paper Chaser," p. 25.

[53] Casey Mahood, "Black buys 19 Thomson newspapers," *The Globe and Mail*, July 28, 1995, p. B3.

[54] Poison pill schemes are designed to thwart takeovers by "killing" companies which swallow them up.

[55] Black, *A Life in Progress*, p. 487.

[56] Cited in Peter C. Newman, *The Establishment Man* (Toronto: Seal Books, 1982), footnote, p. 183. *The National Review* has been an icon of the arch-conservative right in the U.S. since Buckley founded it in 1955.

[57] From a transcript of a question and answer period following a speech by Conrad Black to the Canadian Association of Journalists, annual convention, Ottawa, April 9, 1994.

[58] Mordecai Richler, "Freedom of...ahh...speech," *Saturday Night*, April, 1994, p. 36.

[59] Stevie Cameron, *On The Take: Crime, Corruption and Greed in the Mulroney Years*, (Toronto: Macfarlane Walter & Ross, 1994).

[60] Conrad Black, "Trivial Pursuit," *Saturday Night*, February 1995, pp.78, 80.

[61] Black, *A Life in Progress*, p. 312.

[62] Ibid, p. 326.

[63] Quoted in Peter C. Newman, *The Establishment Man*, pp. 272-73.

[64] Black, *A Life in Progress*, p. 504.

[65] Interview with James Fleming by the author, June 1, 1996.

Chapter Three

PAUL DESMARAIS AND POWER

Not to hire a guy because he has been a politician is
stupid. We want good people in Ottawa and Québec City.
If we can use their talent after they retire, or have been
defeated, I would be the first one to hire them or offer
them a seat on our boards. To hell with the people who say
we do it for political favours. — Paul Desmarais.

Most Canadians are familiar with corporations such as General
Motors, Bell Canada, and Royal Bank of Canada. But what if I were to
tell you that there is one man who owns 117 Canadian companies, and
that the four largest of these companies combined are, by some important
measures such as annual revenues, larger than any of the above giants?
Would you know who this man is? Do you think it is important to know?
Why is it, do you suppose, that we hear so much about GM, Bell, and the
Royal, and so little about these other companies? And what if I were to
tell you that this man has vast holdings in the news media, and that he
has been intimately connected to Canadian prime ministers and political
leaders over the past thirty years? That he was a mentor to Brian
Mulroney, and that he persuaded Pierre Trudeau to run for the Liberal
leadership in 1968? What would you think then?

The man's name is Paul Desmarais Sr. of Montréal. The four
companies are: Power Corp., Power Financial, Great-West Lifeco, and
Great-West Life Assurance Co. When the sixty-nine-year-old Desmarais
announced in the spring of 1996 that he would be handing over the reins
of these major corporations to sons Paul Jr., 41, and André, 39, stories in
the business sections marked the transition with hardly a ripple. The two
sons, who became co-chief executive officers, have been groomed by the
senior Desmarais for the past several years. And, we learned, that as the
controlling shareholder with 62 percent of Power Corp., the senior
Desmarais "will remain a director and be active with Power."[1] He
reminded Power Corp.'s annual meeting in May 1996, that he "still
controls the shares." What that means, Desmarais said, "is that I'm not
really leaving."[2] It is not like Paul Desmarais to take a back seat.

When Southam Inc., Canada's largest newspaper publisher, issued
its quarterly reports for 1994, they were signed by none other than Paul
Desmarais, who, along with Conrad Black was the new co-chair of the

45

board. His signature must have unnerved Southam employees.[3] In March 1993, Desmarais purchased a substantial, 19-percent interest in Southam News Inc., Canada's largest daily newspaper publisher. Desmarais had been sought out by Southam as a counterweight to Conrad Black. He increased his holdings to 21.4 percent, before, like *The Toronto Star* before him, selling his shares to Conrad Black late in May 1996.[4] The three Power directors, including the senior and junior Desmarais and Power Corp. director Michel Plessis-Belair remained on the Southam board following Black's takeover. The $300 million from that sale left Power Corp. With about $750 million in cash for future acquisitions, which might include the Toronto *Sun* chain. Through his broadcasting arm, Power Broadcasting, Desmarais owns three television and 18 radio stations in Ontario, Québec, and New Brunswick. As we will see, in 1995 he was given permission to enter the direct-to-home (DTH) satellite television broadcasting field through Power DirecTv.

Significant though these media holdings are, they form only a tiny portion of the Desmarais empire. In the *Report on Business* top 1,000 companies for 1994, Power Financial ranked number 21 in the country for profits. Great-West Life Assurance Co., a subsidiary, ranked 25th, Great-West Lifeco, another subsidiary, ranked 31st, and Power Corp was 35th. These are the largest amongst the 117 companies held by Desmarais through the holding firms of Power Corp., and Power Financial. But if one simply takes the four largest companies owned by Desmarais, their combined revenues of $26 billion put them ahead of telephone giant BCE Inc. ($22.4 billion), parent company to Bell Canada and the individual leader among publicly-traded companies, and General Motors of Canada ($25 billion) the leading private firm. BCE Inc. does come out ahead when you include *its* subsidiary, Bell Canada. However, Power Corp. appears to be number two in the country; it controls more than a hundred other firms, and is a family controlled business (Figure 5). With these earnings, the Desmarais family overshadows other huge firms doing business in Canada, including Chrysler Canada, with 1994 revenues of $16 billion, and Royal Bank, with revenues of $13.4 billion.

Bu$ine$$ As Usual

In May 1993, following the Southam Inc. annual shareholders' meeting, new board member Paul Desmarais told reporters that newspapers "have to be run as a business." Describing himself as a champion of "efficiency," he said Southam newspapers "have to...find their right level of profitability." No mention of quality here. And no quarrel, except perhaps over timing, with Conrad Black.

Figure 5

Desmarais Family Holdings

Firm	94 Revenue (Billions)	Assets (Billions)	Employees	Profits (Millions)
Power Finan.	6.8B	30.5B	10	273m
GW Life Ass.	6.1B	34.3B	6,864	230m
GW Life Co.	6.1B	34.3B	6,865	210m
Power Corp.	7.0B	31.5B	9,400	186m
Total	26B	131B	23,139	899m

Source: The *Report on Business Magazine*, "The Top 1,000," July, 1995, p. 94.

An indication of Southam's obsession with profits comes from the company's 1992 annual report, which states, "The focus for all operating heads is to maximize the return from their businesses — absolute total focus on maximizing return." It seems clear that maximizing returns benefits shareholders, rather than readers or employees. As regards the latter, Southam planned "to reduce labour costs by approximately 20 percent by the end of 1994," for "total wage savings" of $75 million annually. After the meeting, Harvey Enchin, media reporter for *The Globe and Mail* commented that at Southam "the gentlemen's club...has been overthrown by financiers determined to extract the highest possible return even if it means hacking off a limb or two." According to Enchin, the Southam family culture in which "owning newspapers was a trust" is gone, and "in its place is the profit motive."[5]

Southam demonstrated this when it more than doubled its profits in 1994, to $44 million from $21.6 million in 1993. The company cut about 1,200 jobs from its newspaper division beginning in 1992, saving $21.2 million in labour costs for 1994 alone.[6] The process was described as "a three-year, $129.2 million program to cut labour costs." The 1995 description of further cuts looming at Southam, reported by the *Report on Business,* is instructive. The story headline stated, "Southam may take $40 million hit on jobs." This reads for all the world as though the company is taking a write-off on bad debts, which may not be far from the corporate view on employees. The story included the following information:

> The elimination of approximately 320 jobs would involve a one-time cost of about $35 million, based on the company's experience so far under the program. The current average cost of the downsizing has been $111,000 a worker, with an equivalent annual savings realized of about $81,000, according to the company.[7]

It doesn't take a genius to figure out that the company is in the black about one and a half years after chopping the "excess employee baggage." One example of these kind of cuts came in 1994 when the Southam-owned *Kingston Whig-Standard* fired 12 people, "including the paper's best and most experienced writers and editors." Between them the fired employees had at least seven National Newspaper or National Magazine awards.[8] Southam bought *The Whig,* with its circulation of 37,000, from independent owner Michael Davies in 1990, for a reported $50 million, and quickly set about increasing profits and decreasing quality coverage.[9] By the time Paul Desmarais bought into Southam in 1993, he added Power Broadcasting's two Kingston radio stations as well as the only local TV station, to a media monopoly which included *The Whig.* This kind of cross-media ownership used to be frowned upon by the CRTC, except for "out-of-the-way" places such as New Brunswick, owned by the K.C. Irving family, or London, Ontario, owned by the Blackburn family.

The Boys' Club

An Associated Press wire photo of three smiling men ran on the front page of *The Globe and Mail*'s business section in early October, 1993: Power Corp. Chairman Paul Desmarais Sr. was shown in Beijing, shaking hands with Chinese Vice-Premier Rong Yiren. Looking on approvingly was former Prime Minister Brian Mulroney.[10]

Desmarais was in China to announce a $100 million joint venture between Power Corp., Ontario Hydro and Hydro-Québec, to supply electrical power in Asia. But when it came to identifying Desmarais, and explaining why Brian Mulroney was in Beijing, *The Globe* came up short. It only stated cryptically that "officials of Power and both [hydro] utilities insist the former Canadian prime minister, now a lawyer at Power's long-time Montréal legal firm Ogilvy Renault, is not directly involved in the new venture."[11] As usual, the broader context and history behind events remained inexplicable, another mystery in the news. The brief answer to both questions is that only four of Paul Desmarais Sr.'s family companies now have annual revenues of more than $26 billion — dwarfing Royal Bank of Canada, which got him started in business with his first loan. As indicated, his holdings dwarf almost all of the other firms in Canada as well.

Desmarais is fondly known by senior management as *"Le Patron"* and is the patriarch of the French-Canadian business community. His relationship with Brian Mulroney goes back more than 20 years, to when Mulroney was first hired by Desmarais as a management negotiator in a strike and lockout at the Desmarais-owned Montréal newspaper, *La Presse*. On the surface, the strike was over job protection under automation, but a hidden agenda was the attempt by Desmarais and his managers to rid the newspaper of its separatist journalists. In October of 1971, 15,000 demonstrators marched on the building which housed *La Presse*, many carrying placards which read, *"Desmarais au poteau,"* ("Desmarais to the gallows"), and burned him in effigy.[12] Biographer Dave Greber wrote that, "Desmarais, the staunch federalist, wouldn't allow *La Presse* — or any of the other French dailies he owned — to become a partisan mouthpiece for values he didn't hold."[13] According to Greber, "the labour dispute [was] a cover to purge the newsroom of difficult journalists." As we will see, this is but one example of direct ownership influence.

Much more recently, Desmarais' *La Presse* broke the story of "the lobster affair," which was designed to embarrass the Parti Québecois, specifically Premier Jacques Parizeau. In a speech to European ambassadors in early July, 1995, Parizeau supposedly compared the Québecois to a bunch of lobsters, who, having voted "Yes" in the referendum, could no more escape becoming a sovereign country than lobsters could avoid turning red in boiling water. A federal External Affairs departmental memo was leaked to *La Presse*, which broke the story.[14] The incident proved highly embarrassing for the PQ. It was compared to the infamous "Yvette" comment in the 1980 referendum campaign, when Parti Québecois Cabinet Minister Lise Payette compared the wife of then-Liberal-leader Claude Ryan to the docile girl in Québec primary-school textbooks — a condescending quip which served as a rallying point for federalists.[15] Daniel Latouche, Québec academic and columnist for *Le Devoir* and *The Globe and Mail*, wrote in September 1995 that "many Montréalers, including this one, have now dropped *La Presse* for *The Gazette*; if you're going to read a militant federalist newspaper, you might as well read an English one."[16]

In the winter of 1996, *La Presse* ran a full-page article by Pierre Trudeau, accusing Québec Premier Lucien Bouchard of "hateful demagoguery" in misleading voters in the October 1995 Québec Referendum. Bouchard claimed during the referendum that Québec Premier Rene Levesque was "abandoned" by the other premiers during constitutional negotiations with Trudeau in 1981. This has come to be known as "the night of the long knives" amongst Québec separatists. Trudeau wrote that it was Levesque who abandoned the other premiers, dissolving their united front.

A scant four years after the 1972 strike at *La Presse* Desmarais became the largest single contributor to Mulroney's campaign bid for the leadership of the federal Progressive Conservative Party, apparently one-upping Conrad Black. Mulroney and *Le Patron* have been good friends ever since, gathering at Desmarais' home in the secluded community of Palm Beach, Florida, during winter vacations. But Desmarais' connections extend beyond the PC party. In 1994, Power Corp. and one of its subsidiaries, Great-West Lifeco, contributed $52,148 to the Liberal Party of Canada, putting Desmarais within the top ten contributors. Until his election to head the federal Liberal caucus in 1990, Prime Minister Jean Chrétien served on the board of directors of Power Corp. And Chrétien's daughter France is married to Desmarais' son, André.

Midway through the 1993 federal election campaign, reporters discovered that Liberal leader Jean Chrétien attended a $1,000-a-person fundraiser for wealthy supporters in Montréal. More than 200 people, including financier and Power Corp. board member Charles Bronfman, attended the evening. It was sponsored by the Laurier Club, which promised private meetings and privileged access to Chrétien. Party handlers, leery of negative publicity, tried to keep the event secret and then added insult to injury by having police remove the one reporter who was tipped off about the gathering. Mad as hornets, reporters created a fuss, resulting in a story on the front page of *The Globe and Mail* and the lead item in the CBC National TV news. Chrétien was accused of influence peddling, a charge that he dismissed with the comment: "You know, millionaires vote."

The affair disappeared as quickly as it arose. By Friday, only about a day after the story broke, Hugh Winsor of *The Globe* had dismissed the whole affair as "a part of a regular fund-raising process that both major parties use to tap the wallets of their more prosperous supporters." And that was the end of it.

John Rae, older brother to former Ontario Premier Bob Rae, managed Chrétien's Liberal leadership campaign, and was national coordinator of the Liberal's federal election campaign in the fall of 1993. According to Peter C. Newman, "the man who really fashioned the Liberal victory was John Rae, an executive vice president of Paul Desmarais' Montréal-based Power Corp. Rae spread wisdom and confidence wherever he went."[17] Rae is also a board member of Power Corp., and defended Desmarais' media interests before the Royal Commission on Newspapers, chaired by Tom Kent in 1980. Rae was also executive assistant to Jean Chrétien when he was Minister of Indian Affairs in the Trudeau government.[18]

Federal Liberal Finance Minister Paul Martin, whose personal fortune was estimated at $33 million in 1990, worked for Desmarais as president of Canada Steamship Lines (CSL), until Power Corp. sold CSL to Martin for $195 million in 1981. Martin and Rae were two of the young high-rollers who fished and played poker with Desmarais on Anticosti Island. Power Corp. owned the island, which stretches over 135 miles of the St. Lawrence River, in the early 1970s. Martin was a guest at his friend Brian Mulroney's wedding to Mila Pivnicki.

In July 1995, news came that a powerful consortium of Canada's largest shipping companies, steel mills and grain handlers had begun high level talks with the federal Ministry of Transportation, aimed at taking over operation of the St. Lawrence Seaway.[19] According to *The Globe and Mail*, the federal government reportedly plans to commercialize the St. Lawrence Seaway as part of its "reform of maritime policy." One proposal would see the private sector group take over the daily operation of the Seaway, to increase efficiency and "commercial flexibility," by, for example, looking into "existing labour contracts." The government would retain ownership of the Seaway and the responsibility for "major capital works, such as the upgrading of the aging locks," the report said. Included amongst the consortium of four named shipping companies was Canada Steamship Lines, which the *Globe* did not link to Finance Minister Paul Martin. The report said "Transport Minister Doug Young instructed his staff to deal with the consortium to 'explore the options.'" So, here we had one minister's staff negotiating with a private consortium of companies which included the conglomerate owned by the finance minister, and which was previously owned by the prime minister's in-laws, via a firm on which the prime minister sat as a director. All of these facts go unmentioned by our national newspaper.[20]

Incidentally, a recent House of Commons report described the Seaway as the lifeline of Central Canada's economy, bringing in $3 billion in economic benefits and maintaining 17,000 jobs. According to

Hazen Ghonima, a commodities analyst who monitors the shipping industry, "The St. Lawrence Seaway Authority is doing a very fine job. They are lean and mean — so it's a bit difficult to make it more efficient than that."[21] Although this too was reported in *The Globe and Mail*, one cannot help noticing that the original story was carried at the top of page one, while the sceptical reaction to the proposal was buried the next day on page 12 of the business section.

As Maude Barlow and Bruce Campbell report in *Straight Through The Heart*, in a fiery speech in 1989 Paul Martin told a meeting of the Council of Canadians in Ottawa, "I am a very strong economic nationalist." That year, Canada Steamship Lines, with Paul Martin as its sole shareholder, registered some of its ships under foreign flags. Barlow and Campbell note:

> This practice allows the company to avoid Canadian taxes through loopholes and write-offs. Canadian marine safety standards do not apply to these ships. Crews under foreign registry do not pay Canadian taxes and are not eligible for Canadian social programs. Operating costs are cut by as much as half because of the lower salaries paid to foreign crewmen who have taken the jobs of hundreds of Canadian seamen. One of the reflagged ships, now under Bahamian registry, was renamed the *Atlantic Erie*; the ship was originally named the *Paul Martin*, for his beloved father.[22]

Maurice Sauve, husband to former Governor General Jeane Sauve, was Minister of Forestry in the Liberal cabinet of Lester Pearson in the 1960s. He became executive vice president of administration and public affairs for Consolidated Bathurst, owned by Power Corp., from 1968 to 1981. According to journalist Stevie Cameron, "A story surfaced in January 1989 that [Sauve] made a great deal of money helping Paul Desmarais' Power Corporation find a buyer, Stone Container Corp. of Chicago, for its majority shares in Consolidated Bathurst."[23]

Maurice Strong bounced the young Bob Rae on his knee during the 1950s. Rae's father Saul, a friend to Strong, was in External Affairs, and in the 1960s under Lester Pearson, was appointed Canadian Ambassador to Washington. Strong was president of Power Corp. before its takeover by Desmarais in the 1960s. Strong was appointed as the founding president of Petro-Canada by Pierre Trudeau, in 1976. Later, Bob Rae would appoint Strong as president of Ontario Hydro. Later still, Strong would join the World Bank.

Daniel Johnson, former Liberal premier of Québec, worked for Power Corp. from 1973 to 1981, when he left to run for the Liberal Party. In the last three years with Power Corp. he was a vice president. During the Québec election in late summer of 1994, a scandal briefly surfaced over a surprise Liberal candidate, Yvon Charbonneau. Charbonneau is a former nationalist, described as a "fiery unionist" jailed by the Bourassa government in 1972. More recently, Charbonneau was being sued for $661,595 by Great-West Life Assurance Co., which, as mentioned, is controlled by Power Financial. According to a report in August 1994 in *La Presse*, the suit was settled out of court for "considerably less than $100,000 shortly before Charbonneau declared himself a Liberal candidate." Coincidence? PQ leader Jacques Parizeau thought otherwise, and said so during the election.[24]

Don Mazankowski, former finance minister and deputy prime minister under Mulroney, sits on the board of the Great-West Lifeco., owned by Desmarais. In May 1996, he was added to the Power Corp. Board. Gilles Loiselle, who was finance minister under Kim Campbell's brief tenure as prime minister, is currently employed as an adviser to Paul Desmarais. Gerard Veilleux was appointed by Mulroney as president of the CBC, and was overseer of its extensive cutbacks at the behest of the Mulroney government in 1990. Veilleux resigned in 1993, a year earlier than scheduled. A scant few months later, in 1994, he went to his reward as president of Power Communications, also owned by Desmarais.

These connections are not totally ignored by the mainstream press, but they are presented as isolated incidents and the bigger picture goes unrevealed. When a slightly broader picture is painted, it is framed within a particular perspective, which might be summed up as: "this is business as usual. There is no problem here." For example, in the fall of 1994, *The Globe and Mail* ran an article in the business section concerning the company directorships held by former Conservative cabinet ministers. The gist of the story was that, while some ministers such as Don Mazankowski did very well, holding nine company directorships, others held few or none. Hence, what was at work here was the marketplace: the natural ability of the individuals concerned, rather than a system of rewards, patronage and one hand washing the other. The article quoted Tom D'Aquino, president of the Business Council on National Issues, who made the definitive (and unchallenged) statement: "I don't know of a single time when a politician was rewarded for a job well done."[25]

In early September, 1995, the *Report on Business* indicated that former Tory finance minister Michael Wilson was "back on Bay Street," returning as vice chairman with RBC Dominion Securities. Wilson was executive vice president of Dominion Securities from 1973 to 1979, before he became a part of the Mulroney cabinet in 1984 and before Dominion was taken over by the Royal Bank. (In his autobiography, Conrad Black claims that he helped to launch Michael Wilson's political career, and that Wilson is a longtime friend to himself and his brother Monty). Wilson was quoted as saying that "one of my clients for the last couple of years has been [RBC] Dominion Securities," through his business advisory firm of Michael Wilson International.[26]

The suspicious, nay cynical and perhaps even paranoid reader, may wonder whether these connections have anything to do with the zero inflation, high interest rate policies zealously pursued by Wilson and Bank of Canada governor John Crow during the late eighties and early nineties. Policies which, I might add, contributed substantially to the coffers of the Royal Bank, at the same time that they created the recession of the early nineties. Indeed, one could argue that rather than returning to Bay Street, Wilson never left. We will return to the topic of interest rates and the treatment of Linda McQuaig's best-seller, *Shooting The Hippo*, in the concluding chapter.

"To Hell With the People..."

Liberal Senator Michael Pitfield, who as clerk of the Privy Council was the top bureaucrat in the country under Pierre Trudeau, is vice chairman of Power Corp. Trudeau himself sits on the international advisory board to Power. According to Peter C. Newman, in the offices of Power Corp. at regular Friday night meetings early in 1968, "the plans for Trudeau's leadership candidacy had first been hatched." Just two months after Trudeau was elected prime minister he visited Desmarais' summer home at Murray Bay, near the mouth of the Saguenay River. Newman wrote,

> When Desmarais had picked the P.M. up at the local airport in one of the two Rolls-Royces he keeps there, Trudeau casually inquired about what it was like to drive a Rolls. Desmarais stopped the car, got in the back seat, and,

as Trudeau took the wheel exclaimed, 'This is the first time I've been driven by a prime minister!'[27]

But it is always Desmarais himself who occupies the driver's seat. Pierre Genest, perhaps Desmarais' closest friend, roomed with him as a student at the University of Ottawa in the 1940s. He has noted that "[Paul] loved to get into things, to run things, to influence people. He was treasurer of the student federation, but he remained the man behind the scenes. Candidates who ran for office sort of had to get his blessing, or they wouldn't get in."[28]

Here then, are the roots of *Le Patron*, which began with his student days dabbling in backroom politics, to his role, now stretching over three decades, as the godfather of the Canadian political communities in Ottawa and Québec. According to Peter C. Newman,

> No businessman in Canadian history has ever had more intimate and more extended influence with Canadian prime ministers than Desmarais. He was a good friend and financial supporter of Lester Pearson, who became prime minister in 1963; he was one of the chief backers of Pierre Trudeau's leadership bid and acted as one of his main confidants for his 16 years in office. Desmarais had meanwhile become one of Brian Mulroney's chief mentors, and during the nine Mulroney years, no one outside the prime minister's immediate family had as much influence on the Baie Comeau politician as Paul Desmarais.[29]

This backroom role is in the tradition of the Rockefeller family in the U.S., whose rule is to "operate primarily behind the scenes...laying out the long-range policies while leaving the details to loyal spokesmen of their interests in positions of public power." The Rockefellers' influence in the U.S. dates from the last century, with their founding of the Standard Oil Trust, and more recently Exxon, Mobil, and the Chase Manhattan Bank among other properties. Nelson Rockefeller, who was governor of New York State and then U.S. vice president, was an exception. The Rockefellers founded the Trilateral Commission, of which Paul Desmarais and Conrad Black are members.[30]

As I indicated at the beginning of the chapter, the Power Corp. chairman has defended his penchant for surrounding himself with former and future politicians, and "to hell with the people who say we do it for political favours." Nor, one must presume, does Desmarais make political contributions with the expectation of political favours. As Maude Barlow and Bruce Campbell report, the top 13 contributors to the 1993 federal Liberal election campaign were all banks and financial corporations: Scotia McLeod, Coopers and Lybrand, Wood Gundy, Richardson Greenshields, Nesbitt Thomson, Midland Walwyn, Bank of Montréal, Royal Bank, RBC Dominion Securities Inc., Canadian Imperial Bank of Commerce, Toronto-Dominion Securities, Toronto-Dominion Bank, and the Bank of Nova Scotia. And, note the authors, "The fourteenth was Power Corp."[31]

Desmarais was born in Sudbury, Ontario, where he purchased his parents' failing bus company for one dollar at the age of 24, in 1951. He turned the company around, expanded into Ottawa and Québec and eventually gained prominence with his timely takeover of Power Corp., in 1968, when it held assets in companies worth $1.5 billion. Desmarais' corporate assets are now in excess of $130 billion. In 1994, his two major firms alone, Power Corp. and Power Financial, reported assets of $62 billion. But Desmarais' vast wealth is only one reason why he is a good friend to politicians. He owns 117 companies in diverse areas including finance and insurance services, real estate development, media and energy. Members of the board of directors include Charles Bronfman of the Montréal-based Seagram's, former Ontario premier Bill Davis (and John Robarts before him), and former Ontario Lieutenant Governor John Aird. Additionally, as indicated, he has extensive media holdings.

During his run for the leadership of the Conservative Party in 1976, Brian Mulroney was the big spender amongst the candidates, despite his somewhat humble beginnings as an electrician's son in Baie Comeau, Québec. The rumours that his $2 million campaign was being bankrolled by Paul Desmarais reached such a fever pitch that Mulroney was forced to publicly deny it. "I trust that all of you, when this rumour is raised, I hope that you will ask the person to whom you're speaking exactly for his source. And you'll find that the source is absolutely faceless and groundless and nameless," he said.

Mulroney later confirmed that Desmarais was his largest individual contributor; according to Mulroney he donated $10,000. Afterwards, when Mulroney lost to Joe Clark, Desmarais offered Mulroney a position in upper management with Power Corp., but Mulroney declined, instead joining Desmarais' law firm of Ogilvy Renault, where before becoming prime minister and since leaving office, he has handled the Power Corp.

account. Mulroney is also on the international advisory board of Power Corp.

In her book *On The Take*, Stevie Cameron describes how, when Mulroney was renovating his Parliament Hill office in 1984, Paul Desmarais sent him a trinket, a $6,000 antique for redecorating. According to one source, the bills to renovate Mulroney's law office at Ogilvy Renault exceeded $100,000 when he rejoined the firm after leaving 24 Sussex. In September of 1990, Mulroney appointed John Sylvain, Paul Desmarais' brother-in-law, to the Senate, as one of his eight controversial appointments which ensured passage of the Goods and Services Tax (GST) legislation. In June of 1993, Mulroney appointed *Le Patron's* brother, Jean Noel Desmarais to the Senate, as part of a final flurry of patronage appointments prior to Kim Campbell taking office.

Confederation Life

The example of Confederation Life is instructive as a portrayal of the consolidation of power and the way in which activities and inner workings at the top remain cloaked in secrecy. The media are instrumental in this process, cooperating by burying important questions and ignoring crucial leads. In the summer of 1994, 123-year-old Confederation Life Insurance Co. collapsed in the largest failure of an insurance company in North America. As the fifth-ranked insurer, with assets of $18 billion and more than 2,000 Canadian employees, the collapse of Confederation Life rocked the financial community. Shortly afterwards, Confederation Chairman Adam Zimmerman said the decision not to bail the company out of its financial troubles was made by Power Financial, which owns Great-West Life Assurance Co. of Winnipeg, ranked number three, and which had been negotiating a bail-out with Confederation Life for the previous six months. Zimmerman, himself a business high-roller formerly with Noranda Forest Inc. and a holder of numerous directorships including Southam Inc., stopped short of saying Great-West dealt in bad faith. "I think I probably ought to take the Fifth on that one. You can think a lot of things in the heat of battle. They were very cautious, put it that way. I think everybody has to make up their own mind." According to *The Globe and Mail's* story, "the ultimate decision-makers, in Zimmerman's view, were Power Corp.'s ruling Desmarais clan." Zimmerman claimed that Confederation Life was "led down the garden path" by Great-West, as it looked into an investment in Confederation, in a process that stretched from winter to

summer. Confederation died in August, 1994, after failing to arrange a
last-minute rescue by Canada's major insurers. According to
Zimmerman, the company was probably doomed when Great-West
broke off one-on-one talks earlier that month.[32]

Confederation reputedly collapsed because a subsidiary,
Confederation Trust Co., pumped up the corporation's portfolio with
commercial real estate in urban Ontario. According to Peter C. Newman,
this highly questionable decision was taken with some well-known
decision-makers at the helm. "In 1989, for example, when most of the
questionable investments were being made, Confederation Life's board
included such Canadian Establishment luminaries as...some guy named
Conrad Black." The mistakes made by Black and the other board
members were all the more egregious, writes Newman, because the
company was a mutual rather than a stock company, which means that it
is owned by its 230,000 policy holders, and the company's directors are
supposed to be their "surrogates and protectors."[33]

The collapse of Confederation Life led to the loss of hundreds of
millions of dollars on the part of investors, institutions, and policy
holders. By the end of 1993, Confederation Life and its subsidiaries held
$8.5 billion in mortgages and more than $1 billion in property, including
all or part of 69 Canadian, U.S. and British properties. The company
dropped from a profit of almost $106 million in 1990, to a loss of more
than $29 million in 1993, although its U.S. and British operations
reportedly remained healthy.[34] According to Peter C. Newman, the
company's collapse followed on "Great-West's prolonged hesitation
about whether it should be a white knight or a vulture — to buy into the
company or pick up its pieces."

After Confederation Life collapsed, Great-West Life circled like a
vulture after the entrails. Great-West snapped up the U.S. group life and
health operations, while the Canadian assets went to other competitors.[35]
Although this particular "take" or "angle" on the story was covered, it
was another "one-day wonder," covered briefly by the business section
of *The Globe and Mail,* alluded to in Newman's column, and ignored
elsewhere. Yet, the incident demonstrates the potential for abuse which
comes with the accumulation of power — not only over vast sectors of
the Canadian economy, but also over the information media. If it is true,
then Desmarais may have intentionally allowed Confederation Life to go
under in order to improve the prospects and assets of his own firm,
Great-West Lifeco. When it came to this possibility, somehow we never
got to "read all about it."

Power and DirecTv

A subsequent event is even more chilling, as a demonstration of power and influence at the top: the Power DirecTv affair. This one involves the family and business links between Desmarais and Prime Minister Jean Chrétien. In the Power DirecTv controversy, the federal cabinet took the unprecedented step of overturning a decision by the Canadian Radio-television and Telecommunications Commission. In August, 1994, the mildly protectionist CRTC approved a direct-to-home (DTH) satellite television service. The ruling effectively barred foreign DTH competition by emphasizing Canadian content, and insisting that Canadian satellites be used for delivery. This allowed Expressvu Inc., a consortium of telephone, broadcasting and hardware interests formed in March 1994, to effectively have the field to itself. Alarmed at the impending threat of U.S. satellite "death stars" broadcasting directly into Canada, the CRTC encouraged Canadian companies to form a consortium. Competing companies excluded by the CRTC decision included Power DirecTv, 80 percent owned by Power Corp., and 20 percent owned by a General Motors subsidiary, Hughes DirecTv Inc. of Los Angeles, operator of a 150-channel DTH service in the U.S. The CRTC initially required that the (Canadian) Telesat be used to broadcast *all* programming. Power DirecTv had planned to use Telesat only for its Canadian programming, gaining its big economic advantage from the fact that American Hughes' satellites already carry the U.S. services and pay-per-view movies.

Initially, DirecTv discussed coming into the Canadian market as a U.S. multinational company. Discussions were held with civil servants in the federal Heritage Department and the CRTC. The CRTC told DirecTv that they would get nowhere without a Canadian partner. So, the GM subsidiary turned to people with direct connections to the prime minister. As one former Department of Heritage bureaucrat put it in a confidential interview, "to its credit, DirecTv first tried an approach which was open and above board, before abusing the power structure."

The president and CEO of Power DirecTv is André Desmarais, son of Paul and son-in-law to Jean Chrétien. The company's chairman is Joel Bell, who held numerous government posts under Pierre Trudeau. When the CRTC made its announcement, Bell headed to Ottawa and the office of Eddie Goldenberg, principal secretary to Chrétien. (Ted Johnson, a former Trudeau assistant and a friend and canoeing partner of Goldenberg, is also secretary and legal counsel to Power Corp). Bell also visited Industry Minister John Manley and Minister of Heritage, Michel

Dupuy. Within twelve days of the CRTC decision, the two ministers had announced that the decision would be investigated.[36]

In November, 1994, the government appointed a three-man satellite policy review panel, consisting of former deputy ministers with close professional or personal ties to Goldenberg in the prime minister's office: Gordon Ritchie, André Tasse and Robert Rabinovitch. Rabinovitch is an executive with Claridge Inc., owned by the Bronfman family. By April of 1995, the committee delivered its report to the two ministers, Manley and Dupuy, urging the government to direct the CRTC to promptly license all qualified satellite TV operators, in the interest of avoiding a monopoly. "Monopoly privileges can no longer be justified at a time of rapid technological change and expanded channel capacity," Rabinovitch commented.[37]

In the panel's defense, the CRTC decision was criticized because of its close relationship with Expressvu Inc., including telecommu-nications giant BCE Inc. and Astral Communications, whose co-Chairman André Bureau is a past chairman of the CRTC. The anti-monopoly theme doubtlessly also struck a chord with a government which has promoted the convergence of media in pursuit of the so-called electronic superhighway. In any event, within three weeks the federal cabinet made history by accepting the panel's recommendation and overturning the CRTC decision.

Overturning the CRTC directly benefitted Chrétien's son-in-law, André Desmarais, president and CEO of Power DirecTv, a company in turn owned by Paul Desmarais' Power Corp. Chrétien dismissed the ensuing controversy over his cabinet's interference with the CRTC. "I have absolutely no conflict of interest," he told the House of Commons, saying "the Prime Minister of Canada has the right to have his daughter well married."[38] He indicated that he had personally stayed out of cabinet discussions on the matter, turning things over to deputy PM Sheila Copps. For his part, Bell told *Maclean's* magazine that André Desmarais never lobbied the government on behalf of Power DirecTv, and never talked to his own father-in-law about the issue.[39] The credulity of Canadians has not been so greatly strained since former federal Cabinet Minister Sinclair Stevens said he did not discuss financial matters with his wife.

But whether it was Copps or Chrétien, Manley, Dupuy or Goldenberg who negotiated directly with the people from Power Corp., is not the crucial point. The prime minister's interests are implicit in this situation and neither his principal secretary Eddie Goldenberg, nor Sheila Copps, nor any other minister would overlook that fact. The controversy flared briefly, and then was allowed to die out in a manner which was chillingly reminiscent of the original Teflon man, Ronald Reagan.

One Heritage Department civil servant indicated privately that the Power DirecTv fiasco "was a classic example of undue political interference with a regulatory body." This was a top-down decision, imposed by the cabinet rather than originating with the federal bureaucracy. Hugh Winsor of *The Globe* commented that, "it is an open question ...whether the substance of Power's case could have carried the day without the extensive access guaranteed by its political connections."[40]

These facts bring home the need for closer public scrutiny and regulation of self-serving actions by politicians. As I recall, Brian Mulroney fired Sinclair Stevens from the cabinet, and subsequently refused to sign his nomination papers, over indiscretions such as these. Thanks to Stevie Cameron's book, *On the Take*, Mulroney himself has been vilified for wantonly lining his own pockets at public expense. In the 1993 federal election and in 1995 in Ontario, the public made it clear that it demands honesty and accountability from its politicians. Chrétien pledged his allegiance to integrity, but has failed to live up to that promise. One example was the controversy in the spring of 1996 over the Liberals' failure to deliver on their Red Book promise to scrap the GST. Sheila Copps became a scapegoat. Not that Copps was blameless, but the attention devoted to her promise to resign over the GST detracted from the real story: how Chrétien's Liberals shamelessly lied to the electorate in a blatant case of political expediency.

In early September 1995, it was reported that Gordon Capital Corp., a small brokerage firm which employed Chrétien as a consultant between 1986 and 1990, was chosen to head a list of three firms orchestrating the federal government's sale of its remaining shares in Petro Canada. The shares are worth more than $1.6 billion, which, at the normal underwriting fees of 4 percent, indicate a payday of $64 million for Gordon and the other firms. Gordon Capital made the list of top corporate donors to the federal Liberal Party in 1994 with a donation of $18,336.[41]

A spokesperson for the finance minister's office, Diane Lafleur, denied that the fix was in from the PM's office, in what she described as "a very, very fair process" in which any firm with an interest was invited to make representations and *based on that process and the strengths and weaknesses of each firm*, the coordinating firms were chosen. *The Globe* reported, on the turnover page of its story, that Gordon's long-time chief stock trader Frank Constantini "was barred from the business for life in

1992" after "the most extensive investigation of market cheating yet" conducted by the Ontario Securities Commission. In the winter of 1993-94, Gordon's chief executive James Connacher "sat out a 90-day suspension imposed by the OSC in connection with a billion-dollar bond lending scheme that temporarily put the firm's solvency at risk." In the same case, Gordon's former derivatives chief Eric Rachar "lost his licence to work in the business and was barred from trading securities for 10 years."[42] This story was relegated to the business pages and one-day coverage.

Another example followed almost immediately, this time concerning the attempted privatization of the Pearson International Airport in Toronto. In December of 1992, Paxport Ltd. won a government competition that allowed it to negotiate a contract to operate Terminals one and two at Pearson. Later, Paxport merged with the Claridge Group, a firm controlled by the Bronfman family of Montréal (owner of Pearson's Terminal three), into a consortium called Pearson Development Corp (PDC). This larger firm signed a deal to take over Pearson's two older terminals 18 days before the Mulroney government was defeated. The deal would have leased Terminals one and two of the airport to PDC for 57 years, and let it keep the profits in return for $750 million in renovations. Chrétien said the Pearson deal was "immoral" at the time it was signed by the Tory government, during the 1993 federal election. Following an inquiry by long-time Ontario Liberal Robert Nixon in November, 1993, Chrétien's government cancelled the $750 million deal. PDC is before the courts seeking between $500 million and $2 billion in damages. A Senate inquiry in September, 1995 heard testimony that Chrétien supported the deal to privatize Pearson. The testimony came from Donald Matthews, a former president of the federal Progressive Conservative Party and Tory fundraiser, who was chairman of Brian Mulroney's leadership campaign in 1983. Matthews controlled Paxport Inc., the successful bidder for Pearson. He testified about a meeting between his son Jack Matthews, president of Paxport, and Jean Chrétien. According to the story in *The Globe*,

> Jack Matthews, then president of Paxport, has said that he met Chrétien, before he became Liberal Leader, in late 1989 or early 1990 to ask his advice about approaching Liberal MPs over an unsolicited bid to privatize Pearson. He said Chrétien sounded enthusiastic about the idea of privatizing the airport and that later he inquired about the possibility of a donation to his coming leadership

campaign...The Prime Minister has denied in the House of
Commons that he discussed Pearson with Jack Matthews
"while I was a lawyer."[43]

While *The Globe* reported this story, it is important to examine *the
way* in which it was covered. At first glance, it was a prominent front-
page story. But the crucial allegations against the prime minister were
absent from the article's headlines and lead paragraphs. The main
headline painted the issue with a broad brush: "Developer attacks
Liberals over Pearson affair." The subheading read: "Businessman tells
Senate inquiry he feels he was punished for taking an interest in public
affairs." The lead paragraph stated: "The central figure in the plan to
privatize Toronto's Pearson Airport lashed out yesterday at the
government's handling of the affair, saying he has been punished for his
political connections." Aside from one vague reference in the third
paragraph, the prime minister's role was ignored in the 12 paragraphs on
the front page, and was only brought up beginning with the seventh
paragraph on the turnover page inside, page A10.

Given the importance of the prime minister's office and the serious
nature of the accusations, this *should* have been the subject of the
headlines and lead paragraphs. "Enthusiastic PM gave nod to Paxport,
asked for campaign donation," is an example of an appropriate headline.

In other words, Jean Chrétien was not born with his Teflon coating.
As with Ronald Reagan and others, it is a gift bestowed on leaders by
news media corporations which prefer to tread softly, or look the other
way entirely. In this particular instance the matter subsequently received
some of the appropriate attention it deserved. When Jack Matthews
testified before the Senate committee, his allegations about Chrétien
received front page coverage. We are left to wonder, though, whether
this was a voluntary action on the part of *The Globe*, or if it was merely
because *The Globe* knew the story was going to be covered with some
priority by other news organizations. As the story in *The Globe*
indicated, "Tory senators called news organizations to be sure they knew
that the former Paxport executive was going to repeat under oath his
allegations involving the Prime Minister." To ignore or downplay
Chrétien's role in these circumstances would be difficult, if not
impossible. Although the main headline carried the allegations about
Chrétien, the subheading read: "Claim under oath denied by lawyer..."
who was present. The third paragraph of the story read: "[Jack
Matthew's] account of the meeting and its timing was flatly denied by

Paul LaBarge, a former Paxport lawyer and a former law partner of Chrétien."[44]

The story also reported that Jack Matthews never paid the $25,000 campaign contribution which Chrétien solicited because Matthews was offended when Chrétien's adviser and now principal secretary Eddie Goldenberg, subsequently "tried to double the contribution that had been discussed at the meeting" to $50,000. As a result, Matthews and Paxport instead donated an undisclosed amount to the campaign of Paul Martin. The whole affair dropped from sight as quickly as it arose.[45]

Democracy or Autocracy?

As long as the news media abdicate their public responsibility by underemphasizing or failing to report such information, it is virtually impossible for the public to hold politicians accountable. And as long as the media themselves are controlled by corporations with their own vested interests, it is highly unlikely that this information will be reported or adequately emphasized. The close connections between Chrétien and Desmarais, and the latter's formidable corporate and news media influence, raise serious questions about the ability of the news media to initiate and maintain a critical perspective. Now obviously Desmarais does not control *The Globe and Mail*, either directly or indirectly. But virtually all of the news media are controlled by a few huge corporations with remarkably similar perspectives. As such, Chrétien's Teflon coating has far more to do with the general receptiveness of corporate Canada to his government's neoliberal policies, than it does with his links to Paul Desmarais.

Chrétien has been a Teflon man in the news media, but ultimately of course he remains expendable, just like Kim Campbell, Brian Mulroney, John Turner, Joe Clark and Pierre Trudeau before him. What is important to realize is that ultimately policies are sacrosanct; individuals and even their governments are not. Jean Chrétien's extended honeymoon with the media will end, and they will begin to expose his feet of clay. In his place will suddenly appear Paul Martin, or another virtual clone from somewhere inside the Liberal party.

While the personal greed and unbridled ambition of individuals such as Mulroney and Chrétien are harmful, the nature of the system itself poses the greatest problems. Let's consider the very nature of what we call "democracy." In its simplest form, this stands for one vote each and majority rule. Yet, many of us don't vote and many of those who do wind up without representation even though we voted. I'm referring here to the "winner take all" two-party rules we have in place. In practical terms, we haven't had a true majority government at the federal level for decades. Most of us voted against Jean Chrétien in 1993, and yet he wound up with a landslide victory and a vast majority of the seats in parliament. Here's how it works: with as few as three or as many as a half dozen or more candidates in a riding, the winner is the one with a plurality: more votes than any other. In practical terms this often means as little as 35 or 40 percent of the vote. This person is the "winner" within the riding, and yet 60 or 65 percent cast ballots for other candidates.

Given these rules, on a national scale it's not uncommon for so-called "majority" governments to leave 55 percent or more of the voters, not just in opposition, but totally unrepresented in parliament. At various points there have been discussions about changing the rules to another system which would be more representative, but since the two parties which have governed Canada since our inception are happy with the current system, it remains unchanged. I will discuss some alternatives in the concluding chapter.

There are equally important factors which contribute to the reality that we live in a virtual autocracy, rather than a democracy. Consider the power of the prime minister. The prime minister is a party leader who is elected by a mere two or three thousand party members at a national convention. This position gives him or her the right, under private party rules, to do the following:

1. Decide who will run for the party in a given riding. He/she may sign nomination papers, refuse to sign papers (as Brian Mulroney did with Conservative MP Sinclair Stevens), or simply appoint a candidate who will run in the riding, even over the objections of the local riding association.
2. Decide who will be allowed to sit in the government as a member of caucus (Jag Bhaduria, Liberal MP from north of Toronto, was asked to resign from the caucus by Chrétien because, as a candidate, Bhaduria misrepresented his qualifications in his resume and he earlier wrote intemperate, threatening letters which were made public).
3. Decide who will be appointed to the cabinet.
4. Appoint committee chairs. (Liberal MP and former cabinet minister Warren Allmand was dumped from

his position as chairman of the Commons human resources committee when he voted against the 1995 budget).

5. Appoint parliamentary secretaries to cabinet ministers.
6. Appoint deputy ministers.

In April, 1996, Prime Minister Jean Chrétien expelled Liberal MP John Nunziata from the caucus, and suggested he would prevent the Toronto MP from running for the Liberals in the next election. Nunziata voted against the main budget motion — which amounted to an expression of non-confidence in the government — as a matter of principle. He said it was because of the government's failure to make good on an election promise to scrap the dreaded Goods and Services Tax (GST). This placed Nunziata in good company. Liberal MP and former Cabinet Minister Warren Allmand was dumped from his position as chairman of the Commons human resources committee in 1995 when he voted against the federal budget. He did so because he said the party under Jean Chrétien and Paul Martin had abandoned Liberal principles. The accuracy of Allmand's assessment is borne out by former Conservative Prime Minister Brian Mulroney, who has commented that: "[our] main policies have been maintained intact by the new government, and they're taking them a little further."[46]

Nunziata ran for the Liberal leadership in 1990, placing last. During the 1993 election, he criticized Chrétien's policy of directly appointing riding candidates such as Arthur Eggleton. This might be because in 1984, Nunziata won the York South nomination over former Cabinet Minister Paul Hellyer, who was supposedly being parachuted into a safe seat. Another former member of the so-called Liberal "rat pack," Deputy Prime Minister Sheila Copps previously had said that she would resign if the Liberals did not follow through with their promise to scrap the GST. With a week to go in the 1993 election campaign she told a CBC town-hall meeting that "if the GST is not abolished under a Liberal government, I will resign." For his part, Jean Chrétien said during the election, "the Mulroney GST will disappear. I am opposed to the GST. I have always been opposed to it and I will be opposed to it always."[47] In his letter to Nunziata, Chrétien indicated that "governing with honesty and integrity means recognizing what is possible in reality, examining responsible policy alternatives and choosing what works and implementing whatever is in the best interest of individual Canadians."[48] The fact that Nunziata was expelled while Jean Chrétien stayed on indicates the way in which principles and honesty are punished in our political system, while their counterparts are rewarded.

CBC radio news explained the prime minister's decision to eject Nunziata as being due to the importance Chrétien placed on "loyalty." The CBC TV correspondent who reported Nunziata's expulsion described him as "an accident waiting to happen." In its editorial on the matter *The Globe and Mail* stated that "Jean Chrétien had little choice but to eject" Nunziata. It went on to add that " Nunziata did the honourable thing, and Chrétien did the necessary thing." Liberal Whip Donald Boudria defended the prime minister's decision as a matter of principle. "There is no more fundamental principle of our parliamentary system of government than that governments stand or fall depending on whether they have the confidence of the House of Commons in matters of budgetary policy," he said. If Nunziata did not have confidence in the government, then he could not be a part of that government, said Boudria.

The Globe and Mail, in its news story on the matter, dismissed Nunziata as "an embarrassment," because of his "stridency."

> Nunziata, a 41-year-old lawyer, is no stranger to controversy. But the stridency that made him an effective member of the so-called Rat Pack, a group of Liberal Opposition guerillas who practised hit-and-run tactics against the large Progressive Conservative majority after the 1984 election, is now an embarrassment.[49]

Meanwhile, a call-in poll at CBC TV's *The National* demonstrated overwhelming support for Nunziata. There was a public outpouring of support to his constituency office, on parliament hill, and in the media. Toronto Broadview MP Dennis Mills indicated that he too would leave the Liberal caucus to sit as an Independent over the GST issue. However, that's where the "revolt" seems to have ended. Hugh Winsor of *The Globe* wrote that "other militant MPs have fallen in behind Finance Minister Paul Martin."[50] Ah, those militants.

By virtue of deciding who will be in the government, cabinet, and the senior civil service (all of whom sit at his or her pleasure), the prime minister runs the country. It is conceivable that a caucus revolt could unseat an unpopular leader, as happened to John Diefenbaker in the 1960s, however, it has not happened (at least within memory) to someone in office. This did happen to Maggie Thatcher in Britain, where leaders are responsible to their caucus rather than leadership conventions. In Canada, the caucus alone cannot get rid of the leader. As a result, the rules of the system mean that extraordinary powers rest with the prime minister — or for that matter with the premiers in individual provinces. This opens up the possibility for abuse, either by the leader herself or himself, or by whoever influences them. Now, let's take another look at that quote from popular historian Peter C. Newman, cited earlier.

> No businessman in Canadian history has ever had more intimate and more extended influence with Canadian prime ministers than [Paul] Desmarais. He was a good friend and financial supporter of Lester Pearson, who became prime minister in 1963; he was one of the chief backers of Pierre Trudeau's leadership bid and acted as one of his main confidants for his 16 years in office. Desmarais had meanwhile become one of Brian Mulroney's chief mentors, and during the nine Mulroney years, no one outside the prime minister's immediate family had as much influence on the Baie Comeau politician as Paul Desmarais.[51]

Of course, Jean Chrétien is not just close to Desmarais, he is a member of *Le Patron*'s family.

***

Endnotes

[1] Ann Gibbon, "Desmarais to retire, hand reins of Power to sons," *The Globe and Mail*, April 4, 1996, p. B1.

[2] Quoted in Art Chamberlain, "Power's Desmarais ends a 45-year run," *The Toronto Star*, May 11, 1996, E1.

[3] The 1995 reports are signed by his co-chair, Conrad Black. As indicated, Black bought out Power Corp.'s shares in Southam Inc. in May 1996, as this book was going to press.

[4] *The Toronto Star* was seen as a partner to Southam who would protect it from a takeover by Black, or for that matter Desmarais. But Torstar sold its shares to Black in 1992.

[5] Harvey Enchin, "Financiers running show at Southam," *The Globe and Mail*, May 3, 1993, B1.

[6] Casey Mahood, "Southam getting back to newspaper basics," *The Globe and Mail*, February 10, 1995, B1.

[7] Ibid.

[8] Jamie Swift, "Southamizing the Whig," *The Canadian Forum*, April, 1994, p. 5.

[9] The $50 million figure comes from "a top Southam official," and includes a $20

million penalty paid by Southam to Michael Davies for a drop in the value of Southam shares included in the deal. Southam guaranteed the shares at the 1990 value of $32, but by 1995 the shares had plummeted to the $15-range. This was clearly a costly, over-priced venture for Southam and a boon to Davies. If a newspaper with a circulation of 37,000 can fetch $50 million, what would *The Toronto Star* be worth? See the Canadian Press article, "Southam pays former Whig owner $20 million penalty," *The Globe and Mail*, March 12, 1996, p. B4.

[10] "Utilities Join Power to tap Asian demand," *The Globe and Mail*, Oct. 7, 1993, B1.

[11] In early June 1996 Conrad Black announced that Yves Fortier, chairman of the Ogilvy Renault law firm, was one of five nominees to the board of Southam to replace troublesome independent directors.

[12] Peter C. Newman, *The Canadian Establishment* (Toronto: Seal Books, 1977), p. 47.

[13] Dave Greber, *Rising to Power: Paul Desmarais and Power Corporation*, (Methuen: Agincourt, Ont. 1987), p. 173.

[14] See Daniel Latouche, "The Lobster Affair," *The Globe and Mail*, July 14, 1995, p. A15.

[15] See André Picard, "Québecois Voices," *The Globe and Mail*, July 13, 1995, p. A15.

[16] Daniel Latouche, "The news according to Québec's English media," *The Globe and Mail*, September 1, 1995, p. A17.

[17] Peter C. Newman, "Epitaph for the two-party state," *Maclean's*, November 1, 1993, p. 14.

[18] Peter C. Newman, *The Canadian Establishment*, p. 53.

[19] Robert Williamson, "Big users seek to run Seaway," *The Globe and Mail*, July 13, 1995, p. A1.

[20] A letter to the editor on the topic by this author went unpublished.

[21] Tu Thanh Ha, "Observers sceptical of group's Seaway bid," *The Globe and Mail*, July 14, 1995, page B12.

[22] Maude Barlow and Bruce Campbell, *Straight Through The Heart: How the Liberals Abandoned the Just Society* (Toronto: Harper-Collins, 1995), p. 114.

[23] Stevie Cameron, *Ottawa Inside Out*, (Harper Collins: Toronto, 1990), p. 167.

[24] This controversy received fleeting, one-day coverage in *The Globe and Mail*. See Ann Gibbon, "In the corridors of Power," *The Globe and Mail*, August 5, 1994, A1.

[25] *The Globe and Mail*, October 24, 1994, p. B1.

[26] Douglas Goold, "Michael Wilson back on Bay Street," *The Globe and Mail*, September 7, 1995, p. B1.

[27] Peter C. Newman, *The Canadian Establishment*, p. 44.

[28] Quoted in *The Canadian Establishment*, p. 63.

[29] Peter C. Newman, "Epitaph for the two-party state," *Maclean's*, November 1, 1993, p. 14.

[30] Holly Sklar, ed., *Trilateralism: The Trilateral Commission and Elite Planning for World Management* (Boston: South End Press, 1980), p. 53. As this book is going to press in May 1996, there is an article in *The Globe and Mail* (May 11, D3) titled "More club than cabal," in which those who suspect the activities of the Trilateral Commission are dismissed as conspiracy theorists on the order of the Oklahoma bombers and the

Montana Freemen.

[31] Maude Barlow and Bruce Campbell, *Straight Through The Heart: How the Liberals Abandoned the Just Society,* Harper-Collins, Toronto, 1995, p. 57. The big six banks donated a total of $402,376 to the Liberal Party of Canada in 1994. In all, the Liberals received nearly $6 million in corporate financing from 6800 business firms in 1994, according to figures compiled from the Chief Electoral Officer by the Canadian Centre for Policy Alternatives. This was three times more than corporations donated to the Conservative Party, and 12 times more than they donated to Reform. Power Corp. and Great-West Lifeco donated a combined total of $52,000 to the Liberals in that year, placing Desmarais in the top ten contributors.

[32] John Saunders, "Great-West has explaining to do, Zimmerman says," *The Globe and Mail,* August 17, 1994, p. B1.

[33] Peter C. Newman, "Breaking the unwritten contract," *Maclean's,* August 29, 1994, p. 33.

[34] John Partridge, "Confederation paper probe a whodunit," *The Globe and Mail,* Oct. 22, 1994, p. B1.

[35] Dennis Slocum, "CIBC bids for Confed assets," *The Globe and Mail,* August 26, 1994, B1.

[36] See Hugh Winsor, "Many strings pulled in satellite-TV row," *The Globe and Mail,* May 1, 1995, p. A1, A6.

[37] Lawrence Surtees, "Panel gives nod to satellite competition," *The Globe and Mail,* April 7, 1995, p. B7.

[38] Quoted in Warren Caragata, "Dishing it out," *Maclean's,* May 8, 1995, p.26.

[39] Warren Caragata, "Dishing it out," p. 27.

[40] Winsor, "Many strings" p. A6.

[41] Chief Electoral Officer of Canada, reported in *The Monitor,* CCPA, April 1996 p. 7.

[42] John Saunders, "Ottawa denies Gordon got political kiss," *The Globe and Mail,* September 7, 1995, p. B1, B2.

[43] Murray Campbell, "Developer attacks Liberals over Pearson affair," *The Globe and Mail,* September 14, 1995, p. A1, A10.

[44] Murray Campbell and Paul Koring, "Chrétien solicited campaign funds, Senators told," *The Globe and Mail,* September 22, 1995, p. A1, A6.

[45] *The Toronto Star* buried its short story on the matter on page A16. *The Windsor Star* ignored the matter altogether.

[46] Quoted in Barlow and Campbell, *Straight Through the Heart,* p. 91.

[47] Quoted in Edward Greenspon, "Chrétien relives party battle on GST," *The Globe and Mail,* April 24, 1996, p. A4.

[48] Greenspon, "Chrétien relives" p.4.

[49] Hugh Winsor, "Chrétien gives Nunziata the boot," *The Globe and Mail,* April 23, 1996, p. A1, A9.

[50] Hugh Winsor, "Liberal 'revolt' seems to have ended with Mills," *The Globe and Mail,* April 24, 1996, p. A4.

[51] Peter C. Newman, "Epitaph for the two-party state," *Maclean's,* November 1, 1993, p. 14.

Chapter Four

THE PUBLIC INTEREST

More [news media] commentators than ever are
ideologues of the right. — Jeffrey Simpson, *The Globe
and Mail*, April, 1996.

There has never been a shortage of journalists willing to
toady to the rich and powerful or to cast aspersions on
welfare bums, foreigners and folks who are simply getting
above their place. — Doug Smith, *Canadian Dimension*,
May/June, 1996.

Despite the fact that the news media are owned by a small portion of
the corporate elite, members of the public generally do not view media
content as reflecting corporate interests. Letters to the editor do indicate
that some people consider the news media to be biased, in specific
instances. But generally, people tend to regard the media as reasonably
objective entities which, in most instances, present a fairly diverse
spectrum of views. As a result of this underlying belief on the part of the
public, much of what the news media report tends to be uncritically
adopted as factual. This is a matter for extended debate in academic
circles, but is patently obvious to the casual observer. At the same time,
it is a generalization rather than a universal rule. The rejection of the
Charlottetown Accord in 1993, despite being unanimously endorsed by
the news media and elites, including the labour leadership, is a case in
point.[1] Another is the Canada — U.S. Free Trade Agreement (FTA),
which despite overwhelming approval from the news media, was
rejected in polls by a majority of Canadians prior to being implemented
by the Mulroney government. But for every Charlottetown Accord and
FTA, dozens if not hundreds of other examples show how the public has
either agreed with or tolerated the agenda propagated in the news media.
Indeed, even in the case of the FTA, our own inaction and the failure of
governments to consult us in the decision-making condoned its
implementation, as well as that of NAFTA soon after. The same will be
true for the current free trade agreement being negotiated with Chile.

The example of the Charlottetown Accord is pounced upon with
glee by those who wish to prove that the media have no effect on public

opinion, as if this single example was the ultimate litmus test. In so doing they choose to ignore teensy little examples of media influence such as the way we accept an autocratic system because the news media tell us it represents "democracy," and because they keep alternatives out of sight and mind. Or the way in which wholesale slashing of our social programs has been justified by an obsession with a debt which neither owes its existence to social spending, nor can be addressed by such cutbacks.[2] Or the acceptance of unfettered free market capitalism which has led to a firesale of public assets in recent years, ranging from Air Canada and Petro Canada to CN, and even airports and air traffic control. Or, the acceptance of Iraq's Saddam Hussein as the devil incarnate, in justification for going to war in the Persian Gulf. Or the view that welfare fraud contributes significantly to debt.

Each of these highly questionable views and policies has been tolerated or condoned by the public in large measure because of the way in which the news media promote them. Under relentless bombardment about the superiority of private enterprise, people have come to accept that what is private is, almost without exception, preferable to what is public. We have come to accept an attack on public enterprise, which is a direct attack on workers and jobs. The massive firing of thousands of civil servants adds to unemployment, decreases tax revenues, contributing to the hateful deficit, and yet it is condoned. We are all one job away from unemployment or welfare. As such, attacks on unemployment insurance programs and welfare undermine working people, our ability to bargain with our employers, and our alternatives to exploitation in the workplace. This portion of the social safety net exists to protect workers and to counterbalance the power corporations have to abuse workers with impunity. Even policies which are not as subtle, which are blatantly and demonstrably harmful to the vast majority of the public are accepted: such as undermining our education and health systems. Most of us do not endorse these policies but we tolerate them, because we have accepted the view propagated in the news media, that there are no alternatives. For alternative perspectives on these and other issues we must turn to small independent publishing companies, organizations such as the CAW and union leadership generally, selected academics, the Canadian Centre for Policy Alternatives, the Council of Canadians, and magazines such as the *Canadian Forum, Canadian Dimension, This* magazine, *Briarpatch, Our Times, et cetera* (see Appendix D). Here, we may read about options to social services cuts such as: raising taxes for corporations, the banks, multinationals and the wealthy; lowering interest rates via changes to monetary policies and the

Bank of Canada; the potential for a financial transaction tax, and so forth.[3] All of these go unmentioned in the corporate media.

The news media have successfully portrayed themselves as public advocates, partly through decades of shameless self promotion: a considerably successful propaganda campaign on an immense scale. Of course, we don't see it in this way. We tend to believe that the media are objective and socially responsible watchdogs for the public interest. And while we may realize that in this role the media occasionally let the public down, most of us see these as isolated and unrelated transgressions which "just happen."

There are numerous reasons why this is so. To begin with, as a nation we have bought into this relentless self-promotion by the media. A few years ago, former CBC TV News national anchor Knowlton Nash told an audience of student journalists that journalism is "the hinge of democracy," and "the glue that holds together our democratic society."

> Our job is to try *to reflect reality*, not somebody's self-image...I've always thought that the media are, in effect, *an agent for the public* in seeking out and providing information on what's happening, where, when and why....The heart and soul of our business is our credibility. We get that credibility, and the respect and power that go with it, only *by being a socially and professionally responsible agent for the public*...Our job in the media, be it television or radio or print, is to provide that news, and to provide *a searchlight probing for truth through the confusing, complicated, cascading avalanche of fact and fiction*" (emphasis added).[4]

This statement represents more than just one newscaster who is caught up with his own importance and the mythology of his trade. It is a reflection, broadly speaking, of the public *persona* of journalism, and what has come to be termed a "liberal-pluralist view" of the press.

The Liberal-Pluralist View

Freedom of the press has been essential to "democracy," such as we know it. The Canadian Daily Newspaper Association's Statement of Principles, adopted in 1977 and still in effect, reiterates these notions of social responsibility.

> The operation of a newspaper is in effect a public trust, no less binding because it is not formally conferred, and *its overriding responsibility is to the society which protects and provides its freedom* (emphasis added).

This sentiment provides the very basis for the concept of "freedom of the press" in our society. The press must be free to inform the public in an unfettered fashion. An informed public is, of course, the very basis of democracy. The roots of this idea are much older than Canada itself. But in the Canadian context for example, when George Brown, publisher of *The Toronto Globe* was assassinated in 1880, one newspaper commented that, "like all good journalists, he loved his profession, and he believed in the newspaper as a public educator and *as a power to defend the rights and privileges of the people*" (emphasis added).

And this is not by any means an archaic notion, any more than it is limited to royal commissions and academic work. For example, in the fall of 1992, George Bain, monthly Media Watch columnist for *Maclean's* magazine, wrote that the media "*are ever militant in guardianship of the public interest* and aggressive in the pursuit of truth in government"(emphasis added). And in an article copied and distributed by the Canadian Daily Newspaper Association (CDNA), J.P. O'Callaghan, the former publisher of the *Calgary Herald*, wrote in 1987 that:

> [the newspaper] lives or dies solely by the readers' acceptance of its performance. Its relationship with its readers is the sole reason for that success or failure...In essence, *the newspaper is the reader, in truth and in deed. It is the surrogate for the reader*" (emphasis added).

So, we clearly consider public responsibility—historically and at present—as the *raison d'etre* of newspapers and other news media. Ironically, this popular view of the press has been discarded as fraught with errors, shortcomings and "blindspots" by most academics who conduct research on the news media.[6]

Some evidence suggests that despite this relentless propaganda, members of the public are beginning to look upon journalists with growing suspicion. In August of 1995, Ottawa sports broadcaster Brian Smith was murdered by someone who, according to police, "was angry at members of the media" and chose Smith at random for his target. In its fleeting, momentary search for an explanation of this event, *The Globe and Mail* published an analysis which relied on an opinion poll and interviews, concluding that the "public ranks journalists with lawyers" in terms of the amount of respect they receive. The 1994 opinion poll by Angus Reid indicated that while 48 percent of respondents had "a great deal of respect" for doctors, teachers were at 45 percent, judges, 27 percent, journalists, 15 percent, not far above lawyers at 11 percent and politicians at 4 percent. Peter Desbarats, dean of the graduate school of journalism at the University of Western Ontario, was quoted as saying "people are very inclined to think we are in it for the money and we sensationalize stories to increase circulation and ratings. That's a very common belief."[7]

The Globe reporter went on to editorialize that an increase in salaries for journalists in recent decades placed them in the middle- and upper-middle class. "Most observers say that has translated into journalists being seen less as chroniclers of the establishment and more as members of a powerful elite." But, even if we accepted the totally unsubstantiated view that this low opinion of individual journalists or the "profession" is a reality, it is important to distinguish this from the perceived ideal role of the media. The public's acceptance of that role may contrast with the perceived truthfulness of the reporting and pictures of events supplied by the news media. For example, the poll indicated that only four percent greatly respect politicians. Yet in the apparent absence of alternatives, the public votes for those very same people, gives Jean Chrétien a high approval rating, and has faith in our so-called "democratic" system. Perhaps these examples converge in the way many working-class union members are convinced by the neoconservative news media such as the Toronto *Sun*, to ignore the union leadership and their own class interests and consistently elect conservative or liberal governments.

When Sheila Copps finally resigned over the GST scandal in May 1996, the *Globe* ran a story on how "Confidence in politicians remains low," reporting a poll by Ekos Research Associates. This poll placed the public's "trust" in occupational groups at the following percentages: farmers (80), MDs (70), pollsters (48), civil servants (41), bankers (35), journalists (32), lawyers (24), politicians (15), lobbyists (11), car sales people (7).[8] "Approval" ratings for the Chrétien government were running above 50 percent at the time.

The Press: Lifeblood of Democracy

The basis of democracy is not simply one vote each, but an *informed* vote. After all, as has been demonstrated both historically and at present, to be uninformed is to be at the mercy of dictators and demagogues. The news media function in this alleged free marketplace of ideas as probing "searchlights," in Knowlton Nash's terms, presenting all arguments but highlighting those which have the ring of truth. This ideal has been promoted in part through the misrepresentation of the 17th-century writings of English poet John Milton. Milton asked in his oft-quoted *Areopagitica* of 1644, "Who ever knew truth [to be] put to the worse in a free and open encounter with falsehood?" As a result this work has come to represent a groundbreaking libertarian ideal. But according to Noam Chomsky it is highly elitist:

> Milton himself explained that the purpose of the tract was "so that the determination of true and false, of what should be published and what should be suppressed, *might not be under control of...unlearned men* of mediocre judgement," but only "an appointed officer" of the right persuasion, who will have the authority to ban work he finds to be "mischievous or libellous" "erroneous and scandalous" "impious or evil absolutely against faith or manners," as well as "popery" and "open superstition" (emphasis added).[9]

As the cornerstone, the very lifeblood and oxygen of democracy, the news media supposedly keep the public informed in a full and fair fashion, so that truth and falsehood might grapple. In practice in our society, the central way this is supposedly accomplished is via the media reporting on the rather truncated exchanges between the major political parties, primarily through question period in the House of Commons and the provincial legislatures, but also during election campaigns.

This debate constantly includes accredited "apolitical" or "non-partisan" observers and commentators in the media themselves, in academia, in right-wing "think tanks" such as the C.D. Howe Institute, or in the business community at large.[10] These people function as what Richard Ericson and his coauthors at the University of Toronto call, "normative witnesses" who "uphold the normative order." Ericson concludes, "Thus, journalism is concerned primarily with communications among elite, authorized knowers."[11] Other so-called "special interest groups" representing labour and women are consulted sparingly, providing the appearance of balance and diversity. (Such sparse comments are usually relegated to "the back of the bus" or the latter part of the story, receiving less prominence and little or no attention, though that is seldom acknowledged or even noticed by mainstream journalists).

The media thus present themselves as adversaries of the government of the day, and indeed of so-called "big government" itself, as an unofficial opposition which challenges, questions, investigates and reveals wrongdoings to the public.[12] Based upon these revelations the public may do virtually nothing and freely receive the status quo: the current government for another term. Alternatively, the public is free to choose to punish the party in power by tossing out the rascals, and substituting another one of the major political parties. Increasingly, with the substitution of neoliberals for neoconservatives, this resembles a changing of the guard, rather than a democratic election. The parallel between what is happening today in politics and the picture painted by George Orwell in his book *1984* is striking. One moment we are at war with Eurasia, the next with Oceania. One moment it is the Conservatives running the country, the next it is the Liberals. Eurasia, Oceania, Conservatives and Liberals are all a charade.

Freedom of the press and other media was formally enshrined in our Charter of Rights and Freedoms, as it was much earlier in the U.S. Constitution. After all, the free press is nothing less than the oxygen of our democracy.[13] In an editorial on the occasion of "the third annual World Press Freedom Day," in May, 1995, *The Globe and Mail* decried the infringements by governments around the world (who provide the only possible threat), in places such as Russia, Algeria and Rwanda. *The Globe* argued that governments are ever-willing to infringe on press freedom by, for example, passing privacy laws to prevent intrusions into the privacy of public figures. "Even in the democracies, where it is protected by law, press freedom cannot be taken for granted...As journalists in undemocratic countries are well aware, true press freedom is devilishly hard to achieve."[14]

Devilishly hard to achieve, indeed. Here, as always, the meaning of "true press freedom" is limited to an absence of government interference. By definition, it is not possible for corporations, advertisers, publishers, managers and so forth to impinge on press freedom.

The Journalist as Politician

One outcome of the sanctity of "freedom of the press" is that journalists have enjoyed a special, privileged and protected status, as chroniclers of power, with access to elites and information and indeed even their own special status as minor celebrities. Not infrequently, journalists leave their employers to work as "flacks" or public relations officers for business or the government. Ron Collister comes to mind, who left as CBC's Washington correspondent to serve in PR for Brian

Mulroney. Or Keith Spicer, who left his job as editor of the *Ottawa Citizen* for a Mulroney appointment to head the CRTC. Or former television reporter Bruce Phillips, who was press secretary to Mulroney before being appointed as Canada's Privacy Commissioner. Or Gilbert Lavoie, who stepped down as Muroney's press secretary in January 1992, only to be hired as editor of the Ottawa newspaper *Le Droit*, by its owner Conrad Black. Recently, Giles Gherson of the editorial board of *The Globe and Mail* was seconded to the position of senior advisor on social security review for then-Human Resources Minister Lloyd Axworthy. Gherson drew the wrath of the Ottawa press gallery for favouring *The Globe* with exclusive interviews with his new boss.[15]

As I demonstrated earlier with Peter White, who moved from Conrad Black's side to that of Brian Mulroney, to publisher of *Saturday Night* magazine, the players glide effortlessly from corporate to political to media sites, browsing on their own version of the World Wide Web. In the spring of 1996, columnist Gordon Gibson began appearing each Tuesday in *The Globe and Mail*, writing on "Western issues." Gibson was initially identified as "a senior fellow in Canadian studies at the Fraser Institute." It made him sound like an academic teaching at a university, rather than a representative of a corporate lobby group which is dedicated to free enterprise capitalism. A few years ago the Fraser Institute was regarded as the ultra-right-wing fringe; now it has been welcomed into the pages of the corporate mainstream. (In May 1996, Gordon Gibson provided a lengthy commentary on CBC radio's *Sunday Morning*. Initially he was simply identified on the program as "columnist Gordon Gibson." Afterwards the host mentioned that he was "with the Fraser Institute and a columnist with *The Globe and Mail*.") The lobbyists are becoming inseparable from the journalists, and vice versa. The Thomson Corp., owner of *The Globe and Mail*, is among the corporate backers of the Fraser Institute, as is Southam Inc. Two board members of the C.D. Howe Institute, including its president, are on the board of Southam Inc.

Peter Kent, reporter and anchor for Global TV news, and former boy wunderkind with the CBC, was interviewed about anchors' salaries in the spring of 1996. A controversy arose when it was revealed that Steve Paikin of TVOntario earned $132,500. In response, Kent pointed to what he called the "inconsistencies" of Canadian culture.

> Incentives to excel aren't acceptable. We have a fairly
> narrow-minded view toward the generation of wealth and
> the appreciation of talent. We're an over regulated and

over-unionized society that has all sorts of contradictions. You'll find unionized situations where people are grossly overpaid by society's measure and private-enterprise situations where people are grossly underpaid.[16]

Mike Harris or Ralph Klein would be right at home with this sort of union-bashing and promotion of private enterprise, but how many viewers are aware that the Global TV anchor holds these views?

In the spring of 1996, two related events seemed to reflect the dramatic sea change in the traditional non-partisan role of journalists which had been in place for the past half-century or more. David Frum ("the young Frum," in the words of *Canadian Dimension* columnist Doug Smith, in the column which produced the quote at the head of this chapter), a columnist with *The Financial Post* and offspring of the late CBC journalism icon Barbara Frum, set about organizing the "Winds of Change" conference with the help of Lorne Gunter, a columnist with the Edmonton *Journal*. What was different about this conference, held in Calgary late in May 1996, was that it was designed to discuss the potential for strategic voting between Reform and Progressive Conservative candidates, in an attempt to defeat the Chrétien Liberals in the next federal election. Numerous right wingers were invited, including other journalists. One of the stipulations was that the conference was to be closed to the press. A controversy arose over the secretive nature of the conference and the role played by the journalists. The Edmonton *Journal's* Gunter eventually withdrew, "feeling his continued participation might compromise his role as a political commentator."[17]

Earlier in 1996 there was a gathering of 1,200 Montréalers who were "fiercely opposed to Québec sovereignty." William Johnson, columnist with the Montréal *Gazette*, received a standing ovation when he addressed the crowd. Also on the speakers' platform that day was Andrew Coyne of both *The Globe and Mail* and CBC Newsworld's *Face Off!* While being a Canadian nationalist — or at least being opposed to Québec sovereignty — is probably viewed (in English-speaking Canada) as a lesser crime against the practise of non-partisan journalism, it is one thing to do so in newspaper columns or in televised panel debates, and quite another to speak at a partisan public rally. Both of these activities pale, however, in comparison with organizing a partisan conference, as Frum has done. According to Coyne, who evidently saw no problem with taking part in the Montréal rally, "If you start to be perceived as just a cheerleader, I think your usefulness as a journalist is hampered quite a bit."[18]

Meanwhile, the Toronto *Sun* didn't just send a reporter. The occasion was a $500-a-plate Tory fundraising dinner at the Harbour Castle Convention Centre in downtown Toronto, in April 1996. The *Sun* bought a whole table for the Tories on its staff, at a price of $10,000.[19]

And yet, during the free trade debate in this country, CBC radio journalist Dale Goldhawk of *Cross Country Checkup* was forced to resign his position because he wrote an editorial opposing free trade in his union's newletter. CBC management thought his stance on free trade would compromise his ability to do his job objectively and impartially. Goldhawk was eventually exonerated as a result of the grievance process, but not until after the election of 1988.

In part because of their perceived role of providing a public service, newspapers have benefitted from tax concessions such as avoiding provincial sales taxes, receiving special postal rate subsidies for mailing purposes, free office space, and other amenities in parliament and the provincial legislatures. All of these benefits may be seen to flow, in part, from the mythology of the press as public watchdog. If journalists abandon this tradition to take sides quite openly, then this would be refreshingly candid. But it also calls into question their treasured role. Ontario newspapers went beyond the editorials, columns and news copy in 1993, to take out full-page ads attacking labour law changes proposed by the Ontario NDP government. They did so out of direct political and economic interests, in order to oppose provisions which banned replacement workers during work stoppages. But when they did so they also set a precedent: if newspapers may publish full page ads attacking proposed legislation, what is to prevent them from running ads promoting Reform or Conservative candidates? Is that next?[20]

Left-Libera Biases

In part, the public has accepted this view of the news media as public protectors because — despite its corporate ownership — the news is gathered, written and reported by professional, unionized journalists. Hiring such people allegedly allows corporate owners to maintain an arms-length, strictly financial relationship with their media. Indeed, to a certain extent journalists have a reputation for being left-of-centre, politically speaking. A familiar right-wing refrain dating at least back to former U.S. Vice President Spiro Agnew's attack on the "liberal media" in 1969, claims that the news media have a liberal if not leftist bias.[21] Proof that journalists as a profession are leftist or progressive is decidedly lacking. Indeed evidence points to the contrary.[22] Ironically, as indicated above, much of the academic research on journalists' sources and news and public affairs program guests demonstrates that these people are overwhelmingly conservative.[23] Allegations about left-liberal bias are similar to recent, largely unfounded accusations that academia is being overrun by students and young professors who are "politically correct," and hellbent on stifling academic freedom to further the cause of "special interests" ranging from gays to Blacks and feminists.

These perceptions of journalists and the media as leftist in persuasion and content, respectively, are manufactured by what is known as the major "flak" organizations, one purpose of which is "to harass the media and put pressure on them to follow the corporate agenda."[24] In addition to corporations and the Business Council on National Issues (BCNI), the major source of this particular type of flak is right-wing "think tanks" such as the Fraser Institute in Vancouver, or the C.D. Howe Institute of Toronto, which in part conduct research on media performance.[25] Their allegedly "independent" and "academic" research has been thoroughly discredited in academic literature.[26] This has not prevented the corporate media from a tremendous reliance on them. One study of economic stories over the Canadian Press wire service found that during a one-year period the Fraser was quoted in 140 stories, while the (leftist) Canadian Centre for Policy Alternatives was quoted in 16.

Journalist and author Linda McQuaig recounts how there were a lot of hostile reviews when her best-selling book, *Shooting The Hippo*, came out. One was by Anthony Wilson Smith of *Maclean's*, whom she describes as "another well-known commentator on the right."

> He was absolutely infuriated by the book and one of the things that particularly irritated him was that I referred to the C.D. Howe Institute as a business-sponsored think-tank, which is of course exactly what it is. Instead, he suggested that I should refer to it as an independent non-profit group — which would make it sound like a day-care centre or a home for battered women.[27]

Incidentally, Thomas Kierans, who is the president and CEO of the C.D. Howe, is a member of the board of directors of Southam Inc. (see appendices for a full list).

Right-wing journalists such as George Bain, formerly of *The Globe and Mail*, Conrad Black and his wife Barbara Amiel-Black, and even former Tory Prime Ministers Brian Mulroney and Kim Campbell have taken up the banner, charging journalists with a "left-liberal" bias, and/or with being intentionally "adversarial" toward individual leaders and governments.[28] As Bob Stanfield, Joe Clark and John Turner all discovered before Kim Campbell, the news media can resemble piranhas when they spot the exposed flesh of individual human frailties, or when they smell blood. But their vision and sense of smell are both limited and selective. Highly attuned to (some) individuals, they are oblivious to anything systemic.

Black has written that under the influence of Norman Webster and Geoffrey Stevens at *The Globe and Mail*, "some of the most convinced leftists infested the ROB [*Report on Business*]." Both Webster and Stevens have since left the employ of *The Globe*. Elsewhere, Black has written,

> More important for the decline of interpretative balance with the media is that their opinions and constructions of events are controlled, even in the measure that they ever were, not by publishers, but by the membership of newspaper craft unions. There is an industry-wide, or profession-wide, opinion on most issues, and a uniform slant to public and social questions. It is not a question of one newspaper against another, much less of liberal against conservative reporters, but of the liberal or in some cases radical-liberal press against the other elements of society, the considerable majority, in fact.[29]

For her part, Black-Amiel has complained that former *Globe and Mail* gossip columnist Rosemary Sexton exemplified "Canadian left-lib journalism."[30] In another column she wrote that "ideas are anathema to the left-lib Canadian media, who are not a split camp allowing diversity of views as in Europe and America."[31] Paul Godfrey of the Toronto *Sun* echoes that, "too much of the media portrays [sic] a left-of-centre, sort of bleeding left-wing mentality."[32] I think he meant to say "bleeding heart," but lately, the left wing *has* been bleeding. One of the reasons for this has been the preponderance of right-wing views in the media. As indicated at the beginning of the chapter, *The Globe and Mail's* national columnist Jeffrey Simpson was moved to comment in April 1996 that in the news media, "more commentators than ever are ideologues of the right." Given that Simpson's own views are frequently fairly right wing, this is a significant admission.[33]

***

Endnotes

[1] It is not clear to me why the public resisted the Charlottetown onslaught. Perhaps it was the (anti) Mulroney factor; perhaps because there were a few voices in the wilderness, such as NAC, the Marxist-Leninist Party, the Reform Party. However, it forms an exception to the general rule that perspectives which are absent from the corporate media are likewise missing from public debate.

[2] See for instance Linda McQuaig's *Shooting The Hippo: Death by Deficit and Other Canadian Myths* (Toronto: Viking, 1995) which is discussed in the concluding chaper.

[3] See for example Kathleen O'Hara, "Corporate Wealthfare: How Paul Martin is serving up $90 billion in tax goodies to his fellow wealthy Canadians," *The Canadian Forum*, March, 1996, pp. 16-22.

[4] Knowlton Nash, "The Imperfect Necessity," *content* magazine, Jan./Feb., 1988, pp. 7-11.

[6] For a discussion, see Robert Hackett, *News and Dissent: The Press and the Politics of Peace in Canada* (Norwood, NJ: Ablex 1991), pp. 52-56.

[7] Miro Cernetig, "Public ranks journalists with lawyers," *The Globe and Mail*, August 3, 1995, p. A4.

[8] Edward Greenspon, "Confidence in politicians remains low," *The Globe and Mail*, May 6, 1996, A3.

[9] Noam Chomsky, *Deterring Democracy* (NY: Verso, 1991), p.402, footnote 13.

[10] For an interesting account of the role of such "authorized knowers," see Richard Ericson, P. Baranek and J. Chan, *Visualizing Deviance* (Toronto: University of Toronto Press, 1987). For the U.S., see David Croteau and William Hoynes, *By Invitation Only: How the Media Limit Political Debate* (Monroe, Maine: Common Courage Press, 1994).

[11] Richard Ericson, P. Baranek and J. Chan, *Visualizing Deviance*, p. 351.

[12] Ironically, journalists have created a term which indicates when they actually have investigated something: this is called "investigative journalism," which should be redundant but it is not. There is less investigative journalism all the time. The former Centre for Investigative Journalism in Ottawa changed its name in recent years to the Canadian Association of Journalists, to be more inclusive.

[13] Craig Pearson of *The Windsor Star* deserves credit for coining this phrase.

[14] Editorial, "The unfree press," *The Globe and Mail*, May 3, 1995, p. A18.

[15] Barlow and Campbell, *Straight through the Heart*, p. 119.

[16] Quoted in Kim Heinrich Gray, "Anchors weigh uproar over salaries," *The Globe and Mail*, April 29, 1996 C1.

[17] The quote is from Michael Valpy, in "The journalist as political player," *The Globe and Mail*, April 11, 1996, p. A19.

[18] Ibid.

[19] Richard Brennan, "Mike takes on the media," *The Windsor Star*, May 3, 1996, p. A10.

[20] I participated in a hearing by the Ontario Press Council when the Ontario Federation of Labour complained about the ads, in the fall of 1993. The hearing was nothing less than farcical, with some of the defendants in the case, such as *The Toronto Star*, sitting in judgement over whether their actions were appropriate. These sorts of problems and indeed the entire significance of the case seemed to be lost on the press council.

[21] For both an account and refutation of this perspective, see Martin Lee and Norman Solomon, *Unreliable Sources: A Guide to Detecting Bias in the News Media* (NY: Carol Publishing Group, 1991).

[22] Ibid, pp. 142-143.

[23] See David Croteau and William Hoynes, *By Invitation Only: How the Media Limit Political Debate*; Marc Cooper and Lawrence Soley, "TV's favourite think tanks," *Mother Jones*, March, 1990, p. 26.

[24] Edward Herman and Noam Chomsky, *Manufacturing Consent: The Political Economy of the Mass Media*, (NY: Pantheon, 1988), p.27.

[25] *On Balance*, published by the Fraser Institute, is devoted to assessing media coverage, as is its National Media Archive. According to their literature, Milton Friedman has said of the Fraser Institute, "No organization has done more to help Canadians appreciate the importance of the marketplace - and the consequences of government interference - to their continued enjoyment of that country's standard of living."

[26] For a critique of the Fraser Institute's media research, see Robert Hackett, William Gilsdorf and Philip Savage, "News Balance Rhetoric: The Fraser Institute's Political Appropriation of Content Analysis," *The Canadian Journal of Communication*, 17:1, Winter, 1992, pp. 15-36.

[27] Recounted by Linda McQuaig in , "Gov't. Debt caused mainly by Bank of Canada," *The Monitor*, CCPA, May 1996.

[28] See also George Bain, *Gotcha! How the Media Distort the News* (Toronto: Key Porter Books, 1995); Kim Campbell, "Honour Among Scribes: When Journalists Think They've Crossed the Fairness Line," unpublished paper, 1994, cited in William Johnson, "Campbell's riding the comeback trail," *The Windsor Star*, May 30, 1995, p. A7; Robert Lichter, Stanley Rothman, Linda Lichter, *The Media Elite: America's New Powerbrokers* (Bethesda, Md.: Adler & Adler, 1986).

[29] Conrad Black, "A view of the press," *Carleton Journalism Review*, Winter, 1979-80.

[30] See Black, *A Life in Progress*, p. 389. On Amiel, see Doug Smith, "More Black Humour," *Canadian Dimension*, October 1992, p. 39.

[31] Barbara Amiel, "Public remarks on a private matter," *Maclean's*, January 27, 1992 p. 9.

[32] Quoted in Frances Misutka, "Profile: Diane Francis, Making sure the voice of business is heard," *content* magazine, November/December 1991, p. 14.

[33] See Jeffrey Simpson, "Our industry is chasing its tail," *The Globe and Mail*, April 18, 1996, p. A17, an excerpt from a speech Simpson gave on accepting the Hyman Solomon Award for Excellence in Public Policy Journalism.

Chapter Five

NEWS AS A MANAGEMENT PRODUCT

In the final analysis, the news is not what reporters report but what editors and owners decide to print. — Michael Parenti.

Another problem with the popular representation of journalists as left wing is that it wildly distorts the potential contribution made by individual journalists, especially those who *are* left wing. Here is an account by Nicholas Johnson, former chairman of the Federal Communications Commission in the U.S., the equivalent to our Canadian Radio-television and Telecommunications Commission (CRTC): "The story is told of a reporter who first comes up with an investigative story idea, writes it up and submits it to the editor and is told the story is not going to run. He wonders why, but the next time he is cautious enough to check with the editor first. He is told by the editor that it would be better not to write that story. The third time he thinks of an investigative story idea but doesn't bother the editor with it because he knows it's silly. The fourth time he doesn't even think of the idea anymore."[1]

This tendency toward self-censorship is supported by working professionals in the industry. For example, according to Dennis Mazzocco, who spent 20 years with ABC TV and other broadcast media in the U.S., "when you work in broadcasting, it is very hard not to become an agent for the political-economic interests of those who employ you...There is little room for independence on the job or off, due to the tremendous competition for the ever-decreasing number of jobs available in the broadcast industry."[2]

According to Sandra Precop, a producer with CBC radio in Windsor and a former newspaper journalist, columnist and editor, "you get people within the newsroom anticipating what they think somebody wants. I think that can be a problem. In fact, I've seen that happen. Someone will say, 'Fred will love this story: this is the kind of stuff he really likes.' Fred is the editor, publisher, whatever. And that's the story that they put on the front page. That's a decision made in anticipation that the person who made the decision is going to please someone higher up because this is the kind of story that Fred wants. But Fred never said anything."[3]

Windsor Star reporter Craig Pearson, who wrote an M.A. thesis on the sociology of news and corporate influences, says "most reporters know what the news game is about. Journalism is about the conflicts between people as opposed to the analysis of systemic problems. Those take more time to research and more space." Pearson adds, "there are certain stories that just are not going to be printed. You might as well not even propose a story on newspaper profits — it's not going to get in."[4]

More than forty years of research into the sociology of news supports the anecdotal accounts of Nicholas Johnson, Dennis Mazzocco, Sandra Precop, and Craig Pearson. As U.S. academic Michael Parenti put it in the quote at the head of the chapter, "in the final analysis, the news is not what reporters report but what editors and owners decide to print."[5] In the news industry as in other industries, decisions are made by owners, either directly or indirectly. Here is Nicholas Johnson again, on the implications of ownership: "The First Amendment rights belong to the owners, and the owners can exercise those rights by hiring people who will hire journalists who don't rock the boat, who don't attack advertisers, who don't challenge the establishment. That's a form of censorship."[6]

Owners hire publishers who reflect their views, and who in turn hire and promote managers, who then hire and promote editors and journalists. According to CBC producer Sandra Precop, who was employed at the Southam-owned *Windsor Star* for 19 years, working her way up to assistant city editor, "I think, realistically, people tend to hire or promote people who tend to remind them of themselves...I think publishers hire editors who are like themselves. And editors hire lower level editors who are like them, to some extent, and it's a nice middle class place, like *The Windsor Star*. So you're going to get middle class values."[7]

Journalists who do not demonstrate "the right stuff" simply are not going to go anywhere. They won't be promoted to editor, they won't get the choice assignments, and they are lucky these days if they can even keep their job. The reason for this is simple. In the words of David Radler, president of Hollinger International and right-hand man to Conrad Black, "I don't audit each newspaper's editorials day by day, but if it should come to a matter of principle, I am ultimately the publisher of all these papers, and *if editors disagree with us, they should disagree with us when they're no longer in our employ.* The buck stops with the ownership. I am responsible for meeting the payroll; therefore, *I will ultimately determine what the papers say and how they're going to be run*" (emphasis added).[8]

This is a candid if somewhat chilling admission in an industry where testimonials to the "local autonomy" of chain newspapers have been *de rigueur* during decades of monopolistic expansion which has left only a handful of cities on the continent with independent ownership or competing daily newspapers. For example, in the 1995 Southam Annual Report which bears the signature of Radler's boss Conrad Black, there is a special section on "Corporate Responsibility." Under "Statement of Editorial Independence" it reads:

> For more than a century, Southam has proudly upheld its policy of editorial independence on all matters involving news and opinion. In the widely different environments in which Southam operates across the country, publishers and editors make their own editorial decisions.[9]

Still, Radler's perspective is not unique, as indicated by this comment from Otis Chandler, publisher of the mighty *Los Angeles Times*. "I'm the chief executive. I set policy and I'm not going to surround myself with people who disagree with me...I surround myself with people who generally see the way I do."[10] Or, here is another Canadian example: John Bassett, once publisher of the long defunct *Toronto Telegram*, was asked by a TV interviewer, "Is it not true you use your newspaper to push your own political views?" Bassett replied, "Of course. Why else would you want to own a newspaper?"[11] As we will see momentarily, these little-publicized views are in direct contrast to the mythology normally propagated about themselves by the news media. As indicated above in the chapter on Conrad Black, Radler has changed his tune more recently, and has not been as straightforward. This brings him into line with others in media ownership and management. For example, here is William Thorsell, editor-in-chief of *The Globe and Mail*, in 1994: "Hierarchy once dominated newsrooms — and lines of authority still exist...But authority is also widely distributed in the modern newsroom... Indeed, as the mission of the newspaper diversifies and becomes more complex, discretion about content moves inexorably outward to the writers and section editors."[12]

This seems to be a perspective that is largely peculiar to owners and management in the media. Examples of this can be found in research such as that of Craig Pearson's work on corporate influences in the news. Among the people he interviewed, only one respondent — publisher André Préfontaine — thought that there was no corporate influence on the newspaper's content. Others interviewed not only agreed, but provided their own concrete examples of such interference. Préfontaine, who previously worked for Power Corp., then Hollinger Inc., Southam Inc. under Conrad Black and Paul Desmarais, and now for

Pierre Péladeau's Québecor, replied as follows: "I've worked for three newspaper chains in my day, and I have never to this day seen an example of a corporation picking up the phone and saying write this, or don't write that...It doesn't happen. The notion that some people have that somebody somewhere is pulling levers and strings is a misguided one. And it reflects an ignorance of how corporations work and what are the true objectives of corporations." Asked by the reporter if newspaper staff sometimes might not need to get a phone call, the publisher responded: "You mean self-censorship, or a pro-business slant in management? No, I can't say I've ever seen that. Really, you're talking about a very wide-spread sinister plot. There's no proof or demonstration in our society that any orchestrated group, whether it be business, or labour organizations or political parties, have ever concocted plots to control the media in such a devious way...You work in a newsroom. I mean this is just so unrealistic. This is painting a portrait that someone who has no knowledge of how a newsroom operates would come up with."[13]

Here are some of the other responses to this question from reporters at various newspapers. Reporter A, said "Oh Yeah! (Laughs). Well, I could give one example..." and then went on to elaborate an instance where the publisher blatantly stepped in to delete an opinion column from the second edition that an advertiser might potentially have objected to. Reporter B: (Laughs) "Yes. Sure...Advertisers will often threaten." Reporter C said "We have a number of big-name furriers," and talked about how they influence content, preventing coverage of anti-fur stories. "Over time, it's just got to the point where we just try to avoid doing [the stories] now, because it's not worth the effort." Manager A was paraphrased as saying: 'Corporate influence is inherent.' A former reporter said that "It happens more often in smaller papers," but then described how he left the major Canadian daily he worked for over the pro-business, anti-labour influence.

A columnist said he has witnessed corporate bias "endlessly." Manager B, who worked at the time for the above publisher, said, "Sure there are influences. You would be a fool or a liar to say otherwise." He went on to talk about how "the choice of publisher" and "finances" are the real ways in which corporate influence impacts upon the news department.[14] At the Southam-owned *Windsor Star*, for example, new publisher André Préfontaine was appointed in 1993. He quickly made major cutbacks to staff, brought in many of his own senior people, and then in September of 1995, moved on to a vice presidency in the newspaper division of Pierre Péladeau's Québecor Inc.

Union President Gail Robertson said the new publisher raised expectations but failed to improve things. "We have new faces, new department heads, the new publisher is bringing in his own people — just about every senior management position right now has been brought in by him, or hand-picked. And they are all different faces and they have a friendly veneer, but underneath there are still some of the same problems." As for the publisher's direct influence, Robertson says that under the previous publisher, "I remember one time *wanting* the publisher to step in, when a department head had made a decision. Now we've gone to the complete opposite. Now we've got a publisher who wants to be involved in everything. No one can be involved in every operation of the paper. He is making decisions when he maybe doesn't know the whole picture."[15]

Dave Hall, another reporter on the union executive, spoke to an interviewer during Préfontaine's tenure at the paper. "There is a feeling among our members...I don't know if betrayal is the right word or not. The new publisher arrived, and he's affable and charming, and he laughs and smiles in all the right places, and makes you think he is a great guy to have a beer with and maybe he is...Well we currently have ten active grievances which is the most we have ever had."[16]

According to *Star* reporter Craig Pearson, "For the last two years, since we've had André Préfontaine, there have been a lot of changes. It started within a year of Conrad Black and Paul Desmarais buying control of Southam. They sent down a publisher [Préfontaine] to radically cut back at *The Star*, drastically. Which he did and that included mostly staff reductions and other kinds of budgetary expenses. So we're now a lot fewer journalists." Pearson says that while Préfontaine also improved the appearance of the paper, this was largely a marketing initiative.[17]

Championing The Car Dealers

A prevailing myth of the journalism profession is that corporate ownership may affect profits and the business side of things, but it leaves the editorial or news side untouched. This was evident in the earlier quote from the 1995 Southam Annual Report. To anyone who is not in an advanced stage of denial this is immediately and overwhelmingly false. Two examples from *The Windsor Star*, one under Préfontaine's stewardship and one from his successor James Bruce, are illustrative. In the first instance, on March 1, 1994, Préfontaine pulled from the second, home delivery edition, an editorial page column by regular columnist Gord Henderson. Henderson merely raised some reasonable questions about the wisdom of the Chrysler Corp. paying American executives bonuses ranging from 75 to 100 percent of their salaries. At a time when CAW workers were allowed raises of 1.5 percent, the top 200 American executives were given 100 percent. Shouldn't someone have been allowed to comment?

By censoring Henderson's column from the late edition, the publisher lent credence to those who view the press as a corporate lapdog rather than a public watchdog. Shortly before this incident occurred, Chrysler paid an estimated $300,000 for an advertising spread in *The Windsor Star*. According to Gail Robertson, "Columnists should have the freedom to write opinion pieces. [This example] stands out because a journalist should be able to state an opinion but he couldn't. That was frightening. And our columnists tend to be more right-leaning."[18]

An action by James Bruce, former editor of *The Star* and Préfontaine's successor as publisher, was even more problematical because it applied to the news rather than commentary. On February 5, 1996, *The Star* ran a CP wire service story out of Montréal which mildly criticized car dealers. The story, which ran on Page D7, provided tips on car buying and reported on a study by the Automobile Protection Association, which found in a test that seven out of nine Montréal car dealers mislead customers. Although the story reported on these findings, the criticism was muted, and the story contained a rebuttal by the president of the Canadian Automobile Dealers' Association. Nevertheless, Bruce says "I went ballistic," reportedly screaming at his editors for allowing the story to run.[19] He said he had not received a single complaint. The next day, Bruce published a letter of apology on Page 4, which began: "On rare occasions a story finds its way into the newspaper which does not meet the high ethical and journalistic standards of balance, fairness and factual accuracy which we set for ourselves at *The Windsor Star*." After briefly describing the story, he continued: "The story was a discredit to the dealers and employees of members of the Windsor Essex County Dealers Association, who adhere to the highest of ethical standards and provide their customers with first rate standards of service." Bruce concluded by saying, "*The Star* apologizes to the dealers, their sales people and readers for any false impressions which the story may have created."[20]

The most striking thing about this incident is that it makes it clear that anything which is even remotely critical of advertisers is not going to make it into the newspaper. Additionally, as a letter writer subsequently pointed out, the article in question did in fact meet the three standards of "balance, fairness and factual accuracy" which the publisher said *The Star* sets for itself. It's not at all clear that the publisher's letter meets those same criteria, especially where he asserts by implication that *all* local car dealers "adhere to the highest of ethical standards and provide their customers with first rate standards of service." What is his authority for making this claim? The wire service story was based on a field experiment conducted at nine Montréal dealerships. Publisher James Bruce's sweeping generalization appears to have been based on nothing more than the claims made in the car dealers' advertisements in his own newspaper. I am not aware of any evidence which indicates that car dealers and salespeople are different from other occupational groups. There is however plenty of evidence which indicates that some salespeople mislead their customers. To deny this and apologize to car dealers for what amounts to a balanced and factual story, is to take the business of toadying to advertisers to new heights.

This was not an isolated event. Reporter John Asling, who has worked for the Thomson and Southam chains, recounts numerous incidents of corporate and advertiser influence, in what he describes as "backscratch journalism."[21] Rob Reid, then-city editor of the *Timmins Daily Press* remembers in the 1980s when Maurice Switzer was publisher, and a national story came over the wire which was vaguely critical of McDonalds restaurants. "We ran the story as a small brief. Switzer reamed out the wire editor for running the story," Reid said.[22]

A Newspaper for its Readers

Advertisers pay for 100 percent of private broadcasting, and approximately 75-80 percent of the cost of daily newspapers. As such, publishers have a responsibility to the public whom they supposedly serve, to ensure that advertisers and businesses at large do not receive special treatment. A failure to do so means that newspapers such as *The Windsor Star* and publishers such as Bruce must abandon any claim to serving the public, or to "the high ethical and journalistic standards of balance, fairness and factual accuracy." You can't have it both ways. Stop toadying to advertisers, or cease making the claims about public service and responsibility.

Bruce obviously has not taken this message to heart. In an interview following this incident, he said, "I think that the primary role of a newspaper is to truly reflect the society we live in and to be a mirror of our community." He added, "I think that the ideal newspaper has to be a newspaper that the readers want...You should put out your newspaper for your readers. The ideal newspaper should truly represent their interests, report their interests and reflect their interests."[23]

According to *Windsor Star* reporter Gail Robertson, "I think there was nothing wrong with the first story. I don't think that an apology was necessary at all...We are clearly heading towards writing for advertisers and not for readers...I actually felt ill when I read that. What bothered me the most was that we were giving a stamp of approval to all Windsor-Essex county car dealers. In the letter of apology we said that they all have high standards and I know personally that it's not true."[24]

Journalists at the newspaper were so riled up over the car dealer incident that they demanded a meeting with the editor and publisher, who agreed. According to some who were present, the publisher defended his position by saying that he had recently attended a human rights workshop sponsored by the CAW, and that stereotyping occupational groups such as car dealers was unacceptable. Bruce said afterwards, "I don't believe that any group in society should be stereotyped. Over the years, car dealers have been stereotyped, they have been characterized as a bunch of crooks." He went on to add that "I thought it was a very, very poor piece of journalism, which should not be in our newspaper. I have absolutely no apologies to make for the decision that I personally took at six o'clock the next morning. That decision was to respond and to be pro-active in the situation." To rectify the situation, acting editor Doug Firby vowed that in future, management would read each and every story. This would ensure that no such thing would happen again. Indeed, a column I wrote and submitted on the topic, which criticized the publisher, was rejected because it supposedly may have libelled the car dealerships, since I said, in part, "I'm not aware of any evidence which indicates that car dealers and salespeople are different from other occupational groups. There is however plenty of evidence which indicates that some salespeople mislead their customers."

Bruce says, "I want to assure you that my heart and soul will always remain with the folks in the newsroom." Yet, James Bruce the former editor seems to differ little from André Préfontaine the corporate hit man. According to Bruce, "I believe that we share similar philosophies in terms of what kind of newspapers you should be producing in the 1990s. I think we're quite different in personality and in approach."

"I'm here to run a newspaper and newspapers are only going to exist if they are profitable. The only guarantee that we have that there is going to be a free press is that newspapers are profitable so they can pump resources into the paper in order to have editorial staff to do the kind of job that we want them to do. Profitability at newspapers is not wrong.

We're like any other major corporation even though we're very different in the kind of role we play in society."

This demonstrates that even the publishers from the news side of things have succumbed to corporate pressure, and consider profits ahead of journalism ethics and the community.

Soon after the car dealer fiasco, publisher James Bruce announced the appointment of a new editor, in the spring of 1996. Southam brought into *The Star* an editor from *The Hamilton Spectator*, rather than promoting someone internally. This is the first time that anyone could recall an editor being appointed from outside the newspaper. So now, in addition to appointing publishers, the Southam chain effectively appoints editors as well, tightening the chain's control over individual newspapers. James Bruce denied this. "We had several external candidates and one internal. They were all interviewed by myself and [Southam executive] Gordon Fisher...I hired [*The Spectator's*] Gerry Nott. That's how it [went]. I believe that having someone from the outside in our newsroom is very healthy."[25]

Bruce's opinion happens to coincide with the views at Southam. According to the *Windsor Star's* former editor Doug Firby, "Southam has a policy now in which they [are] trying to implement some cross-pollination between papers. I think they feel as though there's a lot more to be gained by moving people from one paper to another rather than having them spend their entire career at one newspaper."[26]

Bruce sees the changes at Southam as both inevitable and positive. "Going back to the seventies and eighties, Southam newspapers were pretty much operated independently. As we get into the nineties, it became apparent that unlike most other types of corporations, Southam had been left behind," Bruce said. "They decided that they did have to have more of a centralized control of their total operations."

This view is supported by former editor Doug Firby. "Southam has really changed its direction dramatically now, and there is a lot more head-office interest and involvement in local decisions. So the publisher is really a lot less independent than he used to be. There really is a lot of influence from head office, a lot of input in terms of what is acceptable and what isn't acceptable." One result of this centralization is downsizing. According to Bruce, the cuts have not hurt. "I believe that the number of people we have in our newsroom, for a paper our size, is about where it should be. That is, eighty-three. These are divided into about twenty-eight reporters, thirty editors of different levels, seven or eight in the photo department, a couple in the library and five or six people at the *Express* [magazine]." Union Chair Gail Robertson disagrees. She says 105 news and editorial staff were recently reduced by over 20 percent, to 78. Inevitably, this affects the end product: the news. "There is news that we're just not able to cover. There are two things happening: one is the downsizing so we can't do the investigative reporting, what I consider the tougher stories. At the same time, there is the bottom line mentality coming from people like Conrad Black...Those things are happening and you're not getting the tough stories because of the downsizing. You don't want to annoy your advertisers, who are the people who are going to bring in the money."[27]

According to Craig Pearson, Southam now cites "an industry standard" which allows one newsroom employee for every 1,000 copies the paper sells (*The Star's* circulation is 85,000). "I've only heard of this since André Préfontaine came. They try to make it seem like this standard has been around forever, but from what I can tell this is a new thing that they decided because if they do it that way they can cut more staff." He points out that while the number of journalists has gone down at *The Star*, "the marketing department has grown from one and a half to four people."

Publisher James Bruce describes the newsroom at *The Windsor Star* as "excellent." He says that the main impact of André Préfontaine, Southam, and the market researchers is an emphasis on local news, because "people who read our paper said that they wanted more local news." So, the newsroom was restructured into "a more efficient operation." Whereas most of the reporters used to have beats, "as we downsized it became evident that...there had to be fewer specialists and more generalists. In *The Windsor Star's* newsroom right now, you could be the labour reporter but, you could be assigned to cover a fire. Going back a few years, that would be absolutely unheard of. We came to the conclusion that as resources shrink everybody has to work together to do everything."

According to Bruce, the content's quality survived the downsizing. He now sees the biggest quality issue at the newspaper as one of copy editing, and typographical and grammatical errors, a consequence of fewer proofreaders. "In that sense, quality can be impacted because the other set of eyes is not there to function as a backstop. We get complaints all the time," Bruce says. But Gail Robertson says the downsizing means reporters don't even have the time for follow-up calls, let alone investigative reporting. "There was a time when reporters had two days to work on a story. Doing your research, calling around, doing what you were supposed to be doing. Now, they say that it's just a short story so you don't need to spend a lot of time on it."[28]

"At one time, during the day you would be doing one or two stories. Now you're doing three or four and sometimes five, plus checking and doing [photo] cut lines. Instead of working a story and calling more people and really feeling good about those stories, you now have a lot more stories, and you start to feel like you're on an assembly line, churning out another story."[29]

Dave Hall says, "we still have a fifty-to sixty-page paper to put out; we still have a community of readers, and we still have news to gather across a very large area. So I don't see how if you reduce the number of people gathering that news and producing that news, you will not see some drop off in quality. I don't know how you could do that any other way, other than having people work harder and harder."

According to Bill Doskoch, formerly of the Regina *Leader-Post*, "There is no real time for any competent reporting any more, because you are always in a hurry to fill the paper the next day." As a result, he says, "there are few in-depth stories....more wire copy, less news of relevance to Regina readers, a reliance on AP and CP wire features...and fewer stories about the community...People will say at some point, 'why am I spending my money on this thing?'"[30]

"I would like to be able to cover things the way we did," says Craig Pearson. "Both time and space have been reduced. There's not enough time because there's fewer employees and fewer reporters. There's not as much space because there is a higher advertising rate and everything has been squeezed....The stories have to be shorter now and are less in-depth. [Reporters] certainly don't have time to investigate a story."

The Cambridge (Ontario) *Reporter*, with a circulation of about 10,000, was purchased by Hollinger from Thomson in fall, 1995. One reporter with that paper called in to CBC Ontario's *Radio Noon* phone-in program to describe the changes under Hollinger. She spent six years as an editor under Thomson, but was demoted to reporter with the Hollinger cutbacks, which amounted to 30 percent of the staff. Under Thomson, reporters were expected to write 40 stories each, per month. Under Hollinger, this has doubled to four stories a day, "plus editorials and taking pictures and writing opinion columns," she said. As for local news content, she said "They have people there who are doing nothing but rewriting press releases and [they are] tossing these off as local news."[31]

Cutbacks also mean that newspapers such as *The Windsor Star* rely more on freelancers. "I think there are probably thirty to forty freelancers available, but they're probably only using about six on a regular, ongoing basis," says Robertson. Freelancers are paid a paltry sum, with no benefits, and it's piecework. They used to be paid about $40 per story, but now they are paid by the column inch. They can spend the night at a municipal council meeting in the county and if the newspaper doesn't run their story, even though it was assigned, they won't be paid. "Some young people might even work for free because they want to get their portfolios built up."

"Morale was terrible with André Préfontaine," says Craig Pearson. "There were periods for months on end when you didn't know if you were going to lose your job. People would come in and read the [notice] board and would expect to see another announcement of layoffs, reductions or budget cuts that would affect someone in the building. It was terrible."

"There never used to be empty desks in our newsroom," says Gail Robertson. "We'd be two at a desk sometimes, or the afternoon person would share a desk with the evening person." Now, she says, there are empty desks even though some desks and reporters have been moved out of the newsroom to staff a new arts and entertainment magazine.

"There are all sorts of jokes about how there is nobody in the newsroom. I heard one today which was something about not calling across the newsroom to somebody because you get an echo. Or, it's easier to find a desk these days because there is nobody to fill them. That's a reflection of low morale," says Craig Pearson.[32]

One result, according to Robertson, is "a layoff chill" at the newspaper because of firings. She described one human resources person who, the night before had drawn up termination papers for some other managers. The next morning they just told him that he was gone too. "He was anti-union, a destructive person. But it was a callous way to do things. And people said to themselves, if they can be that callous with their own, then..." This results in a kind of fear and loathing in the newsroom. Losses in the senior ranks of veteran reporters, through early retirement buyouts also meant "the loss of a lot of cumulative wisdom," she says.

What's happening at the Southam chain has a definite ring of familiarity. At *The Winnipeg Free Press*, "the paper has been completely Thomsonized," according to one employee who was interviewed confidentially. The newspaper was once a quality paper, the pride of the FP chain. In 1996, the newspaper is on its third publisher since 1991. The previous publisher was having a meeting in the boardroom when the Thomson people flew in. They arrived at 9 a.m., during the meeting, and sent the publisher's secretary in to get him. "He blasted his secretary for calling him out of the meeting. He was a horrible man, really. But they put the new publisher in his chair and within fifteen minutes the former publisher was out in his car on the street."

The picture painted is one of small vignettes reminiscent of the wholesale slaughter orchestrated by Hollinger Inc. at the Saskatchewan dailies. The Thomson people greeted middle managers at the front door and told them they were fired. "It's part of this whole bloodless economy we have created," according to one *Free Press* journalist. "Everyone knows not to keep any notes in their desk," because they won't be allowed to retrieve them. "It's horrendous. I don't understand the motivation or why it has to happen this way. We seem to be living in this nihilistic society where nothing matters except wealth and power for a few."

The centralization taking place at the Southam chain diminishes local employment, which decreases rather than increases the amount of local news, according to Gail Robertson. Since the cutbacks, the film reviews and most book reviews come from news services. Only four Southam papers now have bureaus at the Ontario Legislature. "Eventually, there will be one Queen's Park reporter for Southam," she said, a situation which already exists at the Thomson chain. If one book reviewer doesn't like your book, it will be panned across the country.

The emphasis on chain news at the expense of local news was evident early in 1996, when students across the country protested cutbacks to higher education. About 1,200 students protested and marched at the University of Windsor, about the same number as protested at the Ontario Legislature. In Toronto, a confrontation with police and some property damage ensued. The protests in Windsor and across the rest of the country were peaceful. In its coverage, *The Windsor Star* chose to run a Southam News story across its front page. Although the Windsor protest saw hundreds of demonstrators march through the downtown, rallying first at Solicitor-General Herb Gray's office and later with public service workers who were poised to strike, no *Windsor Star* reporters covered the event. That night, a reporter called Howard Pawley, a political science professor and former NDP premier of Manitoba, who spoke at the demonstration, to ask what happened. *The Star* then ran a paragraph inside the paper on the Windsor demonstration, and splashed the Toronto demonstration across the front page. A community relations official with the University of Windsor subsequently wrote a letter to *The Star* complaining about the lack of local coverage.

Sacred Cows and Management Residues

Hiring, firing and promoting by publishers and management, while obviously crucial, are only the starting points for content control and effective socialization in the newsroom. Story assignments, deciding what gets covered each day from numerous possibilities, is a management function. Producers and assignment editors tell reporters what to cover. Often they indicate to reporters how important a story is. Sometimes this is just a matter of telling the reporter how long the story should be, other times it is more direct. At *The Windsor Star*, an assignment editor has been known to write the notation "Small Moo" (somewhat important) or "Big Moo" (very important) on the reporter's assignment sheet. This indicates that the story is a "must," a sacred cow, a special request by someone higher up in news management. One news manager has commented, "Every newspaper has sacred cows and everyone knows what they are."[33] As American journalist, academic and media critic Ben Bagdikian puts it, "the sacred cows in American newsrooms leave residues common to all cows. But no sacred cow has been so protected and has left more generous residues in the news than the American corporation."[34]

"If someone says 'J.B. [publisher James Bruce] wants this,' you know it's pretty important," says one *Windsor Star* reporter. "If the editor wants it, you know it's important...You get an idea of what makes it onto the front page. A story on the plight of urban poverty would not be deemed that important. Pro-development, or deficit cutbacks are generally seen on the front page." Sociologist David Altheide indicates that management will frequently "frame" a story within a particular news frame or "predefined story angle," or what he calls the "news perspective," which fits the circumstances of a particular story "to prior conclusions, beliefs and practices."[35]

Management also may directly affect the general tone and content of the news. For example, soon after André Préfontaine came to *The Windsor Star*, the paper dramatically increased coverage of crime and accidents. According to one staff reporter, "when Préfontaine came, the coverage of car crashes increased. At one point, people were saying, 'what's going on here?' They were concerned that the roads were unsafe, or whatever. But it was the same number of crashes, we were just putting them on the front page more often."

Here are some other ways in which newsroom management has been found to influence reporters' stories. These are based upon the sociology of news literature,[36] and also field studies and interviews conducted by my students over the years, and my own discussions with and observations of journalists during the course of more than 20 years of research. These are in addition to the above-mentioned management roles of: owning papers, setting policies, and hiring and promoting employees.

1. Management assigns stories, and has a veto over any that journalists themselves initiate.
2. Management decides story "importance," in terms of length, time or play.
3. Management may frame the story within a particular angle or perspective.
4. Management may suggest sources or contacts to interview or leads to follow.
5. When the reporter hands in a story, it may have to be rewritten by the reporter, to the editor's specifications. The emphasis might be changed, new material added, and/or some material dropped.
6. When the reporter is finished with a story, it is copy edited, which may mean significant additional changes.
7. At any time the story may be dropped altogether, for various reasons, without much explanation other than space constraints.
8. If the story makes it into the paper, an editor decides placement: whether it will go on the top of page one, or if it will be buried in the comic section. Additional cuts to content may be made, owing to space considerations or other reasons.
9. Management also decides what the headline will be, which is crucial. This is the first (and sometimes last) thing people learn about the story.
10. At some newspapers, if reporters object to changes made to the story, they may remove their byline. They have no other control over the story at that point, and no right at all to insist that the management version not appear in the paper.

One example illustrates numbers two, three, five, six, eight and nine above. In May, 1994, *Windsor Star* reporter Craig Pearson covered a demonstration and protest against the big five banks, held on Ouellette Ave. in Windsor. I was present and among those who spoke at the demonstration, and was quoted in the story. When he wrote up his article, the opening or "lead" paragraph read as follows: "Big business, particularly banks, are committing the real welfare fraud in our society, and concerned citizens say duplicit politicians had better take heed." By the time this story was edited by management, the lead was changed to the following, which appeared in the paper: "Activists committed to tax reform took aim at big business, banks and politicians this weekend."[37]

At first glance this may seem insignificant. But with a stroke of the editor's pen, "concerned citizens" were transformed into "activists," while corporate "welfare fraud" became the homogenized "tax reform." A specific critique of banks and duplicitous politicians, in the hands of the editor, became a general attack on "business, banks and politicians." In addition, when it came to writing a headline, the editors chose the most emotionally-charged statement in the story, and then distorted it. The headline read, "Protesters say tax system a 'powder keg' set to blow." In fact, one of the spokespersons quoted in the story said "there are cuts to the social welfare system...while corporations remain healthy...People are getting fed up. There's a social powder keg out there and it's going to blow up." Rather than saying the tax system is a powder keg which was set to blow, the spokesperson said that social welfare cuts and the inequities of the tax system threatened to ignite public opposition. However, caught up in the imagery of "protesters" and a "powder keg," the headline writer contributed to the radicalization and marginalization of the demonstrators. In fact, the protestors represented a broad cross-section of the community.

On another occasion, Pearson wrote a story on door-to-door vacuum sales. A complaint had come into *The Star*. The Better Business Bureau told him that many such sales people use high pressure techniques and target older people. His original story was a general warning to the community, but management watered it down and made it seem like only one particular company was doing this, so it would not offend other sales people or companies. "We received about a dozen calls afterwards, reiterating the problem," says Pearson. The company in question left town within two weeks; the high-pressure sales people did not.

As Nicholas Johnson indicated, by the time a reporter endures this process a few times, all but the most dedicated, stubborn and resistant reporters know what is expected and what to do — or else. According to Dennis Mazzocco, when Capital Cities Communications took control of the ABC TV network in the U.S. in 1985, management instituted the usual cost-cutting, efficiency and control measures. "Those who objected to the growing management control seemed to be singled out for disciplinary action by the company. Workers who questioned the rules faced the constant threat of harassment by management and even dismissal."[38]

One example of management control of the news comes from Canada's national news magazine, *Maclean's*, currently under the stewardship of publisher Brian Segal. Since the spring of 1994 the magazine has been owned by Ted Rogers. Segal is brother to Hugh Segal, long-time Tory activist and Principal Secretary to Brian Mulroney during his last year in office. Between the beginning of the federal Conservative leadership campaign to replace Brian Mulroney in the spring of 1993, and the end of the election, Brian Segal devoted five *Maclean's* cover stories to the new Tory leader Kim Campbell. In addition, one cover was devoted to PC leadership candidate Jean Charest and his wife. I mention these facts just to establish the conservative influences at that magazine. According to former *Maclean's* journalist Ian Austen, the previous publisher, Kevin Doyle, was "rabidly pro-free trade....he was obsessed with the idea, personally."[39]

Award-winning journalist and author Linda McQuaig worked for part of the 1980s as a senior writer with *Maclean's*, where she says she was well treated. But this did not prevent her from being very critical in her book *Shooting the Hippo*, of the role played by *Maclean's* in compiling a bogus national panel of "average" Canadians and contributing, along with Eric Malling of CTV's *W5*, to the deficit hysteria. In a talk to a group of communications students in the spring of 1995, McQuaig indicated that when she worked at *Maclean's*, editors would routinely take her articles and those of the other journalists working there and change them to better suit the editors' own biases and expectations and the unwritten policy of the magazine. "They would go through and change the copy all the time to suit their political biases...I remember a million times being enraged with 'my own' writing: with the meaning being fundamentally distorted," she recalled. Making changes even extended to the quotes writers included from people. "What got me was how casual they were about changing quotes. It couldn't be too drastic, of course. If you included a quote from, say, [lawyer] Clayton Ruby advocating human rights they couldn't reverse what he was saying." But, says McQuaig, they made changes, and quotes should be sacrosanct. "As journalists, we should keep them accurate."[40]

On the other hand, editing which is "merely" heavy-handed is a problem faced by most working journalists, at one time or another. Even Barbara Amiel has complained about this to her husband Conrad Black. "I tried to explain to Conrad once how frightful it was to battle with brain-challenged copy editors, and he remarked that he had never encountered anything but the greatest politeness when sending his copy into a newspaper. "'It helps,' I remarked trenchantly, 'to own the newspaper.'"[41]

Linda McQuaig describes how, when she was a reporter for *The Globe and Mail,* she wrote stories about tax policies, discussing how different tax changes favoured the rich. One day she was called into the managing editor's office, and he said, "there's some problems with your tax stories. You've been using some very inflammatory language." McQuaig says that at first she couldn't figure out what he meant. "He was kind of evasive, and finally he said, 'Do you have to use words like 'rich'?' What am I supposed to call them? The financially unchallenged? Eventually he said, 'Whatever you do, just don't make it sound like there's a class struggle going on.'"[42]

Paying the Piper

I want to be very clear that I am not simply reducing the complex process and biases surrounding the news media, to management and ownership alone. There are numerous other factors, many or all of which contribute to similar biases. For example I have described the related area of cutbacks. Then there is advertising, which in addition to its usually subtle and behind the scenes role as paymaster, also plays an essential part in the process of creating media monopolies. Advertisers do this, perhaps unwittingly and ultimately against their own interest as well, because of their relentless short term search for economies of scale — the most cost-efficient vehicle for their ads. Ben Bagdikian has illustrated this phenomenon using the city of Washington as a case study.[43] At the same time, those who feel newspapers are produced for *all* readers would be fascinated with an account buried in the business section of *The Globe and Mail,* in 1990. Under the heading, "Globe cutting circulation in bid to help advertisers," the paper revealed how it was "winnowing" or getting rid of, about 30,000 readers in "smaller cities and towns," in favour of increasing sales in the six largest markets. This would, said *The Globe,* meet the changing needs of advertisers, "providing them with an increased number of better-educated, upper-income readers."[44] Some readers appeal to newspapers and their advertisers more than others: specifically the upscale ones with more disposable income.

According to James Bruce of *The Windsor Star,* he "would be thrown right out of the newsroom" if he suggested that someone write a news story which would intentionally promote business. But at the same time, in his view advertisers may legitimately suggest potential news stories. "Let's say I'm shopping at Freed's [men's store]. Harry Freed would say, 'there's a tremendous change in men's fashion.' This is a fact, the story has been in the newspaper. Then he says, 'men won't buy suits anymore.' There's a business story here; its a lifestyle story; it's a fashion trend story....There's a hell of a story there. Is that an advertiser suggesting a story? I don't think so...If the story is a bad idea you wouldn't pursue it; if it's a good idea you might."[45]

According to one *Windsor Star* reporter, "There's no memo that you are going to read from an advertiser saying 'write this story.' The kind of thing that tends to overtly pop up is a complaint from an advertiser. Like real-estate boards calling up and complaining about a review of a book on selling your own house. Shortly thereafter we wrote a complimentary story on the real estate board."[46]

Among the other influences are also the so-called professional norms of journalism, such as "objectivity" or "fairness," which in practice largely boil down to reliance on official sources. To uphold their neutrality, while simultaneously making their case, journalists often quote official sources. Even where two sides are presented, many other sides are omitted. Seldom does balance exit in headlines and lead paragraphs of stories, where one side is privileged over another. "In short, professional journalism standards introduce a distorted political perspective into the news yet legitimize that perspective as broad and realistic.[47]

News Brought to You By the CAW
In the summer of 1995 reporters at *The Windsor Star* faced an unusual and perhaps unique choice. Reporters and other unionized white-collar workers in advertising, circulation and the business office at the newspaper, voted to leave their U.S.-based union and find a Canadian replacement. Early published reports accurately predicted that the union "will likely be the Canadian Auto Workers (CAW)."[48] The executive of the Windsor Newspaper Guild, representing about 185 workers, recommended a merger with the CAW, which its members subsequently voted on, in late August of 1995. The vote overwhelmingly endorsed joining the CAW, an extremely high-profile player in Windsor. Aside from representing about 30,000 autoworkers in ten locals in the city, the CAW also signed up the workers at Casino Windsor in 1994, and led them out on strike in pursuit of a first contract in 1995. Reporters at *The Star*, like the other workers, were excited about affiliation with a strong, progressive union, at a time when cutbacks were rampant. As one

employee told me, "I guess it will take a Buzz Hargrove to stand up to the likes of Conrad Black."[49]

Unlike the others in advertising and elsewhere, however, the journalists have a concern. *Star* reporters already receive criticism from the Windsor labour movement over the negative coverage of labour in *The Windsor Star*. The paper is notorious for the anti-union stance it takes in a so-called labour town. Reporters realize that owing to the influence of management, labour coverage will not improve in the *Star*, even with its reporters in the CAW. Will community disgruntlement turn to hostility when *Star* reporters in the CAW are seen as demonstrating an anti-union or even specifically anti-CAW bias? Union solidarity and a tendency not to blame fellow workers for management problems would suggest otherwise. CAW organizer Maureen Kirincic is quoted as saying, "if you have a story that's negative toward the labour movement, you've got to write it. Each member's got a job to do."[50] But the matter is still of concern for the reporters. Some may question whether the coverage of the CAW and the labour movement generally will improve with reporters in the union. But a reporter I interviewed disagreed, citing the strong influence of management on the news product. "Being in the CAW won't change the coverage one iota," the reporter said.[51] As for reporters' concerns about a backlash from their sisters and brothers in the CAW, one long-time CAW activist had this advice: "Tell them to come right out and blame management. We've been telling them to do that for years."[52] In this way, reporters would take the heat off themselves and put it where it belongs — squarely on management shoulders.

As for *Star* coverage of labour generally and the CAW specifically, after reporters joined the union, the preliminary indications are that coverage will be "business as usual." A couple of weeks after the ratification vote, *The Star* ran a fairly straightforward story by its labour reporter concerning CAW President Buzz Hargrove's reaction to premier Mike Harris' promise to scrap Bill 40, the mildly favourable labour law reforms brought in by the Rae government. The headline read: "CAW talks tough on Bill 40." In the story we learned that Hargrove actually supported Bill 40: "I just want to remind people what the potential of [scrapping Bill 40] is." He said labour relations could return to "the good old days" when cooperation was unheard of, with "struggles, grievances, overload, wildcat strikes. There was no such thing as working together." To the management headline writer, this became "tough talk." Mark your score card: management one, union zero.[53]

The next major labour coverage in that newspaper involved the September 1995 Labour Day celebrations which coincided with the 50th anniversary of the 1945 Ford strike leading to the (Justice Ivan) Rand Formula arbitration decision. As a result of this decision, Ford union dues now were automatically collected from all workers who benefited from the union, whether or not they were members. This precedent was applied in collective bargaining elsewhere, and meant that union leaders could focus their attention on workers' rights, rather than fundraising. The strike also was of tremendous symbolic significance, representing a moral victory over anti-labour forces. A celebration was planned in Windsor, with CAW President Buzz Hargrove and CLC President Bob White in attendance. *The Windsor Star* carried a special section to commemorate the 1945 Ford strike, with favourable stories written by labour reporter Brian Cross.

In addition, the Saturday edition front and back wraparound pages of *The Star* carried photos and stories, with a giant headline, "A Salute to labour." Underneath a full-page photo of the famous auto blockade of the Ford plant, the cut line read in part, "The labour movement in Windsor and Essex County has raised the standard of living for all of us. Labour helped shape medicare, pensions and politics." This is clearly the most favourable coverage of labour in *The Windsor Star*, and perhaps any Canadian daily newspaper, in recent memory. People in the labour movement to whom I spoke about the coverage were, to say the least, pleasantly surprised.

With no desire to be stingy or mean-spirited, I must point out that the favourable coverage was not without its price. In order to obtain the front and back page wraparound sheets, the labour movement had to purchase ads which filled the two flip side, interior pages, at a cost of thousands of dollars. As for the special section, this is what is known in the newspaper business as a "sucker section," or vendor-support section, one in which the content is specifically written to please and attract specific advertisers. In this case, labour reporter Brian Cross wrote favourable stories about the 1945 strike, and advertisers ranging from credit unions, to restaurants, the United Way, other unions and the mayor's office, took out ads congratulating the labour movement. Normally, these advertising sections help to highlight more traditional topics such as home improvements, fashion, weddings, automobiles, and so forth. But, while *The Windsor Star* might be commended for its entrepreneurial spirit, for managing to turn an anniversary celebration into a profit making venture, we should not confuse this adherence to the bottom line with a pro-labour stance.[54] Indeed, subsequent pieces by columnists Gord Henderson and Karen Hall continued *The Star's* tradition of attacks on labour and working people. For example, Hall belittled labour's one-day shutdown of London, Ontario in December 1995. Henderson accused labour leader Ken Lewenza and the CAW of "barking" and "ranting," of "scorched-earth tactics," and "threatening to kill [the casino] industry." He wrote about "a venomous labour relations problem" at Casino Windsor, and compared the CAW leadership in Windsor to the Communist Red Army.[55]

Despite this, some might view the 1995 labour-day coverage as an example of a pro-labour perspective by CAW-member reporters. In my view, this would be a serious mistake.

Newspaper Awards Reporting Wins No Awards

I quoted *Windsor Star* publisher James Bruce regarding "the high ethical and journalistic standards of balance, fairness and factual accuracy which we set for ourselves at *The Windsor Star*." I'd like to briefly examine those standards as they are applied in a case study of a prominent annual story covered by a number of newspapers. I'm going to focus on the Western Ontario Newspaper Awards, (WONA) because that's where I live, but you can observe a highly similar phenomenon in your own region and community.

Every year, the WONA dinner and awards night is held somewhere in southwestern Ontario. Dozens of reporters, photographers, editors and columnists at 21 newspapers are nominated for 27 awards. The four largest newspapers: *The Hamilton Spectator*, London *Free Press*, *Windsor Star*, and Kitchener-Waterloo *Record* (in that order) normally dominate the awards. Journalists attend the awards, held on the last weekend in April, observe the same events and announcements of winners, and then return to their home cities where someone writes things up for the next edition of the local paper. It's a very straightforward affair, with nominations, winners and honourable mentions in each category. And, it has been going on for 42 years now.

What makes matters less than straightforward is the evident self-interest on the part of the newspapers. When it comes to informing their community about how their journalism peers judged their work— about the relative quality of journalism their readers receive — they are not "factually accurate," or "balanced," or even "fair," in their reporting on this event. For example, at the 1995 awards ceremony in the spring of 1996, the contest was lopsided. *The Hamilton Spectator* won journalist of the year, and top place in six categories, with ten honourable mentions. Of course, the paper reported this with a story headlined:

"*Spectator* staffers win seven top awards: Denise Davy named journalist of year." The story described the awards and honourable mentions won by *The Spectator*, and included praise from the paper's managing editor. Not one mention was made of any competition.[56]

The fact that *The London Free Press* fared poorly in the awards is immediately apparent on reading the headline: "*Free Press* reporter wins praise for writing." This is confirmed by the subheading which refers to "six honourable mentions." Yes, the second largest paper won only one award, given to Jane Sims for entertainment and arts reporting. But that did not prevent the *Free Press* from focusing solely on its own award and honourable mentions, excluding any reference at all to the competition, other than to say that "The Martha J. Blackburn journalist of the year award was won by Denise Davy of the *Hamilton Spectator*. The award is presented in memory of the late *Free Press* publisher Martha Blackburn, who died in 1992."[57]

The Windsor Star headline read, "Star wins 5 newspaper awards." The story did mention in the second paragraph that *The Star's* efforts were "second only to the *Hamilton Spectator's* seven awards." Much further down the story also mentioned that "*The Star* had earned 14 nominations for work done in 1995, second only to *The Spectator's* 17." And, in the final paragraph recognition was given to Denise Davy, the journalist of the year from Hamilton. However, these were the only times another newspaper was mentioned, and one would be at a loss to determine who finished third (or below), or how many honourable mentions *The Spectator* received, *et cetera*. The story included words of praise from the newspaper's editor, and managed to include a reference to an award named after Carl Morgan, a former editor of *The Windsor Star*.[58]

The Kitchener-Waterloo *Record's* headline read: "*Record* first in 2 categories." It went on to describe the two winners and four runners-up at that newspaper, with no mention at all of any other newspapers. Here is a summary of the headlines in the four major dailies covering this same event:

"*Spectator* staffers win seven top awards"
"*Free Press* reporter wins praise for writing"
"*Star* wins 5 newspaper awards"
"*Record* first in 2 categories"

The "national" press, in the form of *The Globe and Mail* and *The Toronto Star*, did not report at all on the WONA awards.

It wouldn't be quite as bad if "all" these newspapers did was to somewhat over-emphasize their own success, which might be seen, after all, as the "local angle" on the story. The problem is that they failed to give readers any context with which to make their own judgements about the winners and losers at the awards banquet. The facts were not just distorted and buried, they were non-existent.

In the 1994 WONA reporting, the four major dailies each captured four first-place awards. In light of this, *The Windsor Star* headline read, "*Star* staff take top honors." The *Free Press* said, "London *Free Press* captures four first-place, four runners-up awards." But the truth of the matter was that the *Hamilton Spectator* was again the winner, with 13 runners-up, compared to eight at the *Star* and four at both the *Free Press* and the *Record*. This information was contained in the last paragraph of the *Free Press* story, but was missing altogether from the *Star*.

I have focused on this case study for a particular reason, although to some it may appear to be relatively harmless. After all, who really cares who won the awards, other than the journalists? The point is that this is an instance where newspapers wear their biases on their sleeves: they have a blatant self-interest. In light of that, how accurate, fair and balanced can they be? Given the results, this may well lead us to wonder about the reporting we get where there are other, perhaps less blatant, examples of self-interest.

***

Endnotes

[1] Martin Lee and Norman *Solomon, Unreliable Sources: A Guide to Detecting Bias in the News Media* (NY: Carol Publishing Group, 1991), p. 98.

[2] Dennis Mazzocco, *Networks of Power: Corporate TV's Threat to Democracy* (Boston: South End Press, 1994), p. 27.

[3] Sandra Precop, from the transcript of an interview with Lanie Hurdle, Brad Milburn and Michelle Pisani, March 18, 1996.

[4] Craig Pearson, from the transcript of an interview with Lanie Hurdle, Brad Milburn and Michelle Pisani, February, 1996.

[5] Martin Lee and Norman Solomon, *Unreliable Sources*, p. 92.

[6] Ibid.

[7] Sandra Precop, interview, March 18, 1996.

[8] Quoted by Peter C. Newman, "The inexorable spread of the Black empire, " *Maclean's,* February 3, 1992, p. 68.

[9] 1995 Annual Report, Southam Inc., Don Mills, ON, p. 18.

[10] Martin Lee and Norman Solomon, *Unreliable Sources*, p. 93.

[11] Allan Fotheringham, "Australian culture imperialism?" *Maclean's*, August 22, 1988, p. 48.

[12] William Thorsell, "Opening Salvo," in *The Globe and Mail: 150 years*, a *Globe and Mail* magazine, Toronto, 1994, p. 8.

[13] Craig Pearson, *Printing News and Money: A Look at Corporate Influence on the Press*, unpublished M.A. thesis, University of Windsor, 1995, pp. 182-183.

[14] Ibid. pp. 180-188.

[15] Gail Robertson, from the transcript of an interview with Mark Crane, summer, 1994.

[16] Dave Hall, from the transcript of an interview with Mark Crane, summer, 1994.

[17] Craig Pearson, interview, February, 1996.

[18] Gail Robertson, interview, February 15, 1996.

[19] James Bruce, interview, April, 1996.

[20] See Ian Jack, "How to drive a bargain when buying a car," *The Windsor Star*, February 5, 1996, p. D7; James Bruce, "Story failed to meet Star's standards," *The Windsor Star*, February 6, 1996, p. A4.

[21] John Asling, "Backscratch journalism on the Bay of Quinte," in Barrie Zwicker and Dick MacDonald, eds, *The News: Inside the Canadian Media*, (Ottawa: Deneau Publishers, 1984).

[22] Quoted in Doug Smith, "Man Bites Newspaper," *This* magazine, Sept., 1992, p. 18.

[23] James Bruce, from the transcript of an interview with students Michelle Pisani, Lanie Hurdle and Brad Milburn, April 1996.

[24] Gail Robertson, interview, February 15, 1996.

[25] James Bruce, interview, April 1996.

[26] Doug Firby, from the transcript of an interview conducted by Brad Milburn, Lanie Hurdle, and Michelle Pisani, March 7, 1996.

[27] Gail Robertson, interview, February 15, 1996.

[28] Ibid.

[29] Ibid.

[30] Bill Doskoch, personal interview, April 4, 1996.

[31] Broadcast live on CBC Ontario's *Radio Noon* call in program, May 30, 1996.

[32] Craig Pearson, from the transcript of an interview with Mark Crane, August 4, 1994.

[33] Craig Pearson, *Printing News and Money*, p. 186.

[34] Ben Bagdikian, *The Media Monopoly*, 3rd Edition (Boston: Beacon Press, 1990), p. 47.

[35] David Altheide, *Creating Reality: How TV News Distorts Events*, (Beverly Hills, CA: Sage, 1974).

[36] See also Warren Breed, "Social Control in the Newsroom," *Social Forces*, May, 1955, 33: 326-35; John Porter, *The Vertical Mosaic*, (Toronto: U. of T. Press, 1965); E.J. Epstein, *News From Nowhere*, (Toronto: Random House, 1973); David Altheide, *Creating Reality*; Wallace Clement, *The Canadian Corporate Elite*, (Ottawa: Carleton U. Press, 1975); Gaye Tuchman, *Making News: A Study in the Construction of Reality* (NY: Macmillan, 1978); Herbert Gans, *Deciding What's News* (NY: Vintage, 1980);

Kent et al, *The Royal Commission on Newspapers*, (Ottawa: Ministry of Supply and Services, 1981). For a further contribution and overview of research, see R. Ericson, P. Baranek, J. Chan, *Visualizing Deviance*, (Toronto: U. of Toronto Press, 1987).

[37] Craig Pearson, "Protesters say tax system a 'powder keg' set to blow," *The Windsor Star*, May 2, 1994, p. A5.

[38] Dennis Mazzocco, *Networks of Power*, p. 22.

[39] Interview with the author, April, 1996.

[40] Ibid.

[41] Barbara Amiel, "Something to be optimistic about," *Maclean's*, November 15, 1993, p. 7.

[42] Linda McQuaig, "Gov't debt caused mainly by Bank of Canada,"*The Monitor*, CCPA, May 1996.

[43] See chapter seven in Ben Bagdikian, *The Media Monopoly*, 4th Edition (Boston: Beacon Press, 1992).

[44] John Partridge, "Globe cutting circulation in bid to help advertisers," *The Globe and Mail*, November 29, 1990, p. B9.

[45] James Bruce, interview, April 1996.

[46] Anonymous personal interview, spring, 1996.

[47] W. Lance Bennett, *News: The Politics of Illusion*, 3rd Edition (NY: Longman, 1996), p. 143.

[48] Brian Cross, "*Star* staff weighs switch to CAW," *The Windsor Star*, July 4, 1995, p. A3.

[49] Anonymous interview, summer, 1995.

[50] Brian Cross, "*Star* staff weighs" p. A3.

[51] Ibid.

[52] Peter Pellerito, interview, summer 1995.

[53] Brian Cross, "CAW talks tough on Bill 40," *The Windsor Star*, August 29, 1995 p. A3.

[54] See Brian Cross, "A Salute to Labor," "Continuing the struggle," and "1945 Ford Strike," in *The Windsor Star*, September 2, 1995.

[55] Gord Henderson, "Feeding off the milch cow," *The Windsor Star*, Feb. 17, 1996.

[56] "Spectator staffers win seven top awards," *The Hamilton Spectator*, April 29, 1996, p. C1.

[57] Peter Geigen-Miller, "Free Press reporter wins praise for writing," *The London Free Press*, April 29, 1996, p. B5.

[58] "Star wins 5 newspaper awards," *The Windsor Star*, April 29, 1996, p. A3.

Chapter Six

MEDIA THINK

> Western industrialized societies seem to have become
> incapable of weighing risks. Whether the 'threat' is from
> PCBs, or asbestos insulation or tainted tuna, any risk, no
> matter how trivial, is considered too great. So we badger
> government and corporations into spending millions of
> dollars of our money to tackle problems that pose no
> significant danger to either humans or the planet. —
> Editorial, *The Globe and Mail*, March 29, 1996.

As we saw in the last chapter, some working journalists have written
articles or books about aspects of corporate and management influence
on the news. Many journalists agree with at least some of this evidence
of corporate influence. On the other hand, some journalists say they
have seldom or perhaps never been unduly influenced in their writing by
their superiors. I argue that they reflect near-perfect conditioning for
their roles, honed by our society, and their employers. They also indicate
the almost seamless beauty of the hiring process. Many of the ideals
which journalists must hold dear are widely embraced by the public at
large: the sanctity of the free market, the symbiosis between capitalism
and democracy, the attraction of and necessity for advertising and
consumerism, the view that businesses are good corporate citizens, *et
cetera*. Why would journalists be an exception to this? Why would it be
necessary for owners and managers to do anything other than a little
fine-tuning and grooming, a little encouragement here and a little
discouragement there? Bill Doskoch, then a reporter at the Regina
Leader-Post, described how things work: "Management appoints people
to certain jobs because they have amply demonstrated they will behave
in a way that is consistent with management's objectives. That isn't
necessarily bad. It depends on the perspective being pushed by the
owners. Therefore, the journalists can quite accurately say they aren't
being censored."[1] So, it would be a mistake to believe that Conrad
Black, Ken Thomson or Paul Desmarais have to call their reporters or
dictate copy to them to keep them in line. This kind of blatant
interference is entirely unnecessary, just as it is unwarranted for large
advertisers to remind news managers that they don't want negative
publicity. Such a thing rarely happens, simply because there is no need
for it.

Perhaps more importantly, I should like to stress that none of the arguments made herein are what academics like to describe as "totalizing" in nature. There are always, to a degree, some exceptions and at least minor contradictions. The commercial media are not absolutely monolithic in the doctrine or ideology which they present, with a few notable exceptions. Nor would it be in their interest to be seen as such. In order for the illusion of diversity to flourish, it is far more effective if there are occasional stories or columns or even one or two journalists themselves who represent dissenting views. Cracks and openings — fissures — can be created by the inventive journalist and exploited, within limits, by the careful reader or viewer.

Hence, the small-l liberal *Toronto Star* can afford the luxury of a columnist such as Tom Walkom, a "leftist" economist and a social critic. Ken Thomson's *Winnipeg Free Press* can carry the progressive views of columnist Frances Russell. For *The Globe and Mail*, with arch-conservative columnists such as Andrew Coyne, William Thorsell, Peter Cook, Margaret Wente and Terence Corcoran among others, it can also afford to carry the small-l liberal views of Michael Valpy, and a weekly column by Rick Salutin. Besides, it also carries some wonderful social criticism as a regular feature of its letters page, which leads one to conclude that (some of) its readers are the best thing about *The Globe and Mail*.

That said, certain matters remain sacrosanct, and must never be questioned: not by columnists; not even on the letters page. These are what we might call "absolute truisms," as contrasted with the somewhat lesser class of "blue-moon truisms," which may be questioned once in a blue moon. While certain doctrines may occasionally be exposed to a little nibbling around the edges, others are so deeply ingrained that even a little nibbling would be too preposterous, too outrageous, and would certainly draw the condemnation of peers, superiors, and the public at large, and quite likely bring on the "people in white jackets" as well. Examples include the role of private enterprise in the economy, which is beyond question. Or the commercial banks. Or the ideal of the "free-market system," by which is meant the absence of government interference with private profits, rather than the absence of government grants, subsidies, tax breaks, laws and other protection for corporations.

Lesser truisms than these may be nibbled at, provided it is only gentle nibbling around the edges and it occurs only once in a blue moon. So, for example, a columnist in the arts-and-entertainment section may concede that the CBC does do some things that are worthwhile, even if it is a publicly-funded crown corporation. Such views are more than offset by higher profile news columns reporting the latest CBC cuts on the road to privatization, and the editorials demanding more cuts and faster privatization. Similarly on the environment, occasionally a frustrated university scientist will be allowed to publish an op-ed column outlining the very real threats posed by the depletion of the ozone layer, the greenhouse effect and global warming. But this hardly compares to numerous news stories and features and editorials which dismiss such fears as conspiracy theories propagated by deluded paranoiacs who, in their spare time, make a practice of ramming Greenpeace boats into innocent whaling vessels.

Agents of Legitimation

The two broad factors outlined at some length above, corporate ownership of the news media and the socialization process in the newsroom, are the predominant influences on news media content, and consequently our perceptions of the world around us. As a result, the broad nature of media content legitimates dominant Western institutions and perspectives, such as corporate capitalism. There is also considerable agreement in the academic literature on similar influences. These include: shrinking newsroom budgets, smaller news and editorial staffs, the focus on the bottom line, direct and indirect advertiser influence, pack journalism, a move towards "infotainment," reliance on "authorized knowers" or legitimated sources within government and business, libel chill, and the role of technological developments.[2] One can hardly overlook the underlying economic influence here.

Critical research in the vein of corporate ownership and newsroom socialization holds that the media frame the news within a particular ideological context. As Bob Hackett puts it in his recent book on peace movements, human rights and the Cold War: "[There is] substantial evidence of news coverage that legitimizes dominant Western institutions and perspectives, and that conversely delegitimizes, depoliticizes, or marginalizes oppositional perspectives and movements."[3]

Whether such framing is intentional or not, and whether it is acknowledged and substantiated or ignored, denied and/or countered by working journalists, hardly matters. Charges of such framing are buttressed by more than forty years of sociological research in Canada, the U.S., Great Britain, and elsewhere. Taken in its entirety, this research presents overwhelming evidence to contradict the prevailing public, liberal-pluralist view of the news media, represented above by Knowlton Nash and others. As discussed, this view sees the media as autonomous and socially responsible institutions which objectively reflect "reality," while serving as protective watchdogs for the public interest.

In contrast, the view of news as a socially "constructed" reality, which is evident from the foregoing body of research, indicates that, in Gaye Tuchman's words, "news obfuscates social reality instead of revealing it. It confirms the legitimacy of the state by hiding the state's intimate involvement with, and support of, corporate capitalism.[4]

Media Think

For the reasons provided and in the ways described above, the news media in Canadian society predominantly may be seen as promoting a narrow ideological "consensus" on the world around us. In previous and ongoing work I refer to this phenomenon as "Media Think." By this I mean a form of group think on a vast scale which permeates the lives of elites, news workers, and much of society at large. It stems from a socialization process that begins at birth. It has its beginnings in a process of enculturation, a value system which stretches through history, across generations and races, classes and gender. The nature and presentation of Media Think is honed, both deliberately as well as unintentionally, in the corporate and editorial boardrooms and newsrooms of the nation's media. It is the process by which the mainstream, corporate media largely function, wittingly and unwittingly, as the delivery system for neoconservative (and neoliberal) dogma. Some writers, including myself, refer to this as a naturalized, "common sense" perspective. It's the means by which the media create particular pictures of the world in our heads, all the while omitting and thereby preventing the formation of alternative, competing pictures. This whole process is so natural, so much taken for granted, that we generally miss it.

The product of Media Think is a conventional wisdom, which is presented as a view of the world that is eminently reasonable, evidently the result of a long process of rational and objective evaluation by policy makers whose overriding concern is the public interest. Anything and everything else is the unthinkable. In recent years, this conventional wisdom has included an emphasis on the glory and inevitability of globalization, free trade, and competitiveness, with the resultant "downsizing" or layoffs and transfer of jobs to still more leaner and meaner economies elsewhere.[5] Most recently we've seen the results of monetarism and the manufacture of deficit hysteria as an excuse for slashing and burning the social safety net (the federal budget, Ralph "Albertosaurus" Klein, Mike "the knife" Harris, etc). But in addition to being used to target social programs, as Linda McQuaig points out, deficit hysteria also is part of a broader, pro-free market strategy for reducing the role of government in society, privatization, increasing unemployment, and driving down wages.[6] All of these goals are synonymous with the neoconservative (and neoliberal) corporate political agenda. They have had ramifications in every area of society, ranging from the environment, to health, education, welfare or "workfare," economic disparity, poverty, and so forth.

A Nation on Drugs

We endure a daily barrage of one-dimensional views on issues whose narrow presentation stands in direct contrast to their importance in our lives. A partial list, as indicated above, would include free trade, globalization, deregulation, rationalization, NDP governments, Native Canadian rights, Constitutional questions, wars,[7] mechanization and technology, the information superhighway, public debt, disparity, poverty, privatization and public ownership, the Mexican Peso devaluation and bailout, the U.S.$500 billion Savings and Loan public bailout, Nicaragua, Panama, Haiti, Cuba, Vietnam and Robert McNamara's memoirs, the Chechnyan "Rebellion," et cetera. The Media Think version of these issues bears little or no resemblance to reality. To gain a different and realistic perspective we must turn to alternative media, or books by outstanding writers such as Linda McQuaig, Tom Walkom, James Laxer, Joyce Nelson, and Noam Chomsky.[8]

Simply put, we are brainwashed. The vast majority of the public is effectively on drugs, addicted to Media Think as surely as if we were taking the *soma* of Aldous Huxley's *Brave New World*. What follows is a brief listing of some of the biased, unquestioned "media truisms" referred to above, which reflect Media Think in operation. It should be noted that this list is intended to be illustrative, rather than comprehensive. Additionally, as indicated above, some of these are "absolute truisms" but many of them are "blue-moon truisms" which may be challenged, provided it is only occasionally, and even then only in a minor way.

Sampling of Media Think Truisms

Economics

1. That which governs least, governs best. The unfettered free market system is the fairest and best guiding principle.

2. Public ownership such as crown corporations is wasteful and inefficient, serving no real useful purpose.

3. Private enterprise, while sometimes given to excess, is the core of our society and is beyond questioning.

4. Democracy and capitalism are synonymous and interchangeable. You can't have one without the other.

5. When it comes to corporation size, the bigger the better.

6. The global economy is as inevitable as the rising sun.

7. We need huge national companies with little or no competition, in order to compete internationally.

8. In order to be lean, mean and competitive, companies must downsize and eliminate inefficiencies.

9. Canadian employees, with (relatively) high salaries and benefits, are the most costly inefficiency of all.

10. Producing goods where labour is cheapest is an inevitable development under globalization and the free market.

11. Transferring jobs to low-wage, no benefit, non-unionized third world countries will help those countries.

12. Job losses in Canada due to company relocations elsewhere are minimal, and where this happens they are menial jobs and people here are better off without them.

13. Job losses under globalization are a temporary thing, during a period of restructuring. Eventually, better paying, high tech jobs will be available for everyone.

14. It's not yet clear what these jobs are, how to train people for them, or who will offer the jobs. These are mysteries.

15. High levels of unemployment are not cause for alarm, but are "structural." High unemployment helps to keep inflation down by putting a brake on unreasonable wage demands.

16. The shift from full-time manufacturing jobs to low paying, part-time service jobs, is another inevitable, short term product of the global economy.

17. A company has to make profits. The more profit it makes, the better the company.

18. People who are wealthy got there because of ability and usually deserve our respect and admiration.

19. People who are poor got there because of their own inability. Still, they deserve some form of charity in the form of food banks.

20. People who are on UI or welfare, with few exceptions, are there because they are too lazy to look for work.

21. Government debts are mostly due to lavish social programs which we can no longer afford.

22. We all pay far too much in taxes, thanks to overspending by bloated governments.

23. Interest rates are determined by complex international forces, over which we have no control.

24. Sometimes the Bank of Canada is forced to raise interest rates to protect the Canadian dollar.

International Affairs

25. Canadians pay out far too much in aid to foreign countries, and most of the time the money doesn't reach its target. Charity begins at home.

26. Occasionally, a tyrant in some part of the world threatens democracy and has to be put in his place, for the good of the world community and those in his own country.

27. Recently, these tyrants have included: Fidel Castro, Saddam Hussein, Manuel Noriega, Daniel Ortega, Ayatollah Khomeini, Muhammar Ghaddafi, and Ferdinand Marcos, among others.

Environment

28. Environmental "problems" are largely invented by hysterical members of radical groups such as Greenpeace.

29. As the economics involved are paramount, we are better off if industry is self-regulating.

Feminism

30. A small group of radical feminists is constantly whining about problems which either don't exist, or which are relatively small problems that we are already doing our best to solve.

31. Violence against women, while unfortunate, is relatively small scale and, let's face it — some women bring it on themselves.

32. Since society "judges" people based on their merits, those who don't succeed, including women, are just not capable enough.

33. Feminists "have it in for" all men, whereas we know that many men are nice guys who neither hate nor abuse women.

Universities

34. A small group of "politically correct" people is trying to turn Canada into a police state, where you can't even think innocent thoughts anymore.

35. Professors on university campuses are a bunch of radical Marxists who are corrupting our youth.

36. Universities have to get more practical and down to earth and train people for jobs rather than all of this pie-in-the-sky stuff.

Culture

37. The CBC is too expensive. It should be sold off to private companies which can do a better job at no cost to the public.

Minorities

38. Native peoples are basically well cared for on reserves, and would be even better off if they would do something for themselves instead of relying on government handouts and complaining.

39. Immigration laws in Canada are too lax. We let people from minority cultures in, and they take advantage of our generous social programs.

40. Because of their small numbers and different views, Gays and Lesbians in Canada only deserve media coverage when they hold demonstrations or if they are dying from AIDS or something.

Working People

41. Labour struggles are senseless, avoidable contests which are created by unions' unwillingness to negotiate in good faith.

42. Companies make wage "offers," while defiant, sometimes even militant unions, will boycott talks and reject management offers.

43. Workers, especially those on strike, are irrational, greedy and self-destructive.

44. Executives and management receive high salaries because they deserve them. There is no point in questioning these, or comparing these to what workers are asking for.

45. Strikes are always caused by greedy unions. What's sad about this is the negative impact strikes have on the public. The fact that unions will inconvenience the public at the drop of a hat is further evidence that workers are selfish.

46. During strikes, the police and other government agencies such as the courts are neutral referees for the public interest. This role includes protecting corporate properties and acting as bodyguards for strike-breakers.

47. Labour unions protect and encourage unproductive, overweight, lazy, and insubordinate workers.

48. Our failure to compete internationally is due to big, powerful unions which have forced employers to pay exorbitant union wages to unproductive workers.

49. Although some very poor and abused workers (particularly women and immigrants) may need to form unions to protect themselves, big unions don't represent workers' interests.

50. Union leaders or "bosses," because they do not come from the educated, cultured and privileged classes, are more likely to be corrupted by the power they achieve than are business or political leaders.

51. Unions have outlived their usefulness. Employers are enlightened and wouldn't abuse their workers. If they do try, there are government laws to protect workers.

52. Unions actually promote conflict with management, as a means of justifying their own existence.

The Media

53.   Freedom of the press is essential to our democracy, and is the basis of an informed public.

54.   The news media are independent, socially responsible watchdogs who look out for the public interest.[9]

In my view, each and every one of these 'truisms' is patently false, with the sole exception of number 14.

***

Endnotes

[1] Bill Doskoch, personal correspondence, June 13, 1995.

[2] These are briefly summarized in Donald Gutstein and Robert Hackett: "Project Censored Canada: Researching the Nation's News Agenda," Simon Fraser University, Burnaby B.C., 1994.

[3] Robert Hackett, *News and Dissent: The Press and the Politics of Peace in Canada*, (Norwood, N.J.: Ablex, 1991), p. 269.

[4] Gaye Tuchman, *Making News: A Study in the Construction of Reality* (NY: Macmillan, 1978), p. 210.

[5] For a critique of this mentality, see James Laxer, *False God: How the Globalization Myth Has Impoverished Canada* (Toronto: Lester, 1993); Robert Chodos, Rae Murphy, Eric Hamovitch, *Canada and the Global Economy: Alternatives to the Corporate Strategy for Globalization* (Toronto:,James Lorimer & Co., 1993).

[6] See Linda McQuaig, *Shooting the Hippo: Death by Deficit and Other Canadian Myths* (Toronto: Viking Books, 1995).

[7] The preceding list was analyzed in my book, *Common Cents: Media Portrayal of the Gulf War and Other Events* (Montréal: Black Rose Books, 1992). Several of the other issues mentioned, such as the debt and deficit, are the subject of a forthcoming book.

[8] For a list of some alternative media, see the appendices. Also, see our alternative media home page on the World Wide Web at:
http://www.uwindsor.ca/newsstad/flipside/index.html

[9] Sources for labour: Michael Parenti, *Inventing Reality*, (NY: St. Martin's Press, 1986), and William Puette, *Through Jaundiced Eyes: How the Media View Organized Labor*, (Ithaca: ILR Press, 1992).

Chapter Seven

PROJECT CENSORED CANADA[1]

The coverage of [Project Censored Canada] was
inadequate last year. Was it due to the corporate press'
continued efforts to suppress news that might reflect on
the economic elite? — Howard Pawley, PCC Judge and
former Premier of Manitoba.

Possibly the most important way in which the news media control the
range of ideas, smothering democracy's oxygen, is through limiting what
Chomsky has called "the bounds of the expressible." They do this by
excluding stories and information or angles on stories which are not to
their liking. These are the real sins of omission. As Michael Parenti notes,
"perhaps the most common and complete form of distortion is
nonreporting." While previous Canadian media research, for example by
Debra Clarke and Richard Ericson *et al.*, examined daily routines in
particular newsrooms, and/or carried out content and/or textual analyses of
news coverage,[2] none of these systematically addressed the information
Canada's news media routinely exclude.[3] Generally speaking, this is the
goal of Project Censored Canada. Project Censored Canada (PCC) is in its
fourth year of operation at this writing. PCC was modelled on Project
Censored in the U.S., which was founded in 1976 by Carl Jensen, a
communications professor at Sonoma State University in Rohnert Park,
California. Former Regina *Leader-Post* reporter Bill Doskoch and other
members of the Canadian Association of Journalists (CAJ) initiated PCC
in the spring of 1993. The 1993 project was conducted in cooperation with
Robert Hackett, Donald Gutstein and others at Simon Fraser University.
By 1994, I and others at the University of Windsor joined the project.

PCC is part of an ambitious attempt by the communication faculty,
students and journalists involved in the project, to accomplish the
following major goals, which are both of a scholarly and public service
nature:

1. To identify and publicize significant but under-
    reported national news stories.
2. To identify systematic patterns in issues and events
    that have been under-reported in mainstream news

media, and to see how these bear upon the validity of different theories of news determinants.
3. To encourage (primarily mainstream) journalists to follow up and report on, under-reported stories.
4. To bring these stories to the attention of the public.
5. To stimulate public awareness and debate concerning filters in Canada's news system, including the extent and meaning of "censorship."
6. To explore perceptions, from a range of Canadian interest groups, about significant omissions in the news agenda, and assess the accuracy of these perceptions.
7. To interview journalists about their perceptions of news filters, and their reaction to the stories identified as under-reported.

Much of the efforts and the resources of PCC have so far been devoted to the first goal above: the identification and publicizing of under-reported stories, although some progress has been made in virtually all areas. To this effect, as with the Carl Jensen and the U.S. project, we have established a rotating panel of national figures as judges for a top ten list of under-reported stories. More on that panel momentarily, but first, a discussion of the research process: how the stories are chosen and evaluated.

Nominating Under-Reported Stories

Several approaches are taken in an effort to cull a large number of story nominations. A brochure is produced and distributed through organizations such as the CAJ and librarians' associations, at public meetings or conferences, and in response to requests from interested individuals. Nominations are solicited by mail from numerous organizations across Canada, including all federal MPs. Alternative media are invited to nominate stories. The current issues of a selection of alternative periodicals are scanned by project members to identify interesting and significant stories which intuitively appear to have received little national media coverage. Included are alternative magazines such as: *Alternatives, Briarpatch, Canadian Dimension, Canadian Forum, Our Times, Peace Magazine, This Magazine*, et cetera.

The above approaches yield a total of about 150 story nominations. Project faculty and staff weed out clearly ineligible entries, using the criteria listed below. In January, story files are distributed to students participating in a seminar at Simon Fraser University, under the direction of Bob Hackett and Donald Gutstein. Students initially present an oral summary of each story, together with the amount of coverage it received in the national media. The extent of coverage is determined through available databases on national media. All stories are searched on CD-ROM through Canadian Business and Current Affairs (CBCA), a computerized bibliographic database. Candidates for final inclusion are eventually also searched on either InfoGlobe or Infomart: full-text online databases.

Evaluating the Stories: the Seven Criteria

The following seven criteria, adapted from Carl Jensen's work, are used by the students in seminars to collectively decide whether stories warrant further research.

1. The story must concern a subject that deserves to be known by a majority of Canadians but has not received sufficient exposure and coverage in the major national news media. While the story might not be "censored" in the traditional sense of the word, it may have been overlooked, ignored or under-reported.
2. The amount of coverage the story received must be minimal (as determined by a search of databases such as CBCA and Infomart).
3. The potential effects of the story must be of major significance, affecting a large number of people.
4. The story should present a clear, easily understand-able concept backed by solid documentation and reliable sources, as opposed to a tangled web of undocumented claims from questionable sources.
5. The scope of the story should be national or international in terms of its impact.
6. The story should be timely, contemporary and ongoing.
7. The exposure of the story through Project Censored Canada should potentially help persuade serious journalists to further explore and publicize the subject of the story and should encourage the general public to seek out more information about the subject.

PCC'S NATIONAL PANEL OF JUDGES, 1995

Donald Benham, professor of journalism, Red River Community College, AB.

Sandra Bernstein, journalist, Toronto, ON.

June Callwood, author and social activist, Toronto, ON.

Michael Clow, sociology professor, St. Thomas University, SK.

David Cohen, Dean, University of Victoria law school, BC.

Clark Davey, former managing editor, *The Globe and Mail*, Ottawa, ON.

Francois Demers, Dean of Arts, Université Laval, Quebec City.

Tom Flanagan, former research director, Reform Party of Canada, U. of Calgary, AB.

Fred Fletcher, professor of political science, York University, Toronto, ON.

Deborah Jones, freelance journalist, Vancouver, BC.

Lawrence Martin, author and journalist, Ottawa, ON.

Linda McQuaig, author and journalist, Oakville, ON.

John Miller, Chair, school of journalism, Ryerson Polytechnic University, Toronto, ON.

Howard Pawley, former premier of Manitoba, U. of Windsor, Windsor, ON.

Pierre O'Neil, P.R., Bombardier Inc., Montréal, QC.

Shirley Sharzer, former assistant managing editor, *The Globe and Mail*, Gloucester, ON.

Maggie Siggins, author, Regina, SK.

Richard Starr, freelance journalist, Dartmouth, NS.

Gillian Steward, freelance journalist, Calgary, AB.

Bruce Wark, journalism professor and former producer, CBC's *Media File*, Halifax, NS.

Barrie Zwicker, publisher, *Sources,* Toronto, ON.

In this manner, the honours seminar at Simon Fraser University selects from among the approximately 150 stories which have been nominated. Additional research and evaluation yields a final selection of about 20. The one-page synopses for these stories are distributed to our distinguished national panel of judges, for the final top ten ranking. The following judges selected the top ten under-reported stories for 1995.

What Can We Expect?

Based upon the foregoing discussion, what might one expect to be excluded from mainstream coverage? Harkening back to the beginning of this book, we have seen that ownership of the news media is concentrated in the hands of corporations owned, controlled and run by wealthy white males with values ranging from the neoconservative to the neanderthal. Their influence extends into the political sphere, via the candidates they support for office; as well as into the newsrooms, through the publishers and managers they appoint. Through the complex process of newsroom socialization the news becomes almost exclusively a management product, despite pretensions to the contrary. All of this would lead us to expect that these components of Media Think would either discourage or preclude entirely, a discussion of views which challenge or oppose corporate ownership values.

Preeminent among these, as discussed, are those which represent the economic underpinnings of the capitalist system: the free market and private enterprise. In *Common Cents*, I explored a number of case studies which demonstrate the way corporate values are reflected in news coverage. These represented what *gets into* the news. I now want to look briefly at what *gets left out*. To do this we turn to an examination of the top ten under-reported stories for 1995 and other years, both for Canada and the U.S. In this way, we can see what perspectives and stories fail to make it onto the news media agenda, given the corporate ownership constraints under discussion.

***

Endnotes

[1] The author would like to acknowledge the significant contributions and assistance of: Robert Hackett, Donald Gutstein, Bill Doskoch, Rick Gruneau, James Compton, Cindy Rozeboom, Kathy Manson, Cheryl Linstead, Tarina Palmer, Michele Platje, the students in the Windsor and Simon Fraser seminars, and our national panel of judges. I would also like to thank Carl Jensen of Project Censored in the U.S., the Goodwin Foundation, and the Social Sciences and Humanities Research Council of Canada, as well as the Windsor and Simon Fraser departments of communication and universities at large, for their support for this project. The contents of this chapter reflect the views of the author alone.

[2] See also Bob Hackett, *News and Dissent: The Press and the Politics of Peace in Canada* (Norwood, NJ: Ablex, 1991); R. Ericson et al., *Visualizing Deviance* (Toronto: U of T Press, 1987); and James Winter, *Common Cents: Media Portrayal of the Gulf War and Other Events* (Montréal: Black Rose Books, 1992).

[3] To my knowledge, only one author has directly addressed this topic, in a theoretical paper. This is John McMurtry, a philosopher at the University of Guelph, who argues that media omit materials which contradict what he calls the "basic social-structural fact" of monopoly capitalism. See John McMurtry, "The Unspeakable: Understanding the System of Fallacy in the Media," *Informal Logic*, 10:3, 1988. A few authors have described the underlying presumptions of the media, or what Dallas Smythe called their "axiomatic propositions," as I did with my discussion of Media Think, in the previous chapter.

Chapter Eight

PATTERNS IN UNDER-REPORTED STORIES

There are times when it seems that the United States and
Canada have only about five or six journalists each, all of
them saying the same things about the same subjects. —
Robert Fulford

Just for your own amusement, see how many of the following under-
reported stories you are familiar with. All received at least some coverage,
but none received very much. This is how a national panel of judges
ranked them.

The Top Ten Under-Reported Stories For 1995

**1. Proposed U.S. Environmental Law could harm Canada's air and
water.** The U.S. House of Representatives passed a bill in May, 1995
which lifted protections for wetlands, made regulators give greater
consideration to costs before requiring water quality improvements from
cities and industry, and allowed states to opt out of environmental water
regulations deemed too expensive or unenforceable. (Source: Ray Ford,
The Windsor Star, Nov. 18, 1994; Chris Vander Doelen, *The Windsor
Star*, Feb. 14, 1995; Brian McAndrew, *The Toronto Star*, June 3, 1995).

2. American-style health care is coming to Canada. With falling federal
transfer payments for Medicare, some provincial governments are turning
to private insurers and health care organizations to help restructure
provincial health care. Many of these organizations are profit-oriented
American companies, such as Liberty Mutual, from Boston, now operating
acute care clinics in Toronto. (Source: Maude Barlow and Bruce
Campbell, *Canadian Forum*, November 1995; Daniel Tatroff, *Our Times*,
May/June 1995).

3. HAARP: The U.S. military's plans to alter the northern ionosphere.
High frequency radio energy experiments by the U.S. military demonstrate
serious consequences for human health, the environment, wildlife and the
weather. The U.S. government is constructing a military radio physics
research facility in a remote part of Alaska. The High Frequency Active

Auroral Research Program (HAARP) will enhance the U.S. military's long-range radio communications and surveillance by injecting high-frequency radio energy into the fluctuating ionosphere, 35 to 500 miles above the earth. Military test results have demonstrated problems. (Source: *Socialist Studies Bulletin* #41, July/Sept. 1995; Mark Farmer, *Popular Science*, Sept. 1995).

4. Social spending not cause of deficits, debt. A Statistics Canada report which debunked this myth was furiously attacked in news media in 1995. Alternative approaches to addressing debt received little media attention, such as taxes on corporations and the wealthy. (Source: Bruce Campbell, *Canadian Dimension*, April/May 1995; Mary Rowles, *Our Times*, Dec./Jan 1995; George Crowell, *Canadian Dimension*, Oct./Nov. 1995; Linda McQuaig, *Shooting The Hippo: Death by Deficit and Other Canadian Myths*, Toronto, Viking, 1995).

5. The untold costs of New Zealand's economic revolution. Although New Zealand's deficit-cutting style is touted by many influential Canadians as a model for debt reduction and economic restructuring, New Zealand's public debt is now twice as large as it was when the country began restructuring in 1985. New Zealand is also facing a high unemployment rate and one of the highest youth suicide rates in the world. (Source: Murray Dobbin, *Canadian Dimension*, April/May 1995; Howard Pawley, *The Windsor Star*, September 18, 1995; Linda McQuaig, *Shooting The Hippo*).

6. Indian Act root cause of violence at Kanesatake. A climate of terror involving violence, drugs, and lawlessness on this Mohawk First Nations community in Québec receives a blind eye from government. Under the Indian Act, the Band Council is responsible to the federal government and not the community, hampering the ability of locals to deal with the problems. (Source: Dan David, *This Magazine*, Dec./Jan. 1995-96; Ben Whiskeyjack, *Windspeaker*, June 1995).

7. Canadian media mum on human rights in Mexico. Two years after the signing of NAFTA, Mexican human rights abuses remain largely ignored in the Canadian news media, including mysterious deaths of babies at a hospital for uninsured poor people in Durango Mexico — a suspected case of organ trafficking. Other examples include: the massacre of 18 peasant farmers in Guerrero; arrests, torture, mutilation, and disappearances. (Source: Rick Salutin, *The Globe and Mail*, August 4,

1995; John Warnock, *The Other Mexico*, Montréal, Black Rose Books, 1995).

8. 'Family entertainment' at Canada's arms bazaar. While Canada has cultivated the image of world peacekeeper, it is one of the world's largest international suppliers of arms and weapons. We rank 7th in sales to underdeveloped countries, and 10th overall in the world. The Biennial Abbotsford International Air Show is billed as "family entertainment," and yet it is a biennial Canadian arms bazaar, to which 70 countries come to buy arms. There were 300,000 visitors in 1995, including 104 military participants. (Source: Ron Dart, *Briarpatch*, Sept. 1995; Kim Bolan, *Vancouver Sun*, Aug 10, 1995; Ken Epps, *Ploughshares Monitor*, June 1995).

9. Exploitation of home-based garment workers. Asian and other third-world immigrant women do home piecework for an average of $4.64 per hour, with no benefits. The garment industry in Canada employs about 60,000 people, about half of whom are unionized. (Source: Dirk Beck, *The Georgia Straight*, April 14-21, 1995).

10. CF-5 jets on the block after $300 million in upgrades. Midway through a costly modernization program, the federal government is taking a heavy loss after putting the squadron of Canada's remaining CF-5 jet fighters on the block. Federal cutbacks to defense spending are blamed. (Source: George Koch, *Western Report*, June 19, 1995).

The above stories may be lumped into four categories: (1) Aspects of the neoliberal economic agenda; (2) Health and the environment; (3) Human Rights; (4) Corporate ethics and profits. On closer examination economic interests (the first category) underlie every story. It makes little sense to distinguish between the neoliberal agenda at large and issues related to health and the environment or human rights, or for that matter economic interests. Aspects of the neoliberal economic agenda include: privatization, cutting back on social programs and the safety net, economic policy, the monetary system, interest rates and the role of the banks. All of these may be seen to be compatible with the corporate interests running the commercial news media in the country. For example, the top-ranked story is about how the weakening of the Clean Water Act in the U.S. would allow States to opt out of environmental water regulations deemed "too expensive," and how this could impact on Canada.

The number two story is about plummeting federal transfer payments and the privatization of our health care system. Number three concerns the health and environmental effects of defense research. Four is about the role of high interest rates as opposed to social spending in creating the deficit and debt. Five, the real story of the down side of neoliberal policies in New Zealand. Six, the continued violation of human rights of Canada's native peoples, specifically the Mohawks of Kanesatake — the site of the Oka standoff in 1990. Seven concerns human rights in Mexico. Eight is about a Canadian arms bazaar, and Canada's role as one of the world's largest suppliers of armaments and weapons. Nine is about the exploitation of home garment workers. Ten is about federal cutbacks to defense spending leading to the sale of CF-5 jet fighters, for less than the costs of upgrading them a few years ago.

Is this just a fluke? Let's examine the 1994 list of PCC's under-reported stories. The top ten stories for 1994 may be collapsed into three closely related and overlapping categories: health and the environment, trade policy, and corporate ethics and profits. All three categories involve money: whether through the expense of environmental cleanup, or reduced taxes on cigarettes, to the long-term costs of fish farming, and banks profiteering through high interest rates. Here are the stories, as rank-ordered by the national panel of judges.

1994 Stories
1. AECL to require $300 million toxic hazard cleanup.
2. Canada's own Inter-provincial free-trade deal.
3. Third world battles GATT over plant patenting.
4. White-collar and corporate crime overlooked.
5. Tobacco companies' complicity in cigarette smuggling.
6. Reducing interest rates; an alternative for debt reduction.
7. The Canadian Wildlife Federation hides its hunting connection.
8. The World Bank funds forced resettlement.
9. Is fish farming a biological time bomb?
10. Chiapas crisis unleashed NAFTA damage control.

How do these stories fit the pattern identified above? In the case of the number one ranked story, AECL, a money-losing Crown corporation, will require a bailout of $300 million for the cleanup of toxic waste at old facilities. Just what economic interests are at issue here is debatable, but the State's commitment to nuclear energy obviously represents powerful economic interests.

At first blush, however, the failure to publicize AECL's problems is inconsistent with a corporate perspective which views public enterprise as an anathema. Why would the privately-owned, corporate media *not* be anxious to undermine AECL, which they readily do with other crown corporations such as Ontario Hydro, *et cetera*? Isn't the omission of this story in fact evidence against one of the very biases being alleged here? Perhaps. But it may also be explained by corporate commitment to nuclear power. Evidence for this assertion comes from the work of Michael Clow and Susan Machum, in their book, *Stifling Debate: Canadian Newspapers and Nuclear Power*. They found that "anti-nuke" arguments rarely were printed. Anti-nuke activists were depicted as irrational or worse by the newspapers. "In sharp contrast, the 'pro-nuke' positions of the governmental power agencies and their commercial allies were advanced in what almost amounts to a public relations exercise by the papers, all in favour of nuclear power."[1] The key here may be "commercial allies," the private firms which benefit from the nuclear industry. To condemn the nuclear industry would bring a pox on both houses, public and private.

Economics also underlie the second story on the provincial trade agreement, with arguments that trade barriers "cost" between $750 million annually, according to one side, and $6.5 billion according to the other. The barriers also, it may be argued, protected jobs and the environment. The third-ranked story highlights the controversy over multinational corporations taking out patents on food and medicinal crops, under GATT, and over the protest of third world countries. The fourth-ranked story concerns the problems of both white collar and corporate crimes, such as tax evasion and monopoly pricing. The fifth story discusses lobbying by tobacco companies to reduce taxes and increase profits, and the windfall profits they realized by setting up shop in the U.S. and selling cigarettes to smugglers, to bring back into Canada. The sixth-ranked story, in part, is about how the commercial banks have profited from the high interest rate policies of the Bank of Canada. The eighth story is about the World Bank forcing people out of their homes by the millions, in favour of mega projects and so-called "development." The ninth story is about how a biological and environmental disaster may result from a lack of policy controls on fish farming. The tenth is about public relations damage control which protected NAFTA from being linked to the Chiapas rebellion. What national and international monetary interests might have benefited from this subterfuge?

This leaves one story: The Canadian Wildlife Federation story (#7) is, in part, about how the federation obtains, from members and the public, millions of dollars in fees and merchandise, under the guise of protecting wildlife, all the while promoting hunting and fishing. Although this last story demonstrates the economic self-interest of the groups involved, it may be stretching things to say that it is about the broader "economic interests" evident in the other nine stories. In any case, nine of ten stories appear to follow the same pattern.

Project Censored Canada is still young, but it appears to support the political-economic or instrumentalist perspectives in the academic literature, which regard ownership and corporate concentration as primary explanations for news media content. As might be expected from a review of the literature, or indeed the simple fact that without exception the news media are owned by large corporations, we seem to be seeing evidence for the *systematic exclusion* of material which presents "free market economics" and "private enterprise" in a negative light. This could be evidence of the news media's "support of corporate capitalism," as American sociologist Gaye Tuchman put it.

One might wish to shy away from definitive conclusions, based upon twenty stories and two years of a larger project. But 1994 did corroborate the results from 1995. The evidence mounts when the top ten stories from 1993 are added. Indeed, it appears as if all ten of the under-reported stories in 1993 revolved around similar economic interests. They were as follows:

1993 Stories
1. Oil prospects in Somalia.
2. Tories forgive wealthy millions in taxes.
3. Canada's cosy trade and aid relationship with Indonesia.
4. Business grabs the environmental agenda.
5. NAFTA: a new economic constitution for North America.
6. Corporate and media ties to political power.
7. The B.C. government giveaway to forestry industry continues.
8. Canadian mismanagement and the cod fisheries collapse.
9. Canada's peacekeeping image: arms exports outpace peacekeeping spending.
10. The environmental and economic costs of military pollution.

Once again, the virtual exclusion of these stories kept material off the public agenda which was critical of private enterprise and the free market economics espoused by the corporate elite.

Since we have only three years of data for the Canadian project, we next turned to the 1995 stories identified by Carl Jensen's group in Project Censored in the U.S.[2] Those stories may be summarized as follows:

1995 U.S. Stories

1. The Telecommunications Bill eliminates virtually all regulation of the communications industry.
2. Balancing the budget on the backs of the poor.
3. Child labour is worse today.
4. Privatization of the Internet.
5. plans to spend $billions on Nukes.
6. Radical plan from Newt Gingrich's think tank to gut FDA.
7. Russia injects earth with Nuke waste.
8. Medical fraud costs the nation $billions annually.
9. Chemical industry fights for toxic ozone-killing pesticide.
10. NAFTA's broken promises.

All of these stories appear to fit within our framework; certainly there are no jarring exceptions. Here is what the 1994 list of U.S. censored stories looks like:

1994 U.S. Stories

1. American workers face on-the-job exposure to hazardous materials.
2. corporate leaders form the right-wing Council for National Policy, to coordinate their political agenda.
3. The Pentagon is secretly subsidizing defense contractor mergers.
4. Giant waste incinerators are producing toxic dioxin.
5. Chemical, auto and appliance industries benefit from Bill Clinton's retreat on CFC's and the ozone crisis.
6. Document reveals human radiation experiments were kept secret to avoid an adverse effect on public opinion.
7. Discarded surplus from fish harvesting wastes 60 billion pounds of fish and seafood annually.

8. The resurgence of tuberculosis, which killed 2.7 million people worldwide in 1993, could be prevented by cheap vaccination.
9. The Pentagon's HAARP project is an attempt to control the ionosphere for military purposes, and carries health risks.
10. News media mask spousal violence in "the language of love."

The first nine of these stories from Project Censored in the U.S. readily reflect underlying economic interests. The last one, about how violence against women is portrayed, is debatable. But consider the Nicole Brown / O.J. Simpson case in the U.S. It reasonably may be argued that this and other cases present the problem of domestic violence "as a matter of individual psychology" and "the victim's personal life," as well as blaming or ignoring the victim and sympathizing with the accused— or at least concentrating almost exclusively on his trials and tribulations. Instead, this may be seen as a societal problem in which "police, prosecutors and judges violate women's civil rights by denying them protection from assault by intimate partners."[3] From this perspective, one could look for motives in our patriarchal system and the economic status quo. To alleviate this problem, many more women would have to be in positions of power in order to change and implement the laws. But additionally, more economic resources would have to be employed to enforce such regulations, and to protect women.

Hence, the top censored U.S. stories for 1994 also reflected the underlying economic motives of the corporate elite— the same corporate elite which, coincidentally, owns the news media.

We are now looking at 50 stories, which were nominated and judged in two separate countries and over the course of three years, and which have been evaluated as important newsworthy stories that have been under-reported or omitted entirely from the mainstream press. In virtually every case, these top censored stories not only contained but were centrally-focussed on views which were opposed to neoliberal economic thinking. These under-reported stories challenge or oppose corporate ownership values: specifically in relation to the economic underpinnings of the capitalist system, the free market and private enterprise. These findings are in keeping with: the analysis provided earlier of corporate ownership and influence, the process of newsroom socialization, and the assertion that the news is largely a management product. It is not surprising to find these stories missing from news media owned by the likes of Conrad Black and Paul Desmarais.

Is this something new? What happens if one goes back 20 years to the first year of Project Censored in the U.S., to look at the stories in that year?[4] I'll leave it to the reader to judge. Here is what the list looked like for 1976:

1976 U.S. Stories
1. Jimmy Carter and the Trilateral Commission
2. Corporate Control of DNA
3. Selling Banned Pesticides and Drugs to Third World Countries
4. The Oil Price Conspiracy
5. The Mobil Oil/Rhodesian Connection
6. Missing Plutonium and Inadequate Nuclear Reactor Safeguards
7. Workers Die for American Industry
8. Kissinger, the CIA, and SALT
9. Worthless or Harmful Non-prescription Drugs
10. The Natural Gas "Shortage"

It should be noted, as several observers have pointed out, that some minimal diversity in mainstream news content is required in order to maintain the illusion of broader diversity in content. In this journalistic equivalent of "been there, done that," the media can both point to evidence of diversity and also rationalize the lack of further coverage of critical perspectives, all the while being filled to overflowing with narrowly-framed, legitimizing content. Thus, occasional and exceptional stories about topics which are otherwise ignored, may be self-serving. (See the discussions on "once in a blue moon" challenges to media truisms and leftist columnists, earlier).

The fact that some of these stories did receive minimal attention from the commercial media is indicative of a number of things. First, as mentioned, it reflects the requirement that the corporate media have some semblance of diversity, in the interest of legitimacy. Secondly, it probably represents success on the part of individual journalists, despite the overwhelming odds of the economic and institutional constraints which are working against them. These are the cracks or fissures in the monolith to which I referred earlier. Journalists can achieve at least limited success in spite of the system which constrains them. I want to clarify that I am not, as I have been mistakenly labelled, a "radical instrumentalist" who sees no avenues for progressive journalists and indeed the public, to struggle against oppressive forces.[5] On the contrary, I remain stubbornly optimistic that we shall overcome.

By this time even the most devoted follower of David Letterman's show will be tiring of lists. Please tolerate just one more. In the spring of 1996, Project Censored Canada released its first so-called "Junk Food News" list, a list of stories which were over-reported in 1995. As we may see from the list below, these may be an important story covered in a sensational manner, with skimpy investigation of the underlying issues (Bernardo); a trivial story that receives more coverage than it deserves (Grant); a superficial approach to a story that ignores more complete information about the same subject (the information highway); or an advertisement in disguise (Microsoft Windows 95, Beatles). The stories were rank-ordered by a national panel of publishers and journalists.[6] American news stories swept the top three places. Here is the list, ranked from most over-covered (1) to least over-covered (10).

Junk Food News
1. The O.J. Simpson Trial.
2. Actor Hugh Grant nabbed with Prostitute
3. Release of Microsoft's Windows 95
4. Dick Assman Promoted by David Letterman
5. Princess Diana's BBC Interview
6. The Information Superhighway
7. The Beatles' Anthology
8. The Paul Bernardo Trial
9. The 1995 Hockey and Baseball Strikes
10. The Toronto Raptors and Vancouver Grizzlies join the NBA

The first thing to note is that American stories took the top three spots, an indication of the degree to which we are inundated by U.S. popular culture. Of course, there are aspects of some of these stories which are well worth reporting. Obviously one cannot avoid coverage of something like the O.J. Simpson or Paul Bernardo trials. But the coverage of the former was on a daily basis stretching over a two-year period. And while the deaths of Nicole Simpson and Ronald Goldman were important, and O.J. *is* after all a celebrity, there remain other possibilities for at least a smidgen of coverage. For example, 1995 marked the 20th anniversary of the Indonesian invasion of East Timor, which resulted in an estimated quarter of a million deaths in just the first five years. In addition, coverage of O.J. Simpson focused on the trial itself, the evidence and the question of O.J.'s guilt or innocence. There should have been more critical analysis of the problems of violence against women and racism in the justice and enforcement systems.

The gruesome sex crimes of the Paul Bernardo trial were portrayed in graphic detail, involving sensational, saturation coverage over a period of several months. In contrast to this, relatively little attention in the news media was focused on important questions such as the issue of violence against women, battered women's syndrome, and the performance of the police. Again, while the deaths involved here were important, we also learned from Statistics Canada in 1995 that for the year before there was one workplace injury every 70 seconds, leading to 724 work-related deaths. That's about two workplace deaths everyday in Canada. Why don't these deaths get more coverage? Two deaths receive blanket coverage, while two deaths everyday go unnoticed. Couldn't we have a little less on Bernardo and Homolka and a little bit about something which affects the lives of so many working Canadians? But it's obviously not in the interest of corporations at large or the corporate news media to play up *these* stories. To do so might lead to a demand for changes in laws and the workplace which would protect workers, at the expense of corporate profits and investors' dividends. Better that people should be fixated on the (admittedly) horrific crimes of Paul Bernardo, or the latest sports event. Nothing needs to be done about the latter, and nothing can be done about the former, except for beefing up police forces and individual precautions, issuing dum-dum bullets to police, staying at home, travelling in groups, and so forth. By focussing on these diversions we are more likely to vent our frustrations on statistically minor incidents, about which we can do little, at least in the short term. We are also more likely to unquestioningly accept the seemingly unrelated and decontextualized deaths of those around us, about which we *could* do a great deal.

In this chapter we have explored the individual stories and patterns in what the news media leave out, and have found these omissions to be logically related to the questions of ownership and management explored earlier. We have also briefly looked at what it is that the corporate media spend much of their time emphasizing: Junk Food News. The former, by their omission, prevent us from obtaining an accurate and realistic view of the world around us. The latter, being ubiquitous, overwhelm us with a barrage of infotainment, and divert us from more important matters— the things that have real meaning in our lives.

***

Endnotes

[1] See Michael Clow and Susan Machum, *Stifling Debate: Canadian Newspapers and Nuclear Power* (Halifax: Fernwood, 1993). For a summary of their work, from which the above quotation is drawn, see Edward Silva, *More Perishable than Lettuce or Tomatoes* (Halifax: Fernwood, 1995, p. 16.

[2] These are drawn from Carl Jensen, *Censored: The News That Didn't Make the New — And Why* (NY: Seven Stories Press, 1996).

[3] This argument is taken from the comments made by Ann Jones, author of *Next Time She'll Be Dead*, quoted in Carl Jensen, *Censored: The News that Didn't Make the News— And Why*, (NY: Four Walls, Eight Windows, 1995), p.76.

[4] Ibid, p. 207.

[5] One author who makes this mistake in what is otherwise an interesting and useful book, is Edward Silva, *More Perishable than Lettuce or Tomatoes* (Halifax: Fernwood, 1995). Silva contrasts what he terms my instrumentalist perspective with the social constructionist view, and develops a synthesis which he terms "socially constrained instrumentalism." Although there is much that I can agree with in his findings, regarding newspaper coverage of new Ontario labour laws, there are a number of problems with any analysis which lumps me in with a liberal pluralist such as John Porter, or lumps Bob Hackett in with a liberal pluralist such as Paul Rutherford (p.15-17). Contrary to Silva's view, my work does "acknowledge the constant creative struggles of the media workers," some of whom are acknowledged as "national media treasures" in the introduction to *Common Cents: Media Portrayal of the Gulf War and Other Events* (Montréal: Black Rose Books, 1992). I write, "By their very existence they prove that the problems described in this book are not monolithic in nature" (p. xv).

[6] The following publishers and journalists took part: Tom Aubin, CBC Radio Windsor, James Bruce, *The Windsor Star*, Lou Clancy, *The Toronto Star*, Bill Doskoch, Regina journalist, R.A. Green, *The London Free Press*, Bob Hughes, The Regina *Leader-Post*, Linda Hughes, *The Edmonton Journal*, George Manz, *Briarpatch*, Craig Pearson, *The Windsor Star*, Frances Russell, *The Winnipeg Free Press*.

Chapter Nine

CONCLUSIONS

VANCOUVER. According to the Fraser Institute, a corporate sponsored west coast think tank, "The best way to resolve Indian land claims in British Columbia is to transfer ownership of all Crown land to individual members of the public, both aboriginal and non-native, and then let the free market prevail." — *The Globe and Mail*, December 14, 1995, p. A6.

Summary

The news media have a tremendous impact in our society. Ultimately, as the late, great communications scholar Dallas Smythe pointed out, the media determine our very consciousness. With this role comes an onerous responsibility. As a result, the media present themselves as highly responsible watchdogs for the public interest. Despite the fact that they are increasingly owned by a small Family Compact of the corporate elite, the news media have managed, by and large, to imbue the public with simplistic and idealistic liberal-pluralist notions about their role in society.

The media have been able to do this, in part, by the sheer force of repetition, through their public utterings and daily writings, their advertising and self-promotion, which now date back for more than a century. Like capitalism itself, over the course of this time the press has come to be seen as virtually synonymous with "democracy." Just as "capitalist democracy" has become redundant, you can't have democracy without the press. Open information is indeed essential in a democracy. But we have neither a free press nor a democracy.

The public tends to accept the glorified role of the media because of the alleged hands-off policy taken by their corporate owners, who allegedly hire independent, professional journalists to run their media. In fact, owners influence the media via what might be called a form of "trickle down theory." News becomes largely a management product, from hiring and promotion to assignment, framing, sourcing, editing, placement and so forth, in a process of newsroom socialization. Far from being independent-minded professionals, most journalists are employees who do the job the boss wants in return for a pay cheque. They have virtually no professional protection akin to that of a medical doctor, a nurse, teacher or a lawyer; none of the academic freedom afforded to professors. Like the rest of us, they have spouses and kids and mortgages, and they want to keep their jobs. Some are well-intentioned and daring, some are excellent journalists, but most are not. Even the outstanding among them are severely limited by economic and organizational constraints.

The resultant news product is not monolithic in nature, but it is overwhelmingly narrow in terms of its range and focus. Alternative perspectives are like so many life rafts on an ocean of news. I listed more than 50 media truisms which illustrate the underlying ideology of the mainstream news on a variety of topics. Some of these are absolute in nature, and must never be questioned. Others may occasionally be challenged, but not seriously or consistently or prominently. The absolute kind pertain to the economic underpinnings of the capitalist system: the free market and private enterprise, and these are sacrosanct. After all, the only possible alternative is communism, and that died an inevitable death in the former Soviet Union, when George Bush "won" the Cold War (!)[1]

The role of the news media in our society may then be seen as one of legitimation. The media are a delivery system for the policies favoured by the corporate elite who own them, and their brethren. Although the media *survive* by making a profit, and delivering audiences to advertisers, they *exist* in order to impart selected information, ideas, opinions and values to their audiences. As Otis Chandler of the *Los Angeles Times* said, "I'm not going to surround myself with people who disagree with me." This is accomplished through what I call "Media Think."

Media Think entails promoting a narrow, ideological perspective on the world around us, in the guise of a common sense consensus with which no right thinking person could disagree. So naturalized do these perspectives become, that anything else is unthinkable, unimaginable. Noam Chomsky, who was arrested and jailed for protesting the Vietnam War, in part by not filing a tax return, uses as one of his many examples the so-called "Vietnam Conflict." To this day, Robert McNamara notwithstanding, that war is explained as the U.S. administration defending a small third world country which was faced with naked communist aggression from the north. Chomsky's dissenting view on this, which he amply supports with documentation, is as follows: The North Vietnamese people came to the aid of the South Vietnamese, who were revolting against a violent and repressive client-state government which was established in South Vietnam by none other than the U.S. government itself.

So ingrained is the first "historical explanation" of what happened in Vietnam, that Chomsky's analysis might as well come from a Martian, rather than someone who is probably the leading living intellectual today.

This example illustrates the power and efficacy of Media Think.[2] It also speaks volumes about motives, ranging from the philosophical and practical desire to suppress democratically-rooted movements, regarded as "viruses" and "rotten apples," to the economic motive played by war in eliciting public subsidies for the armament manufacturers.

Other examples range from globalization and free trade to the role of the deficit as an excuse for dismantling social programs. One cannot help but worry about the unidimensional, doctrinaire perspectives on these issues emanating from the allegedly free, open and diverse corporate media. Of course, the trick is to somehow expose oneself to alternative perspectives, in order to have their separate reality open up for you. It is as though we are collectively viewing a giant hologram, and we need to concentrate our gaze and slowly refocus in order to bring the hidden dimensions of reality into focus.

The annual list of under-reported stories exposes media biases particularly well. Not surprisingly when we examine these lists closely we observe distinct patterns in coverage, or rather the lack of coverage. The patterns are similar to those which emerge from studying corporate news media content, that is, an overwhelming tendency to support free market capitalism.

The Law of the Jungle

As indicated in Chapter one, the view that bigger is better is by no means limited to the media. It is part of the broader neoconservative philosophy which has been adopted by corporations and politicians alike, and has spawned rationalization, free trade and globalization. It represents the triumph of the so-called "free market," or Law of the Jungle. It emphasizes the private over the public, and promotes a minimalist view of the role of government in society. This was evident in Margaret Thatcher's Britain, Ronald Reagan's America, Brian Mulroney's Canada, and latterly in the Alberta of Ralph Klein, Mike Harris' Ontario, and Jean Chrétien's Canada. This view, which is both neocon and neolib, was summed up rather nicely by Andrew Coyne of *The Globe and Mail*, who, along with David Frum is among the new right's recent gurus. Following Mike Harris' election victory in June, 1995, Coyne wrote that the Ontario vote was a message for governments to "get out of our face." He claimed that "for decades, governments of every party have spent their time in office figuring out new ways to interfere in people's lives."[3] For the young neocons, the government and Satan are one. At least in some respects. Of course it is all right for governments to run police forces to protect private property, maintain social control and keep the rabble in line. It is okay to implement tax policies which favour corporations and the wealthy. It is permissible for governments to subsidize private corporations with public money directed at so-called "foreign aid," wars, military armaments, or "research and development." Even subsidies to airports and plane travel for the wealthy go unquestioned. But money spent on social programs, health and education, the so-called government "bureaucracy" which delivers services, or rail subsidies for students and the elderly, are all Satanic interference in the so-called "free market."

Consequently, newly-elected Ontario premier Mike Harris, committed to reducing both the deficit and taxes (which, of course, adds to the deficit), took the highly visible step of dismantling an "in your face" photo radar system which brought in millions of dollars in revenue from speeders, vowing instead to put more police on the streets. His solicitor-general Bob Runciman legalized hollow-point "dum-dum" bullets for use by police officers. At the same time, Harris went about dealing with other "in your face" aspects of government interference, by freezing the minimum wage, cutting welfare benefits by 22 percent, dismantling an employment equity program, and adding thousands of civil servants to the unemployment lines. Eventually, in the tradition of trickle-down economics, he coupled this with a tax cut.

The political elite and their media obviously fear that governments have the potential to actually begin to represent the interests of the public at large which elects them. As American academic Noam Chomsky has noted, wherever even a hint of this takes place around the world, it represents a "crisis of democracy" for the ruling elite. The eighties example of the democratically-elected Sandinista government in Nicaragua is a case in point. By implementing policies which improved the lot of their people, the Sandinistas created a "virus" which had to be removed. The virus was a crisis of democracy which may have spread to other countries. Its removal began with the illicit hiring of a mercenary army of Contra "freedom fighters" with money earned through the illegal sale of armaments to Iran, orchestrated by Ollie North. It was the Contras' job to murder civilians and wreak all-round havoc in Nicaragua, pressuring and distracting the government. The "remedy" involved an economic embargo by the U.S., which ultimately helped to defeat the Nicaraguan government. The ensuing election brought in a government which was more hostile to its own citizens, but more hospitable to the International Monetary Fund and international investors in search of cheap labour.[4]

Consequently, in order to prevent a crisis of democracy from occurring, the elite promotes minimal government "interference," at least when it comes to policies limiting corporations. A weak and ineffective government is not in a position to enact public policies which would benefit the vast majority of citizens, at the expense of the elite. Nor can it serve as a public counterbalance to the huge multinational firms which have run amok. Governments are especially unable to serve these roles if their citizens have been convinced that governments are nothing but wasteful interference, beyond of course, their essential role of effecting social control and ensuring that the rules result in the relentless redistribution of wealth from the many to the few.

Voices in the Wilderness: the CBC Crisis

In the fall of 1995, CBC *Morningside* radio host Peter Gzowski interviewed Maude Barlow, voluntary chairperson of the Council of Canadians. In addition to being a charming and delightful person, Barlow is an author and activist, and Gzowski talked about her latest book (with Bruce Campbell) titled *Straight Through the Heart*.[5] In the book, the authors demonstrate that the Chrétien Liberals are, if anything, *worse* than the Mulroney Tories, in that the Liberals have taken the corporate agenda further and faster, despite promises to the contrary. After talking for a while about the ideas and arguments in the book, Gzowski said, part accusingly and part plaintively, "But Maude, you're a voice in the wilderness!" Barlow disagreed, and she is right in that there is a growing chorus of voices in support. But in the mainstream, Gzowski is right. And just why do you think that is? Could it be because people in the media, including the CBC, are so beholden to corporate views that they treat respectable critics and thinkers such as Maude Barlow like lunatics? In their book, Barlow and Campbell provide an historical context for the current neoliberal economic policies of the Chrétien government, and describe its corporatist policies as an intentional betrayal of an egalitarian and just society. But this is a perspective which is almost totally excluded from the mainstream. The CBC is a case in point. In January 1996 the [Pierre] Juneau report was made public, shortly after Sheila Copps assumed responsibility for the CBC through the federal Heritage Ministry. The 300-page report, prepared by the former CRTC chairman and CBC president, along with TVOntario President Peter Herrndorf and communications professor Catherine Murray, proposed strengthening the CBC by funding it through a tax on cable and long distance telephone charges, while removing advertising from its television service. In the commercial media, the task force report was greeted with a range of reactions from scepticism to outright hostility. It was dismissed as interventionist; as an expensive solution during a time of "economic crisis" rooted in government cutbacks, massive debt, and a withering tax burden.

In terms of a context for a discussion of the CBC, it is instructive to look back at debate over the role of public and private enterprise in broadcasting, which we will do briefly before returning to the present.

Public vs. Private Enterprise in Broadcasting History

At the turn of the last century Canadian elites viewed growing populism with alarm. They could readily envision a time when the army and police might not be able to prevent a mass uprising against property and "order." The newly urbanized and industrialized public was beginning to abandon the moral restraint fashioned by religion and traditional culture, in favour of more democratic pursuits such as "consumerism."[6]

But few amongst the propertied classes could have imagined that a paltry share of consumer bounty would eventually lead to conservativism taking root in the working class. The latter have understandably tended to adopt consumerism and the individualist, free market values of the propertied class, in much the same way that some Native Canadian peoples hundreds of years before adopted firearms and metal cooking pots. As the late historian Christopher Lasch noted in *The Culture of Narcissism*, in this century mass advertising not only advertises individual products, but promotes consumption as a way of life. Lasch argued that this "propaganda of commodities" has served to uphold consumption as an alternative to protest or rebellion.[7] There are limits of course, and when the disparity becomes too great, with the poor unable even to afford staples let alone commodities, things will presumably change.

Historically, each new mass medium, from the telegraph, to newspapers, radio, film, TV, cable, and currently, "deathstars," direct-to-home satellite technology and the Internet, have been measured according to their ability to deliver greater numbers of people to advertisers, to foster greater sales, and to earn ever greater profits.

Individualism and free-market philosophies have combined throughout the past century to lessen the communal, rural, preindustrial influences and benefits of earlier cultures. This was becoming apparent in American society in the last century: when Samuel Morse offered his invention to the U.S. government, the political leaders of the day could not fathom a public, collective role for the telegraph.

When radio became a national medium in the U.S. in the 1920s, it consisted largely of public and educational stations. As American academic Ben Bagdikian writes, radio broadcasting:

> Was not interested in commercials. The most popular stations were noncommercial, operated by universities, states, municipalities, and school districts. Millions of Americans were tuning in to university lectures, taking correspondence courses by radio and listening to drama, music and debates in their communities.[8]

The popular programs of the public radio stations encouraged the sale of radios, which were manufactured by General Electric, Westinghouse, and Western Electric, a subsidiary of American Telephone and Telegraph (AT&T). At that time, commercial radio was run by a private cartel called Radio Corporation of America (RCA), owned by none other than General Electric, Westinghouse and AT&T.

An increased reliance on commercials began in 1922. Rather than being profitable stimulants to radio sales, the educational stations provided a threat: their large audiences reduced the number of those whom commercial stations could sell to merchants. As a result, according to Bagdikian, "commercial stations and the RCA-related corporations used their influence in government to force educational stations to give up popular frequencies and broadcast times, to shift to lower power, and even to move to other communities."[9] Obviously, the same thing occurred with television except that by this time, in the 1940s and 1950s, less thought was given to communal interests.

In Canada, we have long been exposed to rhetoric from politicians and Royal Commissions, to the effect that the airwaves are public property which is regulated in the public interest. In his desire to protect Canadian airwaves from American control, Prime Minister R.B. Bennett intoned in 1932: "I cannot think that any government would be warranted in leaving the air to private exploitation and not reserving it for development for the use of the people."[10] Indeed, heroic efforts by a few individuals maintained a public presence in broadcasting, which has survived into the present. But despite the efforts of Graham Spry, Alan Plaunt and others, the politicians and commissions and regulators have followed what Herschel Hardin has called the "Third Law" of regulatory agencies: "The more elaborate the ritualistic language used by the agency, the more dubious are its actions."[11] Immersed within a private enterprise culture, the public broadcaster is increasingly doomed.

Canadian broadcasting began with the (American) Marconi Company in Montréal, and station XWA, which became CFCF. By 1923 more than 30 Canadian stations were operating, and by 1930 more than 60. According to historian Mary Vipond, "businesses usually became involved in broadcasting as an adjunct to their other activities; many of the early Canadian stations were owned by electrical retailers or by newspapers."[12] Indeed, newspaper baron Roy Thomson initially got into the radio business in Timmins Ontario in order to sell radio receiver sets. Some makeshift Canadian networks developed, such as a chain of stations owned and operated by the Canadian National Railway. But with the establishment of the NBC and CBS American radio networks in 1927, Vipond indicates that the popularity of the best American programming and the consequent eagerness of advertisers to sponsor it made joining these networks attractive to the largest urban Canadian stations. By 1930, CFRB Toronto and CKAC Montréal had joined CBS and CKGW Toronto and CFCF Montréal had joined NBC.

AT&T's Canadian subsidiary, Bell Canada, entered radio in 1922 with licences for stations CKCS Montréal and CFTC Toronto. These licences were not renewed however, owing to an agreement the next year amongst Bell, the Marconi Co., Canadian General Electric and Canadian Westinghouse, respecting each other's media and commercial monopolies. As communications scholar Robert Babe indicates, "signatories to the Canadian agreement were all subsidiaries of foreign parents, again pointing to the high degree of foreign influence shaping Canadian communications."[13]

Vipond notes that the 1932 Radio Broadcasting Act created a government-owned Canadian Radio Broadcasting Commission, forerunner to both the CBC and the CRTC. It was "severely hampered" from the beginning by under funding, which meant that it was unable to build a national public network modelled on the BBC, as envisioned by the Aird Commission of 1929. Instead, time was purchased on private stations. So, historically, despite the lipservice paid to Canadian nationalism and public broadcasting by various politicians and commissions, the reality has been an unfulfilled public promise and encroaching American content and privatization. In large part this has been "dictated" by economic preferences.

The Diminishing CBC

In the more recent context, smaller budgets, less public money, more money from advertising, and deficit hysteria, have steadily eroded the influence and credibility of public broadcasting. Over the years, a greater reliance on advertising support for the CBC makes it harder to distinguish it from the commercial services. At a certain point the argument becomes: why do we need a public broadcaster? What is it doing that is different? Once this argument is plugged into the widely held belief that public enterprise is bad and private is good, especially in a climate of deficit hysteria, combined with the perception that we are already taxed to the max, we are ready to do away with the public broadcaster. The Klein government in 1995 sold *Access Alberta*, the public broadcaster, off to private industry. Federally, can the CBC be far behind? The public broadcaster is not as beholden to corporate interests, and has the potential — not always realized — to carry more balanced and open-minded reporting which may even go so far as to challenge the corporate agenda.

It should be noted that the ability of the CBC to do this is qualified by a number of influences which I discussed earlier in the general context of the news media. First, in the case of CBC-TV, it remains a commercial network in the sense that an increasing proportion of its funding comes from advertising dollars, as public financing dries up. As a result, it is driven by similar economic concerns to those of the corporate media. Second, its upper management and board of directors are appointed by the government of the day, inevitably leading to political appointments, and views at the top which are in sync with those of the corporations, politicians and commercial media. Third, many of the people who work in the CBC move back and forth from corporate to public media, bringing with them the same news values. Fourth, the news decision-makers at CBC rely on wire service sources which are largely compiled by the Canadian Press (CP) news service, which in turn is produced by its member daily newspapers. Fifth, the news workers at the CBC evaluate their own performance by reference to the corporate press and broadcasting outlets. Hence, while Peter Gzowski's *Morningside* program on CBC radio compares quite favourably with the mindless drivel of commercial radio stations, in the final analysis it is little better than a *Toronto Star* or *Globe and Mail* of the airwaves, promoting the same corporate views, frequently coming from the same people in the commercial news media, academia or government. What we really need as I have indicated in personal correspondence with Gzowski, is a *Canadian*

Forum or *Canadian Dimension* or *This Magazine* of the airwaves. (I got back a form letter).

Having gobbled up the independent private stations, the media barons have turned their eyes to the public stations as one of the few remaining areas of expansion. (The other being international opportunities, which are rapidly, if not entirely, diminished). An ad from the Fall of 1995 by Friends of Canadian Broadcasting said the CBC board has begun "crippling cuts" which will begin "dismantling Canada's public broadcasting system."[14] By that December, 639 more jobs had been cut across the country, and the CBC shortwave service, Radio Canada International (RCI), was to be killed after fifty years on the air. As a result, Canada prepared to join the mostly impoverished third world nations which have no international radio service.[15] Early in 1996, the new "Heritage" Minister Sheila Copps evidently found $16 million to rescue RCI from the chopping block yet again, this time for a period of one year.

Working hand in glove with the media barons are the policy makers and their minions on the CRTC and in the Department of Heritage, whom the politicos have appointed. The other private media, such as the newspapers, cooperate by promoting the general ideals and the specific actions needed to undermine the CBC.[16]

As this book was going to press in May, 1996, CBC management and unions were in tense negotiations following a strike vote by 7,000 employees. About a year and a half of fruitless negotiations revolved around the way to deal with major cutbacks. According to CBC management negotiator Alex Mercer, the corporation must cut $224 million from its budget in the 1996 fiscal year, $35 million of which must come through new collective agreements. The main issue in the negotiations was the "out sourcing" of production and services. CBC management says that in view of the cuts it needs greater "flexibility" to contract out to the private sector. The unions say unlimited out sourcing amounts to privatization of the CBC "through the back door."[17]

The Via Rail Model

The public fire-sale model extends to transportation as to elsewhere in the Canadian economy. Take Via Rail as an example. Established at great public expense, it opened up the country. Rail travel has been tremendously popular, but in the face of successful high speed models in Europe, this form of public transit is constantly undermined in Canada. Why? Because it is public. Also, rail is used by students and the elderly: those who are relatively poor. The business elite uses the (heavily subsidized) airplanes and airports. Travel is a tax writeoff, but airports and airlines are subsidized regardless. Ultimately of course, not only Air Canada, but airports and even air traffic control have been privatized. (One wonders if the police and military will be next). Also, the auto industry capitalizes on individualism and independence over public transit, to sell cars, with accompanying inefficiency, pollution, accidents, *et cetera.*

So, with rail, first you transfer all of the expensive money-losing public travel to the public sector (Via) and leave the private (CP) to benefit from the highly profitable transportation of goods. The more profitable sector is skimmed off and privatized, leaving the public service sector to languish. Then, you cut back on service. Let equipment go out of date and break down due to a lack of funding. Have few, irregular and slow trips. Cancel routes. When fewer people use the train, use the drop in numbers to justify making more cuts to funding and routes.[18] Finally, begin to sell off Via Rail to your cronies in private enterprise, as you have done previously with Air Canada, Petro Canada, and so forth.[19]

All of this succeeds because we are bombarded with the view that private enterprise is efficient and good and desirable, whereas public enterprise is inefficient and costly and undesirable. If it is useless, why would public enterprise exist in the first place? The answer is that it is not useless, even to big business. It is important to have public enterprise in the first place, in instances where huge start-up costs can be borne by the public purse. In the rail industry for example, huge public subsidies enabled the startup, and supported initial losses due to our large geographic expanse, to the point where aspects of the enterprise became profitable.

Generally speaking, once a crown corporation is into the black, or profits are just over the horizon and easily attainable through time-honoured traditions such as the wholesale transfer of personnel from company payroll to public unemployment insurance or welfare, then the enterprise is sold off to private interests which, having borne none of the risks and earlier costs, can now reap huge profits. Via Rail, but also potentially the CBC, are cases in point.

Under these circumstances the people of the country invariably move from a situation where they held, collectively through their elected government, sole or controlling interest in sometimes profitable public enterprise which served the public and kept people employed, to one where profits accrue to a small cartel of private interests after the costs are absorbed by the public. The private investors are invariably portrayed in the news media as the public's saviours because they are taking a money pit off our hands, and (generous souls that they are) providing us with some cash to boot. This example extends as well to airports and the air traffic control system, both slated for privatization.

In the spring of 1996, Canada's national newspaper published upwards of eight full pages of lists of public servants earning $100,000 or more. The lists were made public as a result of legislation by the Harris government of Ontario, which required disclosure. But the decision to publish and bring national exposure to every single name on the list was made at *The Globe and Mail* itself. A national debate ensued, with many letter writers and columnists outraged at the "exorbitant" salaries of these public employees. This was but a skirmish in the overall war on public enterprise. About a week later *The Globe* ran a list of the "top" 50 CEOs, earning over $1.1 million. But this was situated in an article that repeatedly justified those salaries as competitively market-driven, derived by human resources compensation committees, and most of all richly deserved by the bold entrepreneurial leaders, one and all.

A Single World Vision

The Law of the Jungle is sacrosanct. Government interference is passé, a relic of a failed leftist experiment from sometime in the past. We are burdened with huge public debts caused by the monetary and fiscal policies of the elite. Among these were, and are, radical "zero inflation" and high interest rate policies, which have created recessions and massive unemployment, all the while filling the coffers of the banks, speculators and the investment community. When journalist Linda McQuaig pointed all of this out in early 1995 in her best-selling book, *Shooting the Hippo: Death by Deficit and Other Canadian Myths*, she was ridiculed on the editorial page of *The Globe and Mail*.[20] As several people indicated subsequently in letters to the editor, columnist Andrew Coyne's attack on McQuaig was reprehensible: it was uninformed, unwarranted and personal.

The Globe's Coyne is a case in point, when it comes to Media Think, the conventional wisdom, and avoiding the unthinkable. In belittling McQuaig, for example, he parodied her book as "Hooting the Dippo," and dismissed her arguments because she doesn't hold a degree in economics. (Earth to Andrew Coyne: Paul Martin is a lawyer, not an economist). Coyne wrote that her "incoherent" arguments put McQuaig in league with Noam Chomsky, "in the intellectual tradition of conspiracy theory." Not bad company to keep, in some quarters. Following yet another great journalistic tradition, Coyne misrepresented McQuaig's thesis, and then proceeded to tear down his own distorted concoction. But in the process he made some revealing observations in defense of what he called "the vast consensus that now exists on certain economic questions," concluding that, "some things are not worth debating." Not if you are a charter subscriber to economic correctness, anyway. Barely three weeks later the Royal Bank admitted McQuaig was right, by releasing its own study attacking the high interest rate policies of former Bank of Canada Governor John Crow as being responsible for the severe 1990 recession. *The Globe and Mail* saw fit to put this on its front page. John McCallum, chief economist for the Royal Bank admitted that, "The primary explanation for declining per capita incomes in the first half of the 1990s lies in the exceptional length and depth of Canada's recession, which was itself due in large measure to the highly restrictive stance of the Canadian monetary policy."[21]

After relating that the Bank of Canada raised its prime rate between 1987 and 1990 "from about 7 percent to over 14 percent in an effort to slow the economy and choke off a rising inflation rate," the *Globe* reporter went on to comment that, "The Bank of Canada *has often come under fire as the primary cause of the 1990-1992 recession*, even from economists who generally support its actions but believe it overdid its high interest rates in 1989 and 1990" (emphasis added). This would appear to be an almost heretical statement which, in the face of mounting evidence and criticism, may be attributed to the desperate desire to find a scapegoat.

Why, just a scant three weeks earlier in his attack on McQuaig, Coyne wrote, "take the continuing furore over the Bank of Canada's 'single-minded' campaign against inflation. The Bank is 'obsessed' with fighting inflation for the same reason that the fire department is 'obsessed' with fighting fires: because that's its job." Of course, according to the Bank of Canada Act it is equally the central bank's job to keep unemployment levels down.

There was no overly restrictive monetary policy, no overly high interest rate levels discussed in Coyne's column. Of course, *The Globe*, The Royal, Andrew Coyne and the Bank of Canada are all seemingly incapable of appreciating the rest of the case put forward by McQuaig and the economists she cites, a case which, coincidentally, is contrary to the interests of the commercial banks. Here is the way that economists Lars Osberg and Pierre Fortin put things:

> We therefore emphasize the importance of monetary policy in solving Canada's debt problem. We do not advocate substantial cuts to program expenditures,

> because the implications of such cuts are now relatively
> minor, compared to the effects of variations in the interest
> rate, and because we think the debate on 'big government'
> has become rather misleading.[22]

What this alternative perspective makes clear is that rarely have so many people been prisoners of such a single world vision.

The Royal Bank's chief economist John McCallum subsequently came under fire from his superiors for making his study public without prior approval. It's one thing for a "weedy" and "leftist" journalist such as Linda McQuaig to point out what has been going on, but quite another thing when the heavy hitters at the Royal temporarily lift the veil and allow the public to have a glimpse of reality, however fleeting.

Almost a year later, in the spring of 1996, the staunchly conservative and pro-free enterprise C.D. Howe Institute weighed in with its own study. It blamed the tight monetary policy of the Bank of Canada for damaging growth and job creation which "added to the severity" of the 1990-91 recession. "The persistence of the [Bank of Canada's] tactical errors has given credence to the critics' argument that the price of price stability is just too high," the study indicated.[23]

So, following the release of McQuaig's book, *The Globe and Mail* in the person of its neocon darling and editorial board member Andrew Coyne, conducted a vicious and sexist attack on the author. Shortly thereafter *The Globe* provided front-page prominence to a study by the Royal Bank which drew similar conclusions, as reported by Bruce Little. A year later, with McQuaig's book now on the paperback best-seller lists, *The Globe's* Bruce Little again reported a study which backed Linda McQuaig's conclusions, this time as reported by the C.D. Howe Institute. And, Little himself previously wrote a column based on Statistics Canada data, which drew the same conclusions. But these perspectives "didn't have weight," and didn't "resonate," to use the terminology of Maude Barlow and Bruce Campbell, and so the news media buried them or excluded them altogether.

As if to undercut the criticism, the central bank began to lower the prime rate, which dropped to about five percent in the spring of 1996. This happened at a time when inflation was running at about one and a half percent, and the Governor of the Bank of Canada began warning about possible "deflation." The apparently low interest rates countered arguments that they were too high, but would have to decline still further and remain in effect over a considerable period — long enough for government debt to be rolled over at a much lower rate. If this were to happen then it would be possible to get the steadily-rising interest rate payments on our accumulated debt under control. It is these payments, which are approaching $50 billion annually on almost $600 billion in debt, that create our annual deficits. Since 1988, government revenues from taxation have exceeded all spending, so except for interest payments on the debt we have been running an operating surplus. This is the key to the damage done by the high interest rate policy.

Politically Correct Government Intervention

These high interest rate policies obviously involved massive, direct interference by government in the marketplace, through its appointee, the Governor of the Bank of Canada. Given the claim by the government and neoconservatives generally that they oppose intervention in the economy, in deference to the so-called free marketplace, this presents a problem. Thus, it is necessary to disguise the fact of massive intervention with a lot of vague discussion about bond rating agencies and demand for government bonds on foreign investment markets. In this way, mysterious international forces are said to be responsible for our economic policies. Thanks to high interest-rate policies and a desire to attract foreign investment, there is some truth in this. But in the first place it is the fiscal and monetary policies of our federal government which created the huge foreign-held debt and our very susceptibility to the mood swings of foreign investors. And, as Linda McQuaig, various economists and even *The Globe and Mail*, the C.D. Howe Institute and the Royal Bank have pointed out, this debt is not the result of overspending by governments, as the media would have us believe.[24]

Economists Pierre Fortin and Lars Osberg argue that the experience of the recession of 1981-82 indicated very clearly that tight monetary policy in the form of higher interest rates resulted in substantially increased government debt. To do so again would have the same effect. So, in 1989, "it should have been easy to predict the consequences of such tight monetary policy."

> If the full political and economic consequences of the zero inflation policy were foreseen, the fact that the Bank implemented the policy implies that an agenda for substantial political change that was never mandated democratically was successfully imposed on Canadian society.[25]

Thus, there exists the distinct possibility that debts were intentionally run up — not just to line the coffers of speculators, investors and the banks — but to justify the current attack on social programs and on the very role of government itself. Linda McQuaig notes that the Mulroney Tories "were ideologically committed to reducing the role of government and, to some extent, having a large deficit was a great way to drive home the need for more spending cuts." She points out that this approach was promoted in the U.S. by some of the Reagan administration's "more extreme anti-government ideologues" who keenly promoted deficit-creating tax cuts. This was revealed by Paul Volcker in his memoirs when he described the "novel theory," prevalent among Reaganites, that "the way to keep spending down was not by insisting taxes be adequate to pay for it but by scaring the Congress and the American people with deficits."[26] According to McQuaig, "the Mulroney government never shied away from using the deficit for such ideological purposes, although it didn't go to the extent of cutting taxes to further the cause of deficit hysteria." Perhaps not intentionally, but the tax breaks afforded by Mulroney to corporations and the wealthy resulted in a revenue shortfall which served that very purpose. She concludes that "there is no evidence that the Mulroney Tories deliberately enlarged the deficit in order to push the need for spending cuts," as advocated by some Reaganites. But as we saw above, economists Osberg and Fortin subsequently seem to be suggesting this is a distinct possibility; that the "evidence" is the fact that the effects of higher interest rates should have been clear to the Mulroney government and the Bank of Canada, based on the 1981-1982 recession.

Intentional or otherwise, the Law of the Jungle is an elite policy which benefits a select few in our society, at the expense of the rest of us. The notion that these elites favour anything which even approaches a free market system is a gross distortion of reality. To advocate a free market is like promoting a hockey game without a referee. Anarchy is as repugnant to the propertied class as is communism. Who among them is opposed to the police, courts, firefighters, road and highway repair, provision of clean water and sanitary sewage, at least *some* environmental protection, and garbage disposal? (Until recently one could have included the health and education systems, or other aspects of the social safety net).

Indoctrinated Intelligentsia

For their part, and contrary to the mythology about politically correct Marxists and feminists taking over university campuses, most academics happily toil away in the service of the status quo. Rather than providing the independent thought and critical perspective which would help to balance the pervasive corporatist view, academics have been almost entirely coopted. As Noam Chomsky, C. Wright Mills, David Suzuki and others have pointed out, academics are the embodiment of corporatism in the classroom. They are charged with the important task of indoctrinating youth and as such must themselves be among the most indoctrinated of all people. This is reflected in part by the seemingly harmless diversion of publishing practically all of their work in jargon-laden language, in obscure academic journals, read by few and understood by fewer still. Thus diverted, academics are preoccupied and rendered impotent, especially the younger, potentially radical ones who desperately seek publications and tenure. By the time they have achieved tenure and promotion they have also been socialized to believe that the academic journals and their colleagues are all that matter. It's also a way of avoiding messy realities. As Chomsky notes,

> Look, it's too hard to deal with real problems, there are a lot of ways to avoid doing so. One of them is to go off on wild goose chases that don't matter. Another is to get involved in academic cults that are very divorced from any reality and that provide a defense against dealing with the world as it actually is...For example, when I would give talks about current realities, even in research institutes dealing with strategic issues, participants wanted it to be translated into post-modern gibberish...These are ways in which intellectuals can separate themselves from actual, ongoing struggle and still appear to be lefter than thou. Nobody's radical enough for them. That way you advance your career, you separate yourself from things that are going on. You don't have to get involved in popular activities. You don't have to learn about the world, let alone do anything about it.[27]

Those academics who are sought out by the media form a part of the in-group of authorized knowers whose studies and opinions make up the common sense perspective on things. They might be conducting research for an "independent think tank," right wing, corporate and free market champions such as Toronto's C.D. Howe Institute, or Vancouver's Fraser Institute. They might tour the country to argue the benefits of free trade, the way University of Toronto industrial relations professor John Crispo did in 1988. Or more subtly, they might be relied upon, on their own initiative, to promote a technological determinism which diverts attention away from the actions of the corporate captains and their political minions. A case in point is professor Derrick de Kerckhove of the McLuhan Institute at the University of Toronto. Like Marshall McLuhan himself, de Kerckhove distracts attention away from people with their nasty motives and profits, and towards the very technology itself. "People appear to be running the show," de Kerckhove warns, "but there may be reasons to ask ourselves to what extent."

> We think, quite naively, that business and government promote computerization in the interest of competition and efficiency. It is the other way around: [technologies] use business and government to proliferate.[28]

As an example, professor de Kerckhove offers that globalization of the economy "is not simply a matter of personal choice or initiative," but "it is the result of the pressure put on by electronic media to effect a global reconfiguration." So, *it is the media technologies themselves* which are behind globalization, according to professor de Kerckhove. As a diversion, this may be even more effective than blaming mysterious international forces. For their part, his contemporaries honour these words of wisdom by including de Kerckhove's work in an edited text of selected writings designed for classroom consumption.

But this example pales in comparison to that provided by the French intellectual Jean Baudrillard, a cult figure of "postmodernism," who, on the eve of the Gulf War predicted it would not occur. "Even if it should," he wrote, "so reliant are we on the pseudo knowledge of media illusions that we are incapable of distinguishing this "hyperreality" from a real-world event."[29] After the war he wrote, "If we have no practical knowledge of this war — and such knowledge is out of the question — then let us at least have the sceptical intelligence to reject the probability of all information, of all images whatever their source." If *all* sources are suspect and the truth is impossible to determine, then not only are we precluded from promoting and fomenting any changes to the status quo, but we are prevented from criticizing it in the first place.

Obviously, not all academics subscribe to academic cults or engage in research whose primary purpose is to shore up the status quo. After all, Noam Chomsky is a professor, and I have cited others, such as Robert Babe. Nevertheless, those taking what might be loosely termed a "critical" perspective in academia are sorely outnumbered by the cheerleaders. In 1994-95 a telling example arose in Robert Babe's own department of communication at the University of Ottawa. Dissatisfied with the lack of critical content in their courses and in protest over the failure by the department and the university to hire additional professors with critical perspectives, a significant body of students in the department formed an independent organization and sponsored their own activities. In the fall of 1994, *CRITICAL*, as they call themselves, organized an international conference-cum-teach-in, inviting international scholars such as Herbert Schiller and Sut Jhally, Canadian scholars such as Vincent Mosco, Robert Babe, Michelle Martin, Heather Menzies, and labour activists of such stature as Madeleine Parent. The students held fundraising activities to pay for transportation and accommodation, while the speakers donated their time. At the conference I found the *CRITICAL* students to be among the very best and brightest, the most dedicated and courageous that I have had the pleasure to meet in more than 20 years of university life. Their continuing efforts, despite considerable opposition from the university hierarchy, are to be lauded. These students' unprecedented efforts serve to both highlight the problems associated with neoliberal perspectives on campuses, as well as pointing toward grassroots solutions.

Dumbing Down

With their mind-numbing control over the mass media, or what the late Canadian communications scholar Dallas Smythe liked to call the "consciousness industries" in our society, the ruling elite has succeeded in spreading its narrow doctrine far and wide. As we saw in Alberta and more recently in the Ontario election, a significant portion of the public bought into the ludicrous neocon view that welfare recipients or "cheaters" are somehow to blame for our current fiscal mess. Ralph Klein responded by giving people on welfare one-way bus tickets to Vancouver; Mike Harris cut Ontario welfare benefits by 22 percent, bringing benefits for a mother and two children on welfare down to $5.83 a day, per person, from $7.44.

Working in conjunction with other ideological institutions in society, such as the education and political systems, the news media have successfully propagated the neoliberal-conservative agenda. For our part, we have been transfixed by O.J. Simpson, Paul Bernardo, and the sports circuses, in addition to tending to the kids and putting food on the table. When we do glance up to take in the world around us, we are inundated with corporate Media Think. This further depoliticizes the populace. It's the "dumbing down" of political thought. Our ability to converse

intelligently is increasingly proscribed, to the point where we are left with
the banal exploits of the previous night's game or murder trial.

In a 1995 poll reported by *The New York Times*, 41 percent of
Americans described foreign aid as the largest single item in the federal
budget, even though it represents just one percent.[30] A columnist for *The
Boston Globe* recently noted:

> In a national survey just undertaken by *The Washington
> Post*, 54 percent of Americans could not name either of
> their U.S. senators; 67 percent could not identify their
> U.S. representative; and 94 percent could not name the
> Chief Justice of the Supreme Court. Only 26 percent of
> the public knew that senators serve six-year terms. Forty
> percent couldn't name the Vice-President, 58 percent
> thought more money is spent on foreign aid than on
> Medicare, and 46 percent didn't know that the Speaker of
> the U.S. House is Newt Gingrich.[31]

I'm unaware of any comparable Canadian study, but research that I did
with university students some years ago demonstrated that they were more
familiar with *American* politicians and media figures than they were with
Canadian ones.[32] A Globe and Mail-CBC News poll taken after the
collapse of the Meech Lake agreement in 1990 found that a majority of
respondents knew "nothing at all" or "not very much" about the accord,
despite saturation coverage by the news media.[33] The combined efforts of
the formal and informal education systems over the years have yielded a
population which is largely politically illiterate. In their rush to provide
advertisers with inoffensive programming, to maintain a "buying mood"
on the part of audiences, and so forth, the information media have served
their corporate patrons and the consumers well, but have neglected the
citizens. And, as the "Junkfood News List" of the previous chapter
indicates, news media audiences are preoccupied with mindless, safe, and
diversionary content.

Dummy Up
One conclusion we may draw is that it is high time for some diversity.
It's time to dummy up, instead. We need to get alternative views out there,
where they can be seen and discussed and numbered amongst the options
facing us. We can't simply be restricted to the narrow, dogmatic and self-
serving ideas of the corporate elite. We need to begin serious discussion of
the things that matter in our lives. It's time for us to "take back" the

thoughts and the talk which reflect our position as communal, interdependent and compassionate human beings.

How can we do this? I am grateful to my students who have helped to bring home to me the need to outline alternatives, to propose solutions, however tentative or otherwise limited these might be, to the problems indicated here. This is an area which has received little attention from critics, for a number of reasons. One is that people must first be aware of the problems, and creating that awareness when corporations have such tight control over the news and information, is a daunting task. Additionally, the problems are so ingrained and widespread that any solutions are either quite intimidating in their scope or seemingly futile. An example of the latter was provided by the Kent Royal Commission on Newspapers which reported in 1981. Its authors attempted to patch up some problems in media ownership with band-aid solutions, and it failed when it fell victim to the broader political forces which were beyond its mandate to consider.

For an example of these broader political forces we can refer to the earlier discussion on Prime Minister Jean Chrétien, his considerable power to single-handedly influence policy, and the real and potential power exercised over him and other prime ministers by Paul Desmarais and other corporate leaders. The overriding problem we face is that we do not have a system of responsible government, in the sense that politicians and leaders currently are not responsible to the public; rather, they are beholden to the corporations, power brokers and lobbyists. As we have seen, corporations contributed about $6 million to the federal Liberal Party coffers in 1994, a non-election year. It is small consolation to us that matters are worse in the U.S., where Bill Clinton's election team raised U.S.$26.5 million in 1995. In January 1996, Pennsylvania Senator Arlen Specter withdrew from the Republican leadership race, indicating [about millionaire Steve Forbes] "when I last looked, someone was trying to buy the White House, and apparently it was for sale."

Inconsequential as TV Wrestling

Our notion of "democracy" is, in reality, a system of elite decision-making. According to the rules, the public is almost entirely reduced to the role of spectators, with allowance for a periodic ratification of the elite rulers every four or five years. Given the narrow political choices, non-ratification votes which supposedly allow us to "throw the rascals out," merely result in the changing of the guard, a substitution of neoliberal policies for indistinguishable neoconservative policies. Within this comfortable two party system, at least in theory the election of an NDP government represents a potential "threat to democracy" in the sense that Chomsky uses the phrase. In theory, truly democratic-socialist NDP policies could conceivably lead to their actually governing in the public interest, thereby throwing the whole system out of whack. The as-yet unrealized potential of this threat to democracy has previously in the province of Ontario reduced the corporate media to near panic, as I have indicated elsewhere.[34] This is one of the reasons why the provinces of B.C. and Saskatchewan have had their own indistinguishable neoliberal NDP policies.

The illusion of diversity in political choices is a powerful one, especially when we can choose amongst three to five main parties. For their part, the Americans have been successfully duped with only two choices, which Chomsky calls corporate party one and corporate party two. Another contributing factor is the way that opposition parties assume a progressive, pro-public stance which is critical of the party in power, only to adopt those same policies, virtually unchanged, upon governing. This is now so apparent that it is even remarked on occasionally by the political columnists. The spectacle of the election campaign leads the observer to conclude that there is a clash of opposing ideologies, but in the quiet following the adoption of the mantle of power, corporatism is revealed to be firmly in place. Maude Barlow and Bruce Campbell quote from Brian Mulroney's approving appraisal of the Chrétien Liberals:

> They've endorsed our agenda pretty well, and I'm very pleased with that. The free-trade agreement with the United States, the North American free-trade agreement, the GST, privatizations and our low-inflation policy. I was very pleased to see that those main policies have been maintained intact by the new government, and they're taking them a little further.[35]

The changing of the guard takes place, noisily and with much public spectacle outside 24 Sussex. Now Jean Chrétien, Paul Martin and Gordon Thiessen stand where before them stood (most significantly, if not most recently) Brian Mulroney, Michael Wilson and John Crow. Inside, glasses are raised in a toast: to *Le Patron*. Some things stay the same. As Michael Lind, senior editor at *Harper's* magazine summed things up, in the American context: "Because the same economic oligarchy subsidizes almost all of our politicians, our political fights are as inconsequential as TV wrestling."[36] In the Canadian context, according to former Trudeau

Cabinet Minister Jim Fleming, "It's a bit scary. People are so proud to think that we have such a democracy. But relatively few people control the economic levers. They're not bad guys, they're just taking care of their interests," he said. "We're back to the Old Boys' Club."[37]

And what does this say about the claim by the news media that their reports are balanced, or fair, or objective, if they manage to include two sides taken by the major political parties? Are there only two sides? As I demonstrated in *Common Cents*, for example, Peter Gzowski of CBC's *Morningside* is not representing diverse views when he has two people debate the Gulf War and one holds that "we" did a great job while the other says "we didn't go far enough, we should have killed Saddam Hussein."

Legitimate Reform

We are sadly in need of reforms which will democratize our political system. For example, the 1990 federal Liberal leadership campaign demonstrated the need to correct the leadership funding problem, requiring changes in political party regulations. During the campaign there was a spending limit of a whopping $1.7 million, a decision which forced out "social" Liberal Lloyd Axworthy, whose anti-free trade and pro-social welfare policies precluded him from obtaining corporate funding. (In retrospect, given his activities as Human Resources Minister, Axworthy demonstrated that he is far from "progressive." However, drastically lower spending limits would at least allow true progressives to run). The wonderful American journalist and satirist A.J. Liebling summed things up very well back in 1947. He indicated that if candidates for the House of Representatives were required to be millionaires, and candidates for the U.S. Senate were required to be millionaires five time over, anybody with the means would be free to try to get nominated. Meanwhile, "the rest of us would be free to vote for our favorite millionaires or even to abstain from voting."[38] Liebling described rather accurately the political situation in which we find ourselves today. The only difference is that the candidates themselves are not required to have the means; they may instead attract corporate backing. This suits the bankrollers very well, as they have a political longevity which mere politicians can only envy. The reign of a Pierre Trudeau or a Maggie Thatcher pales in comparison with the influence of a Desmarais or a Rockefeller.

"In the same sense," Liebling went on to conclude, "we have a free press today." That same corporate backing is now behind the news media, digging furiously for profits all the while it champions freedom of the press and uses its media cash cow as a vehicle for relentless propaganda.

Jean Chrétien raised $2.5 million for his leadership bid, with the help of his chief fund raiser, Paul Desmarais.[39] The difference of $800,000 between what he raised and what he is legally allowed to spend presumably is put aside for a rainy day. Reasonable, more accessible limits could be set by legislation, rather than being left to the whim of the parties.

We require a system of recall, whereby constituents may vote to recall their elected representative if that person no longer protects their interests. This will help to make politicians accountable to the public rather than the corporations. Changes must be made to make governments less hierarchical and more democratic, with shared responsibilities and decision-making. We require a system of proportional representation, which will make for a "messier" and less efficient but far more democratic system. As it now stands, with the winner-take-all system and a large number of candidates, majority governments are obtained with as little as 38 percent of the popular vote, as we saw in Ontario in 1990. Candidates should be nominated by party riding associations, with no exceptions, and the party leader should not be able to overrule the riding. Cabinet ministers and committee chairs should be elected rather than appointed. No members of parliament should be beholden to the prime minister for their job, or perks.

There is some potential for contradictions amongst these recommendations. For example, if a system of proportional representation is chosen which requires that a national slate of party candidates be put forward, then elected politicians might not be attached to a local "riding," which would complicate any recall mechanism. Nevertheless, the world and the minds of political theorists must be scoured for workable, democratic alternatives. Until these political changes are made, little can be accomplished regarding the corporate media. For example, the federal Anti-Combines Act, the Bureau of Competition Policy, and the Canadian Radio-television and Telecommunications Commission should all intervene in the undue concentration of ownership in the news media, indicated in chapter one. It is not in the public interest for one corporation to control all of the daily press in a given province, let alone two or three. Yet, these bodies and the legislation are of no help to citizens because the policy makers are beholden to the perpetrators rather than their victims. The most we could expect to happen under the current system is that a Royal Commission would be set up, which would hold hearings, conduct research, write a report, and languish in obscurity thereafter. After 150 years, we are still in search of representative government.

Another Royal Commission is unlikely to be fruitful. In fact it would prove diversionary, as with the Kent Report, a cathartic venting of frustration which wound up ignored on the shelf. The $3 million that report cost is a lot to pay for an (albeit excellent) journalism textbook— one which the government has allowed to go out of print. As Kent and Jim Fleming demonstrated, tinkering with the media falls victim to the very political and economic forces which are being ignored. In this sense, such an initiative would be more harmful than helpful.

If we cannot rely on "our" lawmakers, what can we do? The Anti-Combines Legislation was toothless at the time of the Kent Commission and is even moreso now. Maude Barlow's Council of Canadians is investigating a Media Watch organization, which would help tremendously. No political change can be accomplished without public education, to publicize current shortcomings. As Ed Finn has commented in *The Canadian Forum*, we need a "concerted, comprehensive, ongoing long-term communications program that reaches down to the grass roots." According to Finn, "there is only one way to win the war of words. That is to make it the number one priority, devise a workable communications-cum-education strategy and then commit whatever is needed in financial and human resources to make it work."[40]

We can only do this if we have our own local and national news media. Not just monthlies, but weeklies and eventually dailies, television, cable and radio stations as well. Impossible? Here's one suggestion. The Action Canada Network is an umbrella organization for five million members, through its affiliated organizations such as the Canadian Labour Congress, the Ontario Federation of Labour, the Council of Canadians, the teachers' federations, and so forth. If we could arrange for a monthly dues checkoff of just one dollar from each of those people, we would have $60 million dollars annually to put towards a progressive, national daily newspaper. The newspaper could employ progressive young writers and operate through an editorial board, and at arms-length from the unions who raise the funding. The labour movement forms the second largest newspaper ownership group in Sweden, with almost 20 percent of national circulation.[41] There is no reason why the working people of this country cannot have one daily newspaper. There are problems. We need to embark on an education program to develop the political will on the part of both union leadership and membership. We need to fundraise. All of the union dues collected by all of the unions in this country in a given year amount to less than the profits of a single corporation such as the Royal Bank of Canada. But despite these and other problems, the unions and social activist organizations represent our greatest hope for developing a balancing force against corporatism.

The major problem here is public misperceptions owing to media mythology. We have been effectively brainwashed about what is going on around us, and even about ourselves: our achievements, responsibilities, and human potential. The public can effect change, can achieve a just and equitable society, once it is aware of the problems and the need for change, and the fact that changes are both desirable and achievable. There is a tremendous amount of collective wisdom and potential power in the hands of the public, ready to be released once that public is free from the cognitive limitations of the current system. So, the first step is: education. To accomplish this we need to work with the mainstream media and educational systems, as well as working around them.

We can reach out to progressive journalists and encourage and assist them in their contributions to our collective struggle. Get to know them. Call them with story ideas. Call them or write with encouragement and constructive criticism. Likewise, we can hammer the neocon and neolib journalists with criticisms, via the letters pages. We can read critically, write letters, write columns, call in to polls and radio talk-back numbers and programs, form a support group for intellectual self-defense. We can join social justice coalitions, and arrange meetings with editorial boards to get out views across. We can demonstrate, boycott media, boycott advertisers. In short, we can get active and go public.

Then there are the alternative media. Between $18 and $29 a year will buy a subscription to *Canadian Dimension, Canadian Forum,* or *This Magazine, Our Times, Briarpatch, Peace, The New Internationalist,* and so many others (see appendix D for a partial listing). By comparison, *The Globe and Mail* costs about $264 a year. So, subscribe. Even students can afford this. Support the CBC. Lobby for the public sphere. In addition, jobless communications or journalism graduates might: start up a Canadian version of the UTNE reader, a monthly with the best articles reprinted from the alternative media; create a World Wide Web site for alternatives, as we have done here at the University of Windsor (Browse our website at: http://www.uwindsor.ca/newsstnd/flipside/index.htm); organize and host a national conference on media and political reforms, inviting alternative journalists, publishers, activists in labour and social movements, with the express purpose of addressing and initiating options; bandy about ideas with anyone who will listen and even some who won't; turn off the spectator sports; follow up the above suggestion with the Action Canada Network, and member labour unions; lobby the CRTC about public access to cable stations, and get on air; take over student newspapers and radio stations and dedicate them to progressive causes; write to progressively-minded leaders in labour, women's movements, education, government, and elsewhere, to suggest solutions and ask for help.

These are just a few possibilities. Once more people recognize the systemic problems, we may begin to seriously examine the democratic means for improving our society. Obviously, long-term goals such as equality, social justice, and serious reform of our political, economic and social systems, require sustained time and effort. The first step, which may be aided by some of the above analysis and suggestions, is a concerted effort towards education to counteract the massive brainwashing by the mainstream corporate media, in which we are all steeped. More broadly, we are in dire need of serious political changes in this country, aimed at representative and democratic government; changes which are constantly asphyxiated by the corporate news media's stranglehold on *Democracy's Oxygen*: our information, ideas and public debate.

***

Endnotes

[1] I previously addressed the fallacies in these arguments. See the chapter on "The Socialist Hordes," in *Common Cents: Media Portrayal of the Gulf War and Other Events* (Montréal: Black Rose Books, 1992).

[2] For more details as well as other examples, including the Gulf War, see *Common Cents*.

[3] Quoted in Rick Salutin, "A Plea For Canada," *Maclean's*, July 1, 1995, p. 42.

[4] For an elaboration of this perspective supported by numerous examples, see Noam Chomsky, *Deterring Democracy* (NY: Verso, 1991); and Noam Chomsky, *Necessary Illusions* (Toronto: CBC Enterprises, 1989).

[5] Maude Barlow and Bruce Campbell, *Straight Through the Heart: How the Liberals Abandoned the Just Society* (Toronto: Harper Collins, 1995).

[6] See William Leiss, Stephen Kline and Sut Jhally, *Social Communication in Advertising: Persons, Products & Images*, 2nd edition (Scarborough, ON: Nelson, 1990).

[7] Christopher Lasch, *The Culture of Narcissism* (NY: W.W. Norton and Co., 1979), pp. 136-137.

[8] Ben Bagdikian, *The Media Monopoly*, 3rd edition (Boston: Beacon Press, 1990), p.138.

[9] Ibid, p. 139.

[10] Quoted in Herschel Hardin, *Closed Circuits: The Sellout of Canadian Television*, (Vancouver: Douglas & McIntyre Ltd., 1985), p. 17. Hardin appeared to be the only credible candidate for the leadership of the federal NDP in the fall of 1995. He did not garner enough support to make it onto the ballot of the leadership convention in Ottawa.

[11] Ibid, p. 302.

[12] Mary Vipond, *The Mass Media in Canada*, 2nd edition (Toronto: Lorimer, 1992), p. 39.

[13] Robert Babe, *Communication and the Transformation of Economics*, (Boulder: Westview Press, 1995), p. 193.

[14] Advertisement in *The Globe and Mail*, Oct. 26, 1995, p. A17.

[15] See Christopher Harris, "CBC cuts 639 jobs across country," *The Globe and Mail*, December 8, 1995, p. C1; and Christopher Harris, "CBC's shortwave service to be killed," *The Globe and Mail*, December 13, 1995, p. C1.

[16] See for example, Editorial, "Good public broadcasting means a leaner CBC," *The Globe and Mail*, October 3, 1995.

[17] Christopher Harris, "CBC rejects union proposal of arbitration," *The Globe and Mail*, May 13, 1996, C1.

[18] See Jo Davis, ed., *Not A Sentimental Journey*, (Toronto: Gunbyfield Publishing, 1990).

[19] See Andrew Willis and Susan Bourette, "Ottawa boosts CN offer price," *The Globe and Mail*, November 15, 1995, B1.

[20] See Andrew Coyne, "Contrary to popular belief, sometimes the conventional wisdom is right," *The Globe and Mail*, May 1, 1995, p. A14.

[21] See Bruce Little, "Royal Bank rips into Bank of Canada," *The Globe and Mail*, May 27, 1995, p. A1.

[22] Lars Osberg and Pierre Fortin, eds., *Unnecessary Debts* (Toronto: Lorimer, 1996), p. 163.

[23] Bruce Little, "C.D. Howe targets high-rate policy," *The Globe and Mail*, April 11, 1996, p. B4.

[24] See Linda McQuaig, *Shooting the Hippo: Death by Deficit and Other Canadian Myths* (Toronto: Viking, 1995). Also: Lars Osberg and Pierre Fortin, eds., *Unnecessary Debts*; J.L. Biddell, *A Self-Reliant Future for Canada* (Thornhill ON: LNC publications, 1993); and Maude Barlow and Bruce Campbell, *Straight Through the Heart: How the Liberals Abandoned the Just Society* (Toronto: Harper Collins, 1995). For another lucid dissection of the role of the Bank of Canada, see Michael Babad and Catherine Mulroney, *Where the Buck Stops: The Dollar, Democracy and the Bank of Canada* (Toronto: Stoddart, 1995). For an isolated commercial media admission that interest rates have created our debt problems, see Bruce Little, "Why the debt is a matter of interest," *The Globe and Mail*, February 13, 1995, p. A11. Of course, the article concludes, " [Paul] Martin is facing a brutal reality. Since he can't cut spending on interest, he has to cut somewhere else or raise taxes."

[25] Lars Osberg and Pierre Fortin, *Unnecessary Debts*, p. 161.

[26] Quoted in Linda McQuaig, *Shooting the Hippo*, pp. 107-108.

[27] Noam Chomsky, *Keeping the Rabble in Line: Interviews with David Barsamian* (Monroe Maine: Common Courage Press, 1994), pp. 163-166.

[28] Derrick de Kerckhove, "The New Psychotechnologies," in David Crowley and Paul Heyer, eds., *Communication in History: Technology, Culture, Society,* 2nd edition (White Plains, NY: Longman, 1995), pp. 329-334.

[29] See Jean Baudrillard, "The Reality Gulf," *The Guardian*, January 11, 1991. For a critique of Baudrillard, see Christopher Norris, *Uncritical Theory: Postmodernism, Intellectuals and the Gulf War*, (Amherst: The University of Massachusetts Press, 1992).

[30] Steven Greenhouse "Smaller helpings of largesse," reprinted in *The Globe and Mail*, May 2, 1995, A13.

[31] Jeff Jacoby, "Democracy for dummies reaches its zenith with elections by mail," *The Globe and Mail*, February 3, 1996, p. D6.

[32] For an overview, see James Winter and Irvin Goldman, "Mass Media and Canadian Identity," in Benjamin Singer, ed., *Communications in Canadian Society* (Toronto: Nelson, 1995).

[33] See James Winter, *Common Cents*, p. 148.

[34] See James Winter, *Common Cents*, especially the chapter on "The Socialist Hordes" of Ontario. For an excellent account of the non-media influences on the Rae government, see Tom Walkom, *Rae Days: The Rise and Folly of the NDP* (Toronto: Key Porter, 1994).

[35] Maude Barlow and Bruce Campbell, *Straight Through the Heart*, p. 91. The authors demonstrate the way in which the Chrétien Liberals betrayed the promises of their Red Book once in power.

[36] Michael Lind, "To Have and Have Not," *Harper's*, June, 1995, pp. 43-44.

[37] Jim Fleming, personal interview, May, 1996.

[38] A.J. Liebling, *The Press* (NY: Pantheon, 1964), p. 15.

[39] Maude Barlow and Bruce Campbell, *Straight Through the Heart*, p. 102.

[40] Ed Finn, "Comes the Revolution?" *The Canadian Forum*, July/August, 1995, p.8.

[41] Staffan Sundin, "Media Ownership in Sweden," *The Nordicom Review*, 1995:2, p.64.

Appendix A

MEDIA CORPORATION ASSETS, 1988, 1994

Corporation	1988 Assets ($Billions)	1994 Assets ($Billions)	% Change
Thomson*	7.3	12.2	67
Rogers/ (+ MHL)[#]	1.1	8.2[#]	646
Maclean Hunter[#]	2.2	n/a	n/a
Québecor*	1.4	6.8	386
Hollinger	1.1	2.8	155
Videotron	0.6	2.1	250
CBC	0.8	1.6	100
TorStar	0.8	1.0	25
Southam Inc.	1.2	0.9	- 25
Shaw	0.2	0.8	400
WIC	0.2	0.7	250
Total	16.9 Billion	37.1 Billion	225%

* Figures for Thomson and Québecor Printing were reported in U.S. dollars, and have been converted by a factor of 1.3.

[#] Includes Toronto *Sun* Publishing, owned by Maclean Hunter (Rogers). 1994 figures for Rogers include Maclean Hunter Ltd.

Copyright: James Winter, 1996

Source: *Report on Business Magazine*, "The Top 1000 Companies," July, 1989, 1995.

Appendix B

MEDIA - CORPORATE DIRECTOR BOARD INTERLOCKS[1]

THOMSON CORP.

Ken Thomson – Hudson's Bay, IBM Canada, TD Bank, Zellers.

John A. Tory – Abitibi-Price, Hudson's Bay, Royal Bank, Sun Life Insurance, Journey's End, Rogers Comm.

William J. Deslauriers – Union Bank of Switzerland.

John Foster Fraser – Air Canada, American West Airlines, Bank of Montréal, CIBC, Shell Canada, Coca Cola, Ford of Canada, Investor's Group Inc.

Ron Barbaro – Prudential Ins., Canbra Foods, Pruca Life Ins., Arizona.

Paul Brett – Thomson Travel Group, Britannia Airways.

Charles Edward Medland – Abitibi-Price, Canadian Tire, Irwin Toys, Journey's End, Seagram Group, Canada Trust, Teleglobe Canada, past Chair Wood Gundy.

Richard Murray Thomson – CEO of TD Bank, Timothy Eaton Corp, Cadillac-Fairview, Prudential Insurance, Union Carbide.

QUÉBECOR INC.

Pierre Péladeau – Donahue Inc.

Raymond Lamay – Donahue Inc., Laidlaw.

Hon. Guy Charbonneau (Senate) – Group Acme Canada, Versa Services Ltd.

Jean Coutu – CIBC and Jean Coutu Group.

Joseph Victor Raymond Cyr – Air Canada, Bell Canada, Northern Telecom, Dominion Textiles, Teleglobe.

Mary Shaefer Lamontagne – CFCF Inc., National Bank of Canada, North American Life Insurance, Quaker Oats.

Pierre Laurin – Cogema Canada Ltd., IST Technical Services.

Claire Leger – The Laurentian Life Inc.

Charles Albert Poissant – Hydro-Québec, National Bank of Canada, Premier-Choix-TVEC Inc.

ROGERS INC.

Ronald Besse – Canada Publishing Corp, Gage Education Publishing, Macmillan Canada, Diffulivre Inc., Global Press, Gage Distribution Co, Handleman Gage Books, RDB Capital Corp, Granite Club, MDC Corp., Cambridge Holding Group.

Bruce Donald Day - Vice President.

H. Garfield Emerson - Rothschild Canada Ltd., CAE Industries, Marathon Realty Inc., Genstar Capital Corp., Live Entertainment of Canada Inc.

Kenneth G. Englehart

The Hon. Francis Fox - (Rogers Cantel) Chairman of the Board.

Albert Gnat - Vitrasan Corp., CCL Industries, AXA Insurance, Boreal Property & Casualty Insurance, CFCF Inc., CamVec Corp, FCMI Financial, GEAC Computer Corp, IKEA Ltd., Leitch Technology Corp, Malofilm Comm. Inc, Regal Greetings and Gifts, SCOR Reinsurance Co, Semi-tech Corp, Slater Industries Inc, Canadian Council for Business.

Gordon Gray – Rio Algom Ltd., Markborough Properties Inc., CGC Inc., OMERS Realty Corp., Stone-Consolidated Corp., AE Lepage Investments, TD Bank, Advisory Board Financial Post, McDonald's Corp.

Philip Lind – St. Mary's Cement Co., Canadian General Tower Ltd., Hees Int'l Bancorp Inc., Toronto *Sun* Publishing, Canadian Cable TV Ass'n, National Cable Television Assoc.

The Hon. David Peterson: – CEO Chapters Inc., Chairman Professional Basketball Franchise, National Life Assurance Co., National Trust, Banque National de Paris (Canada), Speedy Muffler King, Cascades Paperboard Int'l., Industrielle-Alliance Life Assurance Co., Sr. Partner, Cassels Brock & Blackwell, Chairman Cassels, Pouliot, Douglas, Noriega.

Ted Rogers - Toronto Dominion Bank, Canada Publishing Corp., The Hull Group, Mercedes Benz Canada, Teleglobe Canada.

Graham Savage – Alias Research, Vitran Corp., Toronto *Sun* Publishing

John A. Tory – Thomson Corp., Markborough Properties Inc., Royal Bank, Abitibi-Price Inc., Hudson Bay Co.

John H. Tory – Multi-Media Inc & Maclean Hunter Publishing Ltd., Toronto *Sun* Publishing Corp, Rogers Broadcasting Ltd., CamVec Corp., CB Media, Financial Post Company, John Labatt Ltd., Multilingual Television Ltd, Chair, BOG, Canadian Football League.

Colin Watson – Canadian Satellite Comm. (CANCOM), Can. Cable Television Assn, Conwest Exploration Co.

MACLEAN HUNTER LTD.

Donald Graham Campbell – Financial Post, TD Bank, Toronto *Sun*, Key Radio, Canada Life Insurance

Ronald Walter Osborne – BCNI, CTV, Royal Bank, Sun Life Insurance, Toronto *Sun*, Advisory Board, Financial Post

Howard Leighton Beck – Citibank Canada, Paragon Petrolium

John Douglas Creighton – Chm and CEO of Toronto *Sun* Publishing, Financial Post, CAE Industries, McDonalds Restaurants of Canada

Jean R. Douville – National Bank of Canada, Unigesco

Francis William Fitzpatrick – Investor's Group, Interprovincial Pipeline Inc.

Mervin Lloyd Lahn – Canada Trust, Ellis Don, John Labatt, Hayes Danaa, Cameco Corp.

Radcliffe R. Lattimer – Citibank Canada, Algoma Central Corp., Prudential Corp.

Gordon Peter Osler – TD Bank, Trans Canada Pipeline.

Nancy G. Thomson – National Trust

William Price Wilder – Sears, John Labatt, Canada Life, Royal Bank.

SOUTHAM INC. (1996)

Conrad Black – Hollinger Inc., CIBC, Brascan, Eaton's, Argus.
Ronald Laird Cliff* – Royal Bank, Trans-Mountain Pipeline.
Bill Ardell - American Press Institute
Walter M. Bowen – Canada Protection Services, Securitron Canada Inc.
Paul Desmarais – Power Corp., Great-West Life, Power Financial, Petrofina, Seagram Group, Gesca Ltd.
André Desmarais – Power Corp. Bombardier, Great-West Life, Power Communications, Power Financial, Great-West Lifeco, Gesca Ltd.
Hugh G. Hallward* – Avon Canada, Beaumont Shopping Centres, McGill.
David L. Johnston – Canada Trust, Seagram Group, Dominion Textile.
Donna Sable Kaufman – Trans Alta Utilities Corp.
Marnie Paikin* – Acting Chair of Atomic Energy of Canada Ltd., Westcoast Energy Inc.
Michel Plessis-Bélair – VP, Power Corp.
David Radler – Hollinger Inc., West Fraser Timber, Sterling Newspapers.
Thomas Kierans* – C.D. Howe Institute, First Marathon, CFCF, Manufacturers Life, Petro Canada, Trans Canada Pipelines.
Adam H. Zimmerman* – Noranda, MacMillan Bloedel, Maple Leaf Foods, TD Bank, Confederation Life Insurance, C.D. Howe Institute.
Derek Burney# – BCE Inc.
Charles Dubin# – Retired chief justice, Ontario Court of Appeal.
Yves Fortier# – Chair, Ogilvy Renault.
Stephen Jarislowsky# – Chair, Jarislowsky Fraser, money managers, Unimedia Inc.
Donna Kaufman – lawyer, Stikeman Elliott.
*Asked to resign by Black, June 1996.
#Proposed by Black as new director.

GESCA LTD.

Paul G. Desmarais – Great-West Lifeco., Power Corp, Seagram Group.
Marcel Piche – General Trustco of Canada.
Hon. Peter Michael Pitfield - Senate of Canada, Great-West Lifeco.

POWER FINANCIAL

Robert Gratton – Great-West Lifeco, Pratt and Whitney.
Michel Plessis-Belair – Hydro Québec, Great-West Lifeco.
André Bisson – Maxwell Communication Canada, Maxwell MacMillan.
James William Burns – IBM Canada, Investor's Group.
Arthur V. Munro – Atomic Energy of Canada Ltd., CP Hotels, Investor's Group
Sylvia Ostry – Kellog's Canada.
Guy St. Germain – General Electric Canada, Loeb, National Bank of Canada.

POWER CORP.

John Black Aird – Algoma, Mercedes-Benz, Molson Companies, NOVA Corp.
John A. Rae – Paribus Bank of Canada
Charles R. Bronfman – Seagram Group, DuPont.
Hon. William G. Davis – CIBC, Corel Corp., Ford Canada, Magna, Nike, St. Mary's Cement, Seagram Group.

André Desmarais – Power Broadcasting, Gesca Ltee, Bombardier Inc., Great-West Lifeco.

Paul Desmarais – Power Financial, Great-West Lifeco, Seagram group.

Arden R. Haynes – Royal Bank, BCNI

Robert Howell Jones – Trans-Canada Pipelines, Great-West Lifeco.

Robert Parizeau – National Bank of Canada

HOLLINGER INC.

Barbara Amiel Black

Ralph MacKenzie Barford – BCE, Bank of Montréal, The Molson Companies, Union Energy Inc.

Conrad Black – Henry Birks, CIBC, Eaton's, Hees International Bankcorp

Montegu Black – Argus, TD Bank.

Peter Bronfman – Noranda Inc., John Labatt, Hees International Bankcorp, Brascan Ltd.

Tullio Cedrashi – Cambridge Shopping Centres, President & CEO of CNInvest, division of CNR.

Pierre Des Marais II - CEO Unimedia, Goodyear, Imperial Oil, Manufacturer's Life Insurance, Rothman's Inc., Royal Bank.

Marie-Josee Drouin – CIBC, Ford, Seagram Group, Standard Life Assurance Company.

R. Donald Fullerton – CIBC Exec. Committee, Amoco, Coca Cola, IBM, George Weston, Advisory Board Financial Post.

Allan E. Gotlieb – Alcan Aluminum, MacMillan Inc, Burston Marsteller.

Hon. William John McKeague – Investor's Group.

Peter Munk - Horsham Corp, American Barrick.

Paul Reichmann – O&Y, Abitibi-Price, GW Utilities, Gulf Resources Canada.

Peter G. White – Deutsche Bank of Canada.

UNIMEDIA INC.

Micheline Bouchard – Canada Post, Corby Distillers, London Life Insurance.

Hon. Claude Castonguay – Laurentian General Insurance, Eaton's Canadian Airlines Int'l.

Robert Despres – Domtar, National Trust Co., Provigo Distributors, TV Quatre Saisons.

Marie-Josee Drouin – CIBC, Ford, Seagram Group, Standard Life Assurance Company.

Stephen Jarislowski – Abitibi-Price.

Hon. Donald J. Johnston – BCE Inc., Pres. Liberal Party of Canada.

André Monast – CIBC, IBM Canada, Confederation Life Insurance.

Paul-Gaston Tremblay – Abitibi-Price, Bell Canada, National Bank of Canada.

TORSTAR LTD.

Alexander John Macintosh – Stelco Inc.
Robert John Butler – Abitibi-Price, Chm. Gulf Canada Resources.
Martin Phillip Connell – Canadian General Trust.
Dr. John Robert Evans – Alcan Aluminum, Dofasco, Royal Bank, Trimark Financial Corp.

BATON BROADCASTING LTD

Allan Leslie Beattie - Eaton's, Laurentian Life.
Douglas Graham Bassett – Eaton's, Mercedes-Benz.
William Press Cooper – Canadian Malting, CIBC, Laidlaw, Mutual Life of Canada.
Irving Russell Gerskin – CEO of People's Jewellers, Confederation Life Insurance.
Leighton Wilkes McCarthy – National Trust Co., People's Jewellers.
James D. Wallace - Derlan Industries.

WESTERN INTERNATIONAL COMMUNICATIONS (WIC)

Frank A. Griffiths – Canadian Satellite Communications.
Albert Thomas Lambert – Hees International Bancorp, Royal Trust, London Insurance.
Robert A. Manning – Canadian Western Bank.
Peter Paul Saunders – Laurentian General Insurance.
Donald M. Smith – President and CEO of Westcom Entertainment Group.

VIDEOTRON LTÉE.

André Chagon – TD Bank.
Serge F. Gouin – Laurentian Group.
Laurent Picard – Jean Coutu Group.

CHUM LTD.

Fredrick G. Sherratt – CTV.
Robert M. Sutherland – Rogers, Speedy Muffler King.

CINEPLEX ODEON

Allen Carp – Speedy Muffler King
Randolph Peter Bratty – Canada Trust, Financial Post, Toronto *Sun.*
Hon. Ernest Leo Kolber – DuPont, Seagram's, Senate of Canada.
Eric William Pertsch – MCA Canada
James D. Raymond – National Bank of Canada.
Howard Weitzman – MCA Inc.

***

Appendix C

DAILIES BY CHAIN OWNERSHIP[1]

Gesca Inc. (Desmarais, 4 papers plus 20 Southam)
La Presse, Montréal, Qc.
Le Nouvelliste, Trois Rivieres, Qc.
Southam Inc. (17)
La Tribune, Sherbrooke, Qc.
La Voix de L'Est, Granby, Qc.

Hollinger Int'l (Black, 40 papers plus 20 Southam)
Alaska Highway News, Fort St. John, B.C.
Alberni Valley Times, Port Alberni, B.C.
Barrie Examiner, ON.
Belleville Intelligencer, ON.
Cambridge Reporter, ON.
Cape Breton Post, Sydney, N.S.
Charlottetown Guardian-Patriot, PEI.
Chatham Daily News, Chatham, ON.
Cranbrook Daily Townsman, Cranbrook, B.C.
Daily Bulletin, Kimberley, B.C.
Daily News, Prince Rupert, B.C.
Daily Press, Timmins, ON.
Le Droit, Ottawa, ON.
Evening News, New Glasgow, N.S.
Evening Telegram, St. John's, Nfld.
Financial Post (20%)
Guelph Mercury, ON.
Lindsay Post, ON.
Lloydminster Daily Times, SK.
Moose Jaw Times-Herald, SK.
Nelson Daily News, Nelson, B.C.
Niagara Falls Review, ON.
Northern Daily News, Kirkland Lake, ON.

Orillia Packet and Times, ON.
Peace River Block News, Dawson Creek, B.C.
Pembroke Observer, ON.
Peterborough Examiner, ON.
Prince Albert Herald, SK.
Le Quotidien du Saguenay, Chicoutimi, Qc.
Regina Leader-Post, SK.
Sarnia Observer, Sarnia, ON..
Saskatoon StarPhoenix, SK.
Le Soleil, Québec City, Qc.
Southam Inc. (20%, 20 papers).
Standard-Freeholder, Cornwall, ON.
Sudbury Star, Sudbury, ON.
Summerside Journal-Pioneer, Summerside, PEI.
Trail Times, Trail, B.C.
Truro Daily News, Truro, N.S.
Welland Tribune, ON.
Western Star, Corner Brook, Nfld.

Irving Newspapers (4)
Daily Gleaner, Fredericton, N.B.
Telegraph-Journal, Saint John, N.B.
Times-Globe, Saint John, N.B.
Times-Transcript, Moncton, N.B.

Nfld. Capital (3)
Halifax News, Halifax, NS.
Simcoe Reformer, Simcoe, ON.
Woodstock Sentinel-Review, ON.

Québecor Inc. (Péladeau) (4)
Le Journal de Montréal, Qc.

175

Le Journal de Québec, Ville de Vanier,
   Qc.
Record, Sherbrooke, Qc.
Winnipeg Sun, Winnipeg MB.
Southam Newspapers Inc. (20)
Calgary Herald, AB.
Cobourg Daily Star, ON.
Edmonton Journal, AB.
Evening Guide, Port Hope, ON.
Expositor, Brantford, ON.
Gazette, Montréal, Qc.
Hamilton Spectator, ON.
Kamloops Daily News, B.C.
Kitchener-Waterloo Record, ON.
Medicine Hat News, AB.
Nugget, North Bay, ON.
Prince George Citizen, B.C.
Province, Vancouver, B.C.
Ottawa Citizen, Ottawa, ON.
Sault Star, Sault Ste. Marie, ON.
Standard, St. Catharines, ON.
Sun-Times, Owen Sound, ON.
Vancouver Sun, B.C.
Whig-Standard, Kingston, ON.
Windsor Star, ON.

Thomson Newspapers (11)
Brandon Sun, MB.
Chronicle Journal, Thunder Bay, ON
Daily Courier, Kelowna, B.C.
Daily Free Press, Nanaimo, B.C.
Globe and Mail, Toronto, ON
Lethbridge Herald, AB.
Penticton Herald, Nanaimo, B.C.
Times-Colonist, Victoria, B.C.
Times-News, Thunder Bay, ON.

Vernon Daily News, B.C.
Winnipeg Free Press, MB.

Toronto Sun **Publishing Corp.** (10)
(Rogers Communications* Put up for
sale in May 1996, with the leading
contender Québecor Inc).

Calgary Sun, AB.
Daily Graphic, Portage La Prairie, MB.
Daily Herald Tribune, Grande Prairie,
   AB.
Edmonton Sun, AB.
Financial Post, Toronto, ON.
Fort McMurray Today, AB.
Kenora Miner & News, ON.
Ottawa Sun, ON.
Saint Thomas Times-Journal, ON.
Toronto Sun, ON.

Independent Papers (12)
L'Acadie Nouvelle, CaraQct, N.B.
Amherst Daily News/Citizen, N.S.
Beacon-Herald, Stratford, ON.
Le Devoir, Montréal, Qc.
Flin Flon Reminder, MB.
Halifax Chronicle-Herald, N.S.
Halifax Mail-Star, N.S.
London Free Press, ON.
Recorder & Times, Brockville, ON.
Red Deer Advocate, AB.
Toronto Star, ON.
Whitehorse Star, Yukon.

***

Appendix D

ALTERNATIVE MEDIA

Akwasasne Notes
Box 189, St. Regis, PQ H0M 1A0
Published quarterly. Subscriptions: $35

Briarpatch
2138 McIntyre St., Regina, SK. S4P 2R7.
Published 10 times yearly.
Subscriptions: $24.61 individuals, $35.31 institutions,
libraries

Canadian Dimension
401-228 Notre Dame Ave, Winnipeg, MB. R3B 1N7
6 issues $24.50

Canadian Forum
5502 Atlantic St., Halifax, N.S. B3H 1G4.
Monthly, $29.96.

Canadian Perspectives
The Council of Canadians, 904-251 Laurier Ave. West,
Ottawa, ON K1P 5J6. Phone: 613-233-2773. Fax 613-233-
6776. Email coc@web.apc.org http://www.web.apc.org/~coc

Fuse
183 Bathurst St. 1st Floor, Toronto, ON M5T 2R7

Georgia Straight
1235 West Pender St., 2nd Floor, Vancouver, B.C. V6E 2V6.

Monitor
Canadian Centre for Policy Alternatives,
804-251 Laurier Ave. W, Ottawa., ON K1P 5J6. Fax: 613-
233-1458. WWW: http://infoweb.magi.com~ccpa/

New Internationalist
300-1011 Bloor St. W., Toronto, ON M6H 1M1

New Socialist
Box 167, 253 College St., Toronto, ON M5T 1RS.
6 issues. $1.50 at newsstands

Our Times
390 Dufferin St., Toronto, ON M4L 2A3.

Peace Magazine
736 Bathurst St., Toronto, ON M5T 2R7

Ploughshares Monitor
Conrad Grebel College, Waterloo, ON N2L 3G6

Prairie Dog
2201 Hamilton St., Regina, SK. S4P 2E7.
Monthly. Free locally.

This magazine
35 Riviera Drive, Markham, ON L3R 8N4.
$23.99 8 x yearly.

Windspeaker
17-318 Cooper St., Ottawa, ON K2P 0G7

***

Appendix E

1995 COMPENSATION FOR CEOs

CEO	Company	Compensation ($ Millions)
Ken Thomson	Thomson Corp.	334.5
Frank Stronach	Magna Int'l	47.2
Gerald Pencer	Cott Corp.	13.0
Brian Hannan	Methanex Corp.	12.9*
John Doddridge	Magna Int'l	10.8
David Walsh	Bre-X Minerals	10.0
Paul Desmarais	Power Corp.	5.7
Ted Rogers	Rogers Comm.	4.4*
Stephen Hudson	Newcourt Credit	4.2
Brent Ballantyne	Maple Leaf Fds	3.6
Donald Walker	Magna Int'l.	3.6
Conrad Black	Hollinger	3.5*
Clayton Woitas	Renaissance	3.5
Richard Thomson	TD Bank	3.4
Bernard Isautier	Can. Occidental	3.4
Lawrence Bloomberg	First Marathon	3.3
Michel Perron	Uniforet Inc.	3.3
Gerald Schwartz	Onex Corp.	3.2
Charles Childers	Potash Corp.	3.1
David O'Brien	PanCanadian	3.1
William Holland	United Dominion	3.1
Peter Munk	Barrick Gold	2.6
Brian Steck	Nesbitt Thomson	2.5
Edgar Bronfman	Seagram Co.	2.5
Matthew Barrett	Bank of Montréal	2.5
Richard Currie	Loblaws	2.4
John Cleghorn	Royal Bank	2.3
Purdy Crawford	Imasco Ltd.	2.3
James Buckee	Talisman Energy	2.3
Jean Monty	Northern Telecom	2.2
Anthony Fell	RBC Dominion	2.0
Peter Godsoe	Bank of Nova Scotia	2.0
Brian Colburn	Magna Int'l (VP)	2.0
Al Flood	CIBC	1.9
Jacques Bougie	Alcan Aluminum	1.8
Graham Orr	Magna Int'l (VP)	1.8
Edward Newall	Nova Corp.	1.7

Franklin Pickard	Falconbridge	1.6
Michael Sopko	Inco Ltd.	1.6*
Brent Belzberg	Harrowston Inc	1.6*
Lynton Wilson	BCE Inc.	1.5
Reto Braun	Moore Corp.	1.5
Robert Ogilvie	Toromont Industries	1.5
Ken Thomson	Thomson Corp.	1.5
James Stanford	Petro-Canada	1.3
Israel Asper	Canwest Global	1.3
André Berard	National Bank	1.3
Hollis Harris	Air Canada	1.3
James Bullock	Laidlaw Inc.	1.3
William Shields	Co-Steel Inc.	1.3
Garth Drabinsky	Livent Inc.	1.2*
David Galloway	Torstar Corp.	1.2
Robert Peterson	Imperial Oil	1.2
George Kosich	Hudson's Bay Co.	1.2
William Casey	Coca-Cola	1.1
Gwyn Morgan	Alberta Energy Co.	1.1
Wayne Lenton	Canada Tungsten	1.1
Ronald Oberlander	Abitibi-Price Inc.	1.1
Donald Shaffer	Sears Canada	1.1
John Wilson	Placer Dome Inc.	1.1

* 1994 compensation, as 1995 figures were unavailable.

Sources: John Saunders, "A league of their own," *The Globe and Mail*, April 13, 1996, p. B1; Jim Turk, ed., *Unfair $hares* (Don Mills: The Ontario Coalition for Social Justice, 1996).

Appendix F

NEWSPAPER OWNERSHIP BY PROVINCE

Alberta: 9 Dailies. Toronto Sun 4, Southam Inc. 3, Thomson 1, Independent 1.

British Columbia: 17 Dailies. Hollinger 8, Southam 4, Thomson 5.

Manitoba: 5 Dailies. Thomson 2, Sun 1, Québecor 1, Independent 1.

New Brunswick: 5 Dailies. Irvings 4, (English) Independent 1 (French).

Newfoundland 2 Dailies, both Hollinger.

Nova Scotia: 6 Dailies. Hollinger 3, Dennis Family 2, Nfld. Capital 1.

Ontario: 42 Dailies. Hollinger 18, Southam 12, Toronto Sun 4, Thomson 2, Nfld. Capital 2, Independent 4.

PEI 2 Dailies, both Hollinger.

Sask. 5 Dailies, all Hollinger.

Québec 11 Dailies. Power Corp. 4, Québecor 3, Hollinger 2, Southam 1, Independent

Yukon 1 Daily, Independent.

Appendix G

SELECTED WEALTHY CANADIANS

Name	Company	Net Worth
Kenneth Thomson	Thomson Corp.	$10.0 billion
The Irving Family	Irving Oil	$7.5 billion
Charles Bronfman	Seagrams	$2.9 billion
The Eaton Family	Eaton's	$1.7 billion
Ted Rogers	Rogers Comm. Inc.	$1.4 billion
W. Galen Weston	George Weston Ltd.	$1.3 billion
H.& W. McCain	Maple Leaf Foods	$1.2 billion
Paul Desmarais	Power Corp., Finan	$1.0 billion
Israel (Izzy) Asper	Canwest Global	$632 million
André Chagnon	Le Group Videotron	$394 million
Pierre Péladeau	Québecor Inc.	$359 million
Conrad Black	Hollinger Inc.	$303 million
Southam/Fisher Families	Southam Inc.	$201 million
Peter Munk	Horsham, Barrick	$188 million
Blackburn Family	The Blackburn Group	$185 million
J. Allan Slaight	Standard Broadcasting	$171 million

Sources: Jim Turk, ed., *Unfair $hares* (Don Mills: The Ontario Coalition for Social Justice, 1996); *The Financial Post Magazine*, January 1996. Note: this list contains all eight billionaires from these sources, but only selected, communications industry multi- millionaires who were listed in the top 50.

***

Endnotes

[1] These are current as of company reports in the spring of 1994. Some, such as Rogers and Thomson, have been updated for 1995, and Southam is current as of May 1996. The list of directors is not comprehensive, and includes only those directors with significant additional directorships.

[2] Supplied by the Canadian Daily Newspaper Association, March 1994. Revised, by the author, August 1995, January 1996, April 1996, May 1996.

Author Index

Subject Index

MANUFACTURING CONSENT
Noam Chomsky and the Media,

2nd printing

Mark Achbar, ed.

Manufacturing Consent Noam Chomsky and the Media, the companion book to the award-winning film, charts the life of America's most famous dissident, from his boyhood days running his uncle's newsstand in Manhattan to his current role as outspoken social critic.

A complete transcript of the film is complemented by key excerpts from the writings, interviews and correspondence.

Also included are exchanges between Chomsky and his critics, historical and biographical material, filmmakers' notes, a resource guide, more than 270 stills from the film, and, 18 "Philosopher All-Stars" Trading Cards!

...philosophical documentary bristling and buzzing with ideas.
Washington Post

You will see the whole sweep of the most challenging critic in modern political thought.
Boston Globe

One of our real geniuses...an excellent introduction.
Village Voice

An intellectually challenging crash course in the man's cooly contentious analysis, laying out his thoughts in a package that is clever and accessible.
Los Angeles Times

...challenging, controversial...the unravelling of ideas.
Globe and Mail

...a rich, rewarding experience, a thoughtful and lucid exploration of the danger that might exist in a controlled media.
Edmonton Journal

...lucid and coherent statement of Chomsky's thesis.
Times of London

...invaluable as a record of a thinker's progress.
Guardian

Mark Achbar has applied a wide range of creative abilities and technical skills to over 50 films, videos, and books. He has worked as editor, researcher and production co-ordinator.

264 pages, 270 illustrations, bibliography, index
Paperback ISBN: 1-551640-02-3
$19.99 within Canada
$22.99 outside Canada
Hardcover ISBN: 1-551640-03-1
$48.99 within Canada
$51.99 outside Canada

COMMUNICATION
For and Against Democracy

Marc Raboy, Peter Bruck, eds.

Addresses different aspects of the 'communication question', bringing out the ways in which communication serves at times as an instrument of repression and domination, and at other times as a support for human emancipation. Essays written by international scholars and activists.

These essays do much to increase reader awareness of the "mediatization" of society.
Choice

248 pages
Paperback ISBN: 0-921689-46-2 $19.99
Hardcover ISBN: 0-921689-47-0 $48.99

COMMON CENTS
Media Portrayal of the Gulf War and Other Events

James Winter

Objectivity is the theme of these five case studies which deal with how the media covered the Gulf War, the Oka standoff, the Ontario NDP's budget, the Meech Lake Accord and Free Trade.

Winter provides strong evidence of a corporate tilt in the mass media...it is impossible to dismiss [his] arguments.
Vancouver Sun

Like Chomsky, he enjoys contrasting the "common-sense" interpretation with views from alternative sources. As facts and images clash, we end up with a better grasp of the issues at hand.
Montréal Gazette

Winter's analysis of why the media fail to tell us all, in greater, more useful depth, gives basis for hope and humor.
Peace Magazine

304 pages, index
Paperback ISBN: 1-895431-24-7 $23.99
Hardcover ISBN: 1-895431-25-5 $52.99

ECONOMY OF CANADA
A Study of Ownership and Control

Jorge Niosi

2nd revised edition
It is refreshing to come upon a book that discounts the theory of the American control of Canada.
Financial Post

179 pages
Paperback ISBN: 0-919618-75-8 $12.99
Hardcover ISBN: 0-919618-49-9 $41.99

PASSION FOR RADIO
Radio Waves and Community

Bruce Girard, ed.

A project of the World Association of Community Radio Broadcasters, this book tells the stories of alternative radio projects around the globe, from First Nations in the Canadian North, to punks in Amsterdam, progressives in California, and guerrillas in El Salvador.

The stories in this book are both moving and inspiring.
Media Development

This impressive book is an exciting window into the increasingly diffuse world of participatory media.
Media Information Australia

212 pages
Paperback ISBN: 1-895431-34-4 $19.99
Hardcover ISBN: 1-895431-35-2 $48.99
L.C. No. 91-72979

BANKERS, BAGMEN, AND BANDITS
Business and Politics in the Age of Greed

R.T. Naylor

Based on Naylor's widely read column, this book is designed to give the news behind the news, to put back into the stories the 'awkward' details the main stream media find convenient to omit.

An eminently readable book, with outré insights into the corrupt underside of world affairs in each chapter.
Canadian Book Review Annual

250 pages
Paperback ISBN: 0-921689-76-4 $18.99
Hardcover ISBN: 0-921689-77-2 $47.99
L.C. No. 90-83630

CULTURE OF TERRORISM
Noam Chomsky

Closely argued, heavily documented...will shake liberals and conservatives alike.
Publishers Weekly

...argues powerfully that the elite groups in the U.S. are committed to furthering their own interests by the use of force.
Queen's Quarterly

...a penetrating analysis of American foreign policy and practice in Central America. It should be read.
Books in Canada

296 pages, index
Paperback ISBN: 0-921689-28-4 $19.99
Hardcover ISBN: 0-921689-29-2 $48.99

ON POWER AND IDEOLOGY
Noam Chomsky

Five lectures on U.S. international and security policy that examine U.S. foreign policy in Central America. The arguments are concise, the information overwhelming, and the presentation particularly moving.

... an impressive range of sources, a thought-provoking analysis.
Kingston Whig Standard

146 pages
Paperback ISBN: 0-921689-04-7 $18.99
Hardcover ISBN: 0-921689-05-5 $47.99

PIRATES AND EMPERORS
International Terrorism in the Real World

Noam Chomsky

revised edition

This work deals with terrorism, both State and 'retail', with special attention given to the scandal surrounding the Iranian arms deal. With meticulous research and documentation, it demonstrates the true motifs of U.S. foreign policy.

...raises provocative questions about U.S. diplomacy.
Maclean's Magazine

215 pages
Paperback ISBN: 1-895431-20-4 $19.99
Hardcover ISBN: 1-895431-21-2 $48.99

REAL TERROR NETWORK
Terrorism in Fact and Propaganda

Edward S. Herman

A scathing analysis of the U.S. media's unbalanced coverage of terrorism and its impact upon the public's perceptions of the problem.
Choice

252 pages, index
Paperback ISBN: 0-920057-25-X
Hardcover ISBN: 0-920057-24-1

RETHINKING CAMELOT
JFK, the Vietnam War, and U.S. Political Culture

Noam chomsky

For those who turn to Hollywood for history, and confuse creative license with fact, Chomsky proffers an arresting reminder that historical narrative rarely fits neatly into a feature film. A thoroughly researched background.

...a particularly interesting and important instance of media and power elite manipulation.
Humanist In Canada

172 pages, index
Paperback ISBN: 1-895431-72-7 $19.99
Hardcover ISBN: 1-895431-73-5 $48.99

LANGUAGE AND POLITICS
Noam Chomsky, Carlos P. Otero, ed.

A series of previously unpublished interviews, spanning the twenty year period from 1968 to 1988, that looks at the connection between Chomsky's linguistic studies and his political analysis. Prepared for Chomsky in celebration of his sixtieth birthday.

For those who know [Chomsky] only as media analyst and critic of foreign policy, this wide-ranging book offers glimpses of his studies on language, anarchist theory and critiques of radical politics.
NACLA Report on the Americas

779 pages
Paperback ISBN: 0-921689-34-9 $28.99
Hardcover ISBN: 0-921689-35-7 $57.99

UNDERSTANDING TECHNOLOGICAL CHANGE
Chris DeBresson

with Jim Peterson
A fresh look at technological change, highlighting labour's role in creating these new technologies.

An indispensable guide. Accessible, thoroughly documented, highly original.
CND Jrnl of Political & Social Theory

This book is one of the best available treatments of such a topic in a Canadian context.
Labour/Le Travail

272 pages, index, illustrated
Paperback ISBN: 0-920057-27-6 $19.99
Hardcover ISBN: 0-920057-26-8 $48.99

IMAGINING THE MIDDLE EAST
Thierry Hentsch

translated by Fred A. Reed
Recipient of the Governor General's Literary Award for Translation, this book examines how the Western perception of the Middle East was formed and how we have used these perceptions to determine policies.

For readers who want to understand the world of plural identities. A very rich and necessary book.
Montréal Gazette

This remarkable book...could be seen as advancing our understanding beyond professor Edward Said's Orientalism.
Crescent

...a stimulating work.
Journal of Palestine Studies

...a thorough and valuable account.
Arab Studies Quarterly

218 pages
Paperback ISBN: 1-895431-12-3 $19.99
Hardcover ISBN: 1-895431-13-1 $48.99

BLACK ROSE BOOKS

has also published the following books of related interest

Beyond O.J.: Race, Sex and Class Lessons for America, *by Earl Ofari Hutchinson*
Perspectives on Power: Reflections on Human Nature and the Social Order,
  by Noam Chomsky
The Trojan Horse: Alberta and the Future of Canada,
  edited by Gordon Laxer and Trevor Harrison
Complicity: Human Rights and Canadian Foreign Policy, *by Sharon Scharfe*
Free Trade: Neither Free Nor About Trade, *by Christopher Merrett*
The Other Mexico: The North American Triangle Completed,
  by John Warnock
Bringing the Economy Home From the Market, *by Ross Dobson*
The Sun Betrayed: A Study of the Corporate Seizure of Solar Energy
  Development, *by Ray Reece*
The Myth of the Market: Promises and Illusions, *by Jeremy Seabrook*
The Political Economy of the State: Canada/Québec/USA,
  by Dimitrios Roussopoulos
Statistics for Social Change, *by Lucy Horwitz and Lou Ferleger*
Critical Teaching in Everyday Life, *by Ira Shor*
Writers and Politics, *by George Woodcock*
Working in Canada, *edited by Walter Johnson*
The Political Economy of International Labour Migration,
  by Hassan Gardezi
Toward a Humanist Political Economy, *by Phillip Hansen and Harold Chorney*
Dissidence: Essays Against the Mainstream, *by Dimtrios Roussopoulos*
Voices from Tiananmen Square: Beijing Spring and the Democracy Movement,
  by Mok Chiu Yu and J. Frank Harrison

send for a free catalogue of all our titles

BLACK ROSE BOOKS
P.O. Box 1258
Succ. Place du Parc
Montréal, Québec
H3W 2R3 Canada

To order books in North America: (phone) 1-800-565-9523
(fax) 1-800-221-9985
In Europe: (phone) 081-986-485 (fax) 081-533-5821

Printed by the workers of
Les Éditions Marquis
Montmagny, Québec
for Black Rose Books Ltd.